# CRADLE *of* VIOLENCE

*As townspeople gloat (left) and seamen jeer (right), customs informer John Malcolm is tarred and feathered, threatened with hanging, and prepared for carting through the streets in this British caricature of a 1773 event in Portsmouth, New Hampshire. Entitling his work* A New Method of Macarony Making as Practiced at Boston in North America, *the artist included the Boston Tea Party of 1774 in the background, as an additional scandal.*

Carnegie Museum of Art, Pittsburgh; Eavenson Fund

# CRADLE *of* VIOLENCE

## How Boston's Waterfront Mobs
## Ignited the American Revolution

RUSSELL BOURNE

WILEY

John Wiley & Sons, Inc.

Published by John Wiley & Sons, Inc., Hoboken, New Jersey
Published simultaneously in Canada

Design and composition by Navta Associates, Inc.

*Library of Congress Cataloging-in-Publication Data:*

Bourne, Russell.
    Cradle of violence : how Boston's waterfront mobs ignited the American Revolution / Russell Bourne.
        p. cm.
    Includes bibliographical references and index.
    ISBN-13 978-0-471-67551-8 (cloth)
    ISBN-10 0-471-67551-2 (cloth)

    1.  Boston (Mass.)–History–Revolution, 1775–1783. 2. Boston (Mass.)–Politics and government–1775–1783. 3. Boston (Mass.)–Social conditions–18th century. 4. Mobs– Massachusetts–Boston–History–18th century. 5. Riots–Massachusetts–Boston–History–18th century. 6. Violence–Massachusetts–Boston–History–18th century. 7. United States– History–Revolution, 1775–1783–Causes. 8. United States–History–Revolution, 1775–1783– Social aspects.  I. Title.

    E215.B68 2006
    973.3'115—dc22

    ISBN 978-1-68162-391-7 (hc)
    ISBN 978-1-68442-152-7 (pbk)

                                                                    2005026870

For I have heard the whispering of the crowd;
Fear is all around;
They put their heads together against me;
They plot to take my life.

                        — PSALM 31:13

# Contents

# Preface

## Boston's "Jack Tars" and the Birth of Rebellion

When Boston's best lawyer, John Adams, was persuaded by his conservative merchant clients to defend the British soldiers who had slain five waterfront characters on King Street on the cold night of March 5, 1770, he devised a strategy that would both calm the town and satisfy the Crown. As shrewd a politician as he was a lawyer, he solved the delicate matter of excusing the soldiers by making their victims appear to have been of little account. That way, the court would arrive at a minimal sentence (which it did), and the concerned people of Boston could go on decrying the so-called Massacre without worrying much about the personal situations or the actual motivations of the fallen.

As will be related further in chapter 7 of this book, Adams carried out that strategy brilliantly, referring to the five slain individuals as "A Rabble of Saucy Boys, Negroes and Mulattoes, Irish Teagues, and Outlandish Jack Tars." By such colorful, prejudicial language, he not only won both his goals but also persuaded even history to look the other way—to look not at those who had fallen (for they, because of their low rank, might as well be ignored) but at the abstract circumstances and the legal considerations of that occasion. American historians, until recently, have tended to follow Adams's advice.

That is regrettable. Lost to subsequent generations has been any personal knowledge of the dynamic men and women who really brought about the Massacre and other formative events of the Revolution. In the case of the port of Boston—which has been called the Cradle of Liberty because of the formative events that took place there before Americans declared independence in 1776—this means a loss of acquaintanceship with a unique group of individuals, often violent, who existed at the bottom of society.

More specifically, these were the sailors who feared impressment, the unemployed dockworkers, the exploited apprentices, the runaway slaves, the fishermen not permitted to sail, the stressed-out ropewalk spinners, the oystermen beaten up by soldiers, the career smugglers and sometime pirates—in short, a host of highly charged men and boys who, joined by their wives and mothers, teamed up in mob action against local authorities. Their spontaneous uprisings and planned maneuvers steered America toward enormous change, even toward the awful risk of revolution. For they were the people who applied the tar and feather to the backsides of British customs officials; who, in one wild night of havoc, gutted the mansion of Lieutenant Governor Thomas Hutchinson; who armed themselves with marlinespikes and cudgels for street fighting against soldiers of the British occupation; and who flung the contents of 350 chests of British East India Company tea into Boston Harbor under the very guns of the anchored British fleet.

They were indeed daring and violent—yet purposeful. Though few of them had gone far in Boston's schools, they were fully conscious that their deeds involved consequences. In taverns and at dockside, they had heard or read the popular arguments about "Tyranny" and "Liberty." Indeed, they employed words and symbols themselves, providing Boston with its historic Liberty Tree on the eve of the Stamp Act riots of 1765—an elm near Chase and Speakman's distillery at the corner of Essex and Newbury (today's Washington) streets. They gave the tree its resonant name by means of a plaque so inscribed, securing the plaque to the trunk with "large deck nails." These industrial-size fasteners had clearly come out of the ditty bags of seamen or shipyard workers; they declared that the people carrying out the Stamp Act demonstration that day were

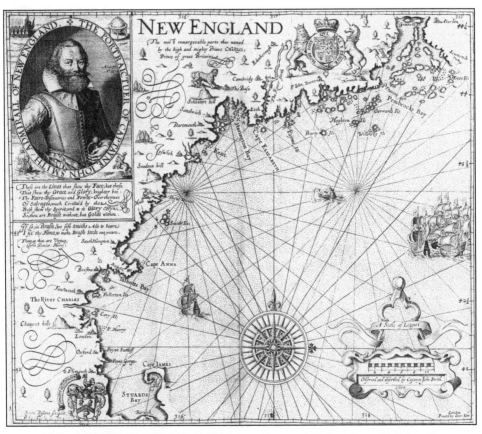

*Explorer John Smith prepared this fairly accurate, partially imaginary depiction of his route along the coast of Massachusetts Bay in 1614. The first to identify the region as New England, the map is peppered with names from England and Scotland suggested by King Charles I, including "Plimouth." Boston would be located at the mouth of the river named for the king himself.*

Rare Books Division, New York Public Library Collection, Astor, Lenox and Tilden Foundations

from the waterfront, and that they were determined to strike a blow for liberty.

We know all this because a new generation of American historians has dared to buck the tradition, that is, to contradict John Adams's dismissal of the laboring-class participants and to discover who really did the dirty work of the Revolution. Chief among these explorers is the historian Alfred F. Young, now a professor emeritus of history at Northern Illinois University. It was he who recognized those deck nails as important clues and who went on to describe Boston's Liberty Tree as central to an understanding of what the Revolution signified politically. For the territory around that tree, in his words, "became a public space" that rivaled other established institutions in the city; here, townspeople "could take part in public life in both a legislative and judicial capacity." Professor Young has also made the point that in saluting the mariners who gave all Americans this revolutionary sense of rightful involvement in government, we should indeed hail certain leaders but need not be excessively concerned that the actual names of many others will never be known. They were all parts of a shifting but powerful force of working men and women and youngsters who were recognized as "the people out of doors." They were not romantic personages looking for baroque monuments.

Other historians have also made enormous contributions to this new understanding of who swung America's wheel toward Revolution. Many of them will be named and thanked for their assistance in this book's acknowledgments, but because their pursuit of scholarship at the lower levels of society involves sources strange to many, I would like to highlight here a few of those historians and their modus operandi. By probing the records of jailhouses, almshouses, and magistrates' courts, Paul A. Gilje of the University of Oklahoma has sought to discover the roots and the racial character of rioting in America, including colonial port cities. By delving into the logbooks of shipboard life, the ledgers of counting houses, and ship manifests, Marcus Rediker of the University of Pittsburgh has succeeded in showing how fundamentally important the exploited seamen were in carrying out these waterfront actions. Finally, by working his way through the registers and the graduation records of Boston's schools, the scholar John L. Bell has produced a clear picture of the astonishingly large role that boys played in the mob actions of the town.

On the basis of their deep researching and profound reevaluation of the Revolution's origins, I have been able to splice together the narrative that follows, as if it were a hawser of many strands. The narrative is intended to counter John Adams's suggestion that the people involved in the mob actions along Boston's waterfront in

the eighteenth century were nothing but unthinking, easily manipulated "Rabble." It is also intended to show that those actions could
not have occurred anywhere else but in the salty social circumstances of this peculiar seaport.

In the words of yet another great historian, Pauline Maier, "Seamen gave the ideal of . . . equality to the rest of the nation." They
deserve no longer to be hidden down below, but to appear on deck,
in the sun.

# CRADLE *of* VIOLENCE

Part One

# THE ANCIENT IDEAL OF SEAMEN'S EQUALITY

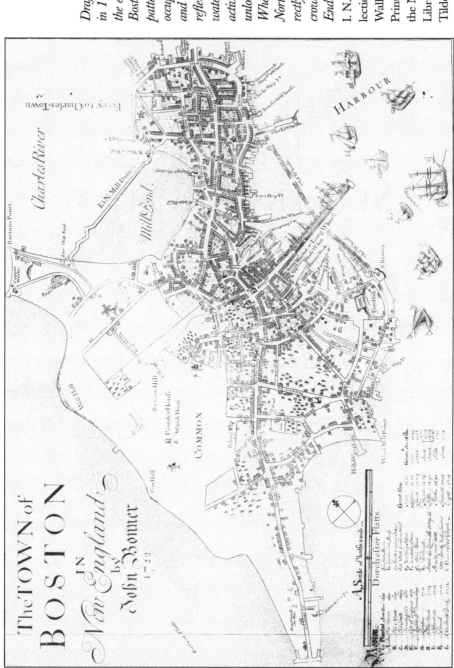

Drafted by John Bonner in 1722, this map was the earliest map to show Boston's shape and street pattern. Bonner's previous occupations as navigator and shipwright are reflected in his attention to waterfront features and activities, such as the ships unloading at the "Long Wharfe." The fist-shaped North End (right) correctly appears as more crowded than the West End (center).

I. N. Phelps Stokes Collection, Miriam and Ira D. Wallach Division of Art, Prints and Photographs, the New York Public Library, Astor, Lenox and Tilden Foundations

# 1

# The Maritime Origins of a Mutinous Town

T he ambitious and well-connected British foreign service official Francis Bernard, who had served competently as the governor of New Jersey during the French and Indian wars, believed that to assume the governorship of prosperous Massachusetts would be to attain the pinnacle of his career. It was a post that he considered much deserved and quite in keeping with his talents. The appointment was arranged in 1760, that apparently wonderful year in which Montreal was captured and the French were totally defeated in North America. Little did Bernard know that the War of American Independence was only fifteen years in the future and that the elegant colonial capital to which he so expectantly moved with his wife and ten children—Boston—would be the locus of mob violence whose sparks would leave him scarred forever and would help to ignite the American Revolution.

It all happened with amazing speed. Within less than five years of his arrival, Bernard was writing home that in order to defeat the hated Stamp Act, Bostonians were "combining in a body to raise a rebellion." Not only did he see the aroused citizens of America's leading seaport as violent and savage and determined to destroy royal authority, but also he accused them of "general

Leveling"—that is, desiring to take away "the distinction of rich and poor." In an effort to alert the most powerful officials in the king's administration and to make himself appear the victim of more than a passing storm, he wrote ominously that "the real authority of government is at an end." Civilization itself was threatened.

Painting a picture of anarchy let loose, a picture that might be compared with Dickens's later view of the French Revolution, Bernard went on to report that "Some of the principal ringleaders of the late riots walk the streets with impunity. No officer dares attack them, no witnesses appear against them, and no judge acts upon them."

Indeed, Bernard's lieutenant governor, Massachusetts-born Thomas Hutchinson, chose this moment in 1765 to resign timorously his secondary position as chief judge of the province. Hutchinson's mansion in the North End of Boston—a structure of Inigo Jones–style beauty, one of the peninsular town's few architectural gems—was viciously ripped apart as the Stamp Act riot burst all expectable bounds. The mob sweated for a full three hours before toppling the building's lofty cupola, after which they turned their frenzied, drunken attention to stripping and wrecking the interior, including the wine cellar. Hutchinson, in the years of unceasing riots that followed, seemed to join Bernard in abandoning all hope of ever restoring orderly, not to mention royal, government to the province. He had always loved Massachusetts Bay, but he had never comprehended the salty ways of its capital's people.

## Violence and Consciousness on the Waterfront

Who could understand the contradictory citizens of Boston, with its excess of steeples and its Puritan ethos, now turning to violence? Who then or in subsequent generations had an adequate explanation or a rationale for these inbred, antiauthoritarian people whose Stamp Act riots exploded into the most damaging of all such protests staged throughout the American colonies? One purpose of this book is to provide an interpretation of their mutinous spirit, its roots and its consequences. And this chapter, with its brief introduction of Bernard and Hutchinson and others who will be portrayed more fully in later chapters, sets the scene for their extraordinary personalities and rebellious actions. The total of Boston's riots, which began near the end of the preceding century and lasted well into the 1700s, exceeded thirty—far surpassing comparable disturbances in all other colonial ports. Yet however earthshaking their results, they continue to appear as the quixotic actions of a very idiosyncratic, curiously stressed people. That was certainly the conclusion of Nathaniel Hawthorne, the deeply probing, deeply ironic writer who demonstrated his understanding of (as opposed to sympathy for) stressed New England characters in *The Scarlet Letter* and *The House of the Seven Gables*. Hawthorne wrote a remarkable short story in 1837 called "My Kinsman, Major Molineux" that reveals his fascination with Boston's pre-Revolutionary mobs. This grotesque and cruel sketch of Bostonians in a tarring-and-feathering incident is drawn from historical research, as well as, presumably, from the author's tribal memory. Here is the most vivid part of the story:

> A mighty stream of people now emptied into the street, and came rolling slowly towards the church. A single horseman wheeled the corner in the midst of them, and close behind him came a band of fearful wind-instruments, sending forth a fresher discord, now that no intervening buildings kept it from the ear. Then a redder light disturbed the moonbeams, and a dense multitude of torches shone along the street, concealing by their glare whatever object they illuminated. The single horseman, clad in a military dress, and bearing a drawn sword, rode onward as the leader, and, by his fierce and variegated countenance, appeared like war personified; the red of one cheek was an emblem of fire and sword; the blackness of the other betokened the mourning which attends them. In his train, were wild figures in the Indian dress, and many fantastic shapes without a model, giving the whole march a visionary air, as if a dream had broken forth from some feverish brain, and were sweeping visibly through the midnight streets. A mass of people, inactive,

except as applauding spectators, hemmed the procession in, and several women ran along the sidewalks, piercing the confusion of heavier sounds, with their shrill voices of mirth or terror.

Another Yankee who thought he understood the troublesome people of Boston, and one who lived at the actual time of the pre-Revolutionary events, was the rationalistic Congregational clergyman Jonathan Mayhew, heir to a long line of appropriately eccentric Massachusetts Bay colonists. In the pews of his affluent West Church sat such liberal-minded citizens as James Otis, Samuel Adams, and Robert Treat Paine (the last of whom would later prosecute the British troops on trial for the Boston Massacre and who would even later sign the Declaration of Independence). Paul Revere, in his younger years, had received a harsh parental whipping for attending Mayhew's church; the pastor had been judged by other Congregationalists as excessive in his view of human freedom. Although Mayhew was not one of the "New Light" enthusiasts in this era of individualistic Christian renewal that came to be called the Great Awakening, he dared to preach the novel message that civil and religious liberty were both mandatory and inseparable.

On the Sunday before the Stamp Act riots, it happened that Mayhew had delivered a particularly fiery sermon, basing it on the text "I would they were even cut off which trouble you, for, brethren, ye have been called unto liberty!" Yet on hearing of the wreckage of Hutchinson's house and other associated acts of violence, the preacher was immediately seized by a Puritanical guilt spasm, a reaction not unlike that of the town's well-to-do merchants, who, however much they may have disliked Hutchinson and his high-and-mighty manners, feared that something even more consequential than property destruction had occurred. They saw that the people involved in the affair had been of the lowest sort—fishermen and dockworkers and seamen.

In one voice, the merchants condemned this "licentious" action of the lesser orders, this outrageous presumption on the part of riffraff and outcasts that they could muscle their way into what was truly a grave political matter. The merchants' words echoed those of their fathers back in 1747, when popular riots against the Royal Navy's impressment actions had impelled them to react conservatively against the rioters. They had heaped blame for what had truly been a community uprising on "Foreign seamen, Servants, Negroes, and other Persons of Mean and Vile Condition." Order, or the semblance thereof, must be preserved, whoever the disturbers might be. Such people must not mutiny against God's community.

In this same spirit of denial, Jonathan Mayhew penned a personal letter of regret to his neighbor Thomas Hutchinson. Deploring the action of the mob and wondering whether his own understanding of Bostonians of all sorts and conditions might have been in error, he wrote that henceforth he needed "to moderate and pacify [them rather] than to risk exciting so sensitive a people." By "sensitive," did the preacher mean "hysterical"? Mayhew's view of his fellow citizens was restrictively that of the pastor in his high pulpit looking down on the erratic sheep below. Much more attentive to God's wishes than to those of man or woman, he should perhaps be excused for not knowing much about persons of "Vile and Mean Condition"—Bostonians who lived on the edge of starvation, in terror of impressment, or at the call of brutal masters.

Yet a man of such aloof intelligence must have pondered, even as he castigated himself and consoled his neighbor, how people of that condition could have taken so fierce an interest in an international issue like the Stamp Act. As Hutchinson himself remarked, many of those in the mob—he called them the "cudgel boys"—never knew what a Stamp Act was. Were they not, by their rioting, really making a mockery of the exalted liberty that Mayhew advocated? Were they making Boston not a cradle of liberty but a cradle of violence and licentiousness? An exploration of their town's history may help reveal their intentions.

## The Triumph of the Codfish Aristocracy

Boston, the high-rising peninsula that European explorers called Trimontaine for its three hills but that Native Americans called Shawmut for its "living fountains," was first beheld by English settlers as they approached it in an open sailboat. That roomy little shallop, resembling a lifeboat, had sailed north from Plymouth along the shores of Massachusetts Bay in September of 1621, just ten months after the *Mayflower*'s landing. Aboard the shallop were thirteen men, ten Europeans and three Native Americans acting as their guides, one of whom was the linguistically talented Squanto. The whole party operated under the command of red-bearded Captain Myles Standish, whose purpose was not only to reconnoiter the coast but also, as Charles Francis Adams Jr. later wrote, "to establish trading connections with the inhabitants"—meaning to swap something of very little value for the Native Americans' much-needed produce, be it harvested corn or trapped beaver.

Because of shifting winds, the Pilgrim explorers could not quite reach land; they were required to spend the night on board. In the morning, they anchored in the lee of Thompson's Island and attempted negotiations with a party of Massachusetts tribesmen they met on shore. Reassured that the situation was not hostile, they reboarded the boat and sailed into what is now Boston's inner harbor. There they noted and admired many of the "plantations" glimpsed by the far-roving Captain John Smith seven years earlier. Now abandoned by Native American farmers who had been hit by European plagues, these sites looked well cleared and ripe for occupation.

Standish and his crew then rounded the tip of Boston's North End, anchoring at the mouth of the Mystic River. On landing, they heeded Squanto's advice that the chiefs of the region could be located and should be contacted in the interior. But instead of a Native American ruler, they encountered a countryside still recovering from recent attacks by the Tarratines from the north. Concluding nonetheless that the well-watered territory was pacified and available for European settlement, the explorers sailed home to Plymouth with good news.

Ten more years were required, however, before English settlers established themselves on the three-summited peninsula, and these settlers were not Pilgrims but Puritans. The distinction was not only one of faith—the Pilgrims believing that a total break with the ritualistic Church of England was necessary, the Puritans trusting that they, with their carefully wrought Calvinist credo, could reform and reshape the church*—but also one of means. Whereas the Pilgrims tended to be families of farm-village background and modest expectations, the Puritans were regarded as gentlefolk "of consideration," provident townspeople whose servants and retainers would do the work in farm or forest that would let them go about their business as proper managers. Having moved from their initial landing site in Salem to what is now Charlestown in the late summer of 1630, they soon determined that the supply of spring water there was inadequate. So they floated across the harbor to the place of the rumored fountains, where they established themselves in tents and rude shelters. They numbered some five hundred settlers, including the gentle families' servants and workmen, all covenanting together under the authority of the king's Great Patent of New England (1620) and under the stern but creative direction of Governor John Winthrop.

Among the first acts of the governor's so-called Court of Assistance was to order "that Trimontaine shall be called Boston" (after the English church town of one of their backers, Isaac Johnson). Here they set about building a New Zion, a tightly controlled community of hard work and religious dedication whose intellectual brilliance and social harmony would be an example to the iniquitous Old World left behind. This "Cittie on a Hill" would embody and would demonstrate God's purpose on earth. The Puritans saw themselves as defined by their hardships, removal, and future mission. After the first winter of starvation, in which some two hundred of the colony died and many others vowed to take the first boat back home to England, inland farms began to produce bountifully. The survival of God's people seemed assured.

Word spread swiftly abroad that in a harbor of Massachusetts Bay was a safe and commodious haven for Englishmen of the Puritan persuasion (certainly not for others). Soon, emigrants fleeing from the wrath of God in the corrupt Old World arrived by the hundreds. Land sales and house-building were the prime businesses of those first challenging years, though certain would-be merchants strove to get a leg up by dealing in fur and timber. A retail store was

---

*Puritan magistrates did not declare the Massachusetts Bay Colony independent of the Church of England's ecclesiastical authority until 1648.

licensed and established by 1633. By 1640, a mere decade after Boston's founding, the population numbered twelve hundred. Some of the city's short streets followed the shoreline, some fanned out from the center of town, and many of them were named for basic needs (like Water and Milk streets). They soon set the irregular pattern that would forever identify Boston, to the confusion of visitors. Many historians have commented that the original 2.8-mile-long peninsula was shaped like a polliwog; one more geometrically inclined observer saw it as a diamond-shaped quadrilateral. However viewed, it measured little more than a mile at its widest, containing less than a thousand acres of solid land. Indeed, Boston's miniature size must be judged as inversely proportional to the extraordinary human energy that went into its development, as well as into its fundamental values.

The multigabled wood-frame house of small windows and an overhanging second story that Governor Winthrop built for himself and his family in that first decade was notably sturdy; it stood fast down through the years until the severe winter of 1775–1776. Then, old and decayed and having served as the parsonage of the nearby Old South Meeting House, the house was torn down. The destruction was carried out not by rampaging mobs but by freezing British soldiers of the occupying force in search of firewood. "Old South," as Bostonians fondly called the venerable neighboring structure, had been built in 1669 and stood almost exactly at the center of the town.

Old North Meeting House had been built about twenty years earlier near the very tip of the peninsula at North Square (and thus near the still-standing Paul Revere House). It was surpassed in steeple height by a grander structure built on Salem Street in 1723— an Anglican church known as either Christ Church or North Church. It was from this lofty steeple that two lanterns would be displayed in 1775 to signal the secretive setting forth of British troops up the Charles River on their way northwest to Lexington. In either old or new form, this church served as the heart of the North End—a tightly congested and fiercely diverse community of merchants and whores, fishermen and townspeople, loyalists and revolutionaries.

Originally, before all the levelings and the landfills that reshaped Boston over the years, the North End seemed to exist as an island on its own, nearly cut off from the rest of the town by the canal running between Mill Pond and the harbor. It was in this remarkably insular North End (very similar to the human condition depicted in the movie *Mystic River*) that a mob of ruffians would coalesce in the next century, when the prosperity of early years was long past. This mob would combine with one or two others across the town to provide muscle for the riotous actions leading to the Revolution. The South End, less densely populated but home to many of the ropewalks and shipyards in which the maritime laborers worked, led to the Neck that joined the mainland. Both the North End and the South End fronted on the Great Cove, the crescent-shaped, quickly built-up harbor. Here one found the docks, the chandleries, and the counting houses that supported Boston's industry of the future—shipping—and that helped it become North America's richest colonial port in the years before 1750.

"Two strong arms reached out at either end of the Great Cove," explained an early guidebook. At the tip of the harbor's northern arm rose Copp's Hill, near which settlers built the North Battery (whose guns would lob cannonballs across at American soldiers at Breed's Hill in 1775). At the end of the southern arm was the even higher Fort Hill, at whose foot authorities established the much stronger South Battery. To build a secure haven between those two defense points, the settlers constructed a kind of breakwater out of timber and stones, the so-called Barricado. Its prime purpose was to prevent enemy fire ships from storming in against Boston's still primitive wharves. At certain points, breaks in the Barricado allowed the passage of ships, in or out. Not until 1710 was a major wharf built out into deep water from the waterfront. This was the famous Long Wharf, stretching out nearly half a mile in length, a wonder in its day. In 1768, British troops marched up it toward the town's center in order to calm down anticustoms rioters.

The British government's official presence in town had made itself known long before that. Winthrop's rival and eventual replacement, Thomas Dudley, had ordered the construction of an offshore battery for the king's emplaced commanders at Castle William three miles south of town (now Castle Island, connected to the mainland). This outpost, for reasons forgotten long ago, always flew the royal flag, as opposed to the stripped-down version of the British flag flown by authorities in Boston. Out of that latter flag, the cross of St. George had been slashed by the sword of a particularly spirited Puritan forefather. Ship captains entering the harbor, on scanning the two flags and noting their differences, received a hint of Boston's bifurcated view of itself and its not quite autonomous identity.

By the time the Long Wharf was built, the harbor's ancient Barricado was falling apart, remaining little more than a hazard. Yet the line it once marked is still visible today as the course of Boston's Atlantic Avenue. Another heritage of those early Puritan days, along with savage intolerance and public schools, is the peculiar accent of Bostonians. This much-ridiculed, grating, chronic nasal condition—with the long *a* and the gone-missing *r*—may be traced back, linguistic experts say, to the speech of the town's first immigrants from East Anglia.

All too soon, the wealth-producing influx of land-hungry immigrants came to an end. This occurred partly because the success of Cromwell's 1644 seizure of power from the Stuarts had made life in England more secure for Puritans, and partly because the land resources of tiny Boston had been severely depleted. And so, in 1637, Massachusetts Bay Colony warriors, booted and spurred, rode out to win control of the region's fur industry, carrying out a brutal campaign against Connecticut's Pequot tribe. Although the war was successful in destroying the Pequots and in demonstrating the Puritans' inhumane attitude to Native American peoples, it accomplished little economically. The fur industry soon reached its apex; wampum would serve as the coin of trade for only a few more years. The town was forced to turn not to the land but to the sea for economic survival.

As far back as when Captain John Smith had surveyed the coast, he had urged that fishing outposts be established. The silver of the cods' glistening sides seemed to be the only metal of real value in this part of North America. And already certain coastal towns—Beverly and Marblehead among them, but not Plymouth, which never seemed to get the hang of the art—were prospering as a result of fisher families' successful harvests. There were two difficulties about Boston developing itself on a seaward course, neither of them insoluble. The first of these was social: fishermen tended to be wandering, irreverent types, subject to multiple vices, and unwilling to live and work within the tight framework of Puritan governance. Winthrop and the colony's founders had conceived of Massachusetts Bay as a "commonwealth," with prices, wages, and the exchange of all goods strictly controlled by the authorities. Fishermen found ways to avoid such regulations, scorning even the concept of a public market; carelessly, they failed to pay taxes and attend worship service. For all that, they were so valuable to the town at this point that they, along with carpenters and very few others, were exempted from military duty. Surely, by dint of public pressure and communal norms, they could be controlled, as captains always controlled their crews—so thought the town's fish-rich elite.

The governor named a committee of six Puritans to "consult and advise" him on the financially and socially tricky business of "setting forward and managing the fishing trade." By 1653, that committee had grown to a full-fledged commission; its laws attempted to maintain standards of quality in the marketing of fish and to prevent the taking of cod and mackerel during the spawning season. Official encouragement and flexible regulations seemed the only way to manage the infant industry and its contentious personnel.

The second problem was technical: how to construct a fleet of fishing vessels large enough to bring the harvest to port and carry it out to wider markets? Just one year after Governor Winthrop's arrival, he had built a small ketch of thirty tons' burden (probably some forty feet long) on the banks of the Mystic River, naming her *Blessing of the Bay*. Records indicate that she had two masts, the forward one rigged with square main and topsail, and the mizzen mast rigged most likely in the lateen mode (meaning with a long, slanting spar that held a loose-footed, triangular sail). In a coincidence that might be called providential, she was launched on July 4, 1631, just 145 years to the day before the Declaration of Independence was signed.

Winthrop realized that ships far more commodious than the *Blessing* would be needed if the town were to compete with New England's other seafaring communities. By 1640, a shipbuilder in Salem had built a craft of 300 tons' burden (more than a hundred feet long). Challenged, Winthrop urged public investment in ship-yards and the recruitment of talented carpenters. Captain Nehemia Bourne responded with a trading vessel named *Trial*–the first com-mercial ship built in Boston–which, at 160 tons, was a respectable beginning. In building the *Trial*, Bostonians of all ranks seem to have pledged themselves to work together for the common purpose. That attitude declares itself in Winthrop's diary: "The work was hard to accomplish for want of money, &c, but our shipwrights were content to take such pay as the country could make."

Gradually, Boston constructed and acquired a fishing fleet. The ships of all sizes that were built in shipyards like Gillian and Com-pany's in the North End provided work for hundreds of carpenters, caulkers, and riggers. Like the building of *Trial*, this was a commu-nity enterprise. The Puritans' shrewd manipulation of factors that included private enterprise and government regulation allowed Boston to surpass other towns, both in fishing and in allied mar-itime industries.

Many of Boston's craft were rather primitive, open boats for coastal work; others were more ocean-worthy, developing into the large-sterned, blunt-bowed ketches and pinkies and sloops that are shown in paintings of New England harbors at this time. Later would come the schooners and the brigantines–originally, "brig-andines," named after the brigands who extended fishing and fish-shipping into piracy aboard sleeker, faster ships–that crowded New England harbors in the Revolutionary era.

An important point about the fishermen who worked in these early craft was that they functioned as a team but in a highly indi-vidualistic spirit. That is, they were paid not in wages (as sailors on merchantmen would be) but in shares of the entire crew's combined catch. Of the four men aboard the smaller fishing vessels–namely, the master, the midshipman, the foreshipman (their ranks indicating the position of their fishing stations), and the cook–each and every one "hauled his own line" (a phrase of the day), teaming with the others but on his own. On going to sea, the master or captain would forge a consensual decision with his men about course and destination, a decision that would affect all of their lives and fortunes. It was a regular and unquestioned process, with unsuspected political consequences for later generations. Having sailed back to Boston with their catch, the fishermen would argue about which fish were whose and what the promised share had actually been, creating frequent dockside uproars. Flocking fisher wives added their opinions and passion to the debate: the voice of the people could be heard on the waterfront.

Wealth and the apportioning of it were and would forever be a discomforting ethical problem for this Puritan town, pulled in different directions as its leaders were by their communal principles and by their desire to do well unto themselves. The Puritan administration sought to ensure that all merchants charged a "just price," but that covenant was often honored in the breach. Take the famous example of waterfront storekeeper Robert Keayne, who won fame as the first entrepreneur (or, by a modern analogy, the first executive officer) to have the law book thrown at him for having tried to grab too much. Governor Winthrop charged that in some of his dealings, Keayne had taken "above six pence in the shilling profit"; in others, "above eight pence. And in some small things, above two for one." It should be remembered that there were twelve pence in the shilling (twenty shillings in the pound), so the charge that he was getting a monstrous 50 percent profit seems accurate. Keayne survived this encounter with the colony's finger-wagging governor sufficiently well to bestow upon the town, in his will of 1665, three hundred pounds for a market shelter—an indication that he, like many contemporaries, was a community-minded Puritan through and through but also a profit-directed businessman looking for whatever advantage he could take.

Even before the first decade of Boston's life had concluded, Francis Higginson, the chief clergyman of the community, was scolding his contemporaries for their tendency toward commercialism. He reminded them of the Puritans' "Original Errand" of a

*Although Boston's earliest fishing and merchant vessels were crude and limited in range, its shipyards were producing ships for overseas trade before 1700. This handsome schooner, the* Baltic, *sketched by an unknown artist as she headed out under full sail from the island of St. Eustatius in 1765, is typical of Boston's successful but not necessarily legal West Indies traders.*

Photograph courtesy of Peabody Essex Museum

Christian commonwealth. Increase Mather continued this theme after his installation as the pastor of Old North Meeting House in 1664. But by then, a perceptible change had taken over the town: the commands of the fish-shipping merchants could be heard more loudly than could the commandments of the divines. This had happened in large part because of the gradual mastery by a few Boston families of the American colonies' trade with the West Indies. On the strength of that trade, the city had set forth on its period of greatest success and expansion, to the apparent benefit of one and all. But, in fact, the intermarrying group that came to be called the "Codfish Aristocracy" (a term that by no means embarrassed its members) dominated the people of the town, its members feeling themselves mighty enough to pursue aristocratic pretensions and to abandon no-longer-pertinent Puritan precepts.

# The Lure of the Triangle Trade

As if they were all parts of a single body, Bostonians from old and new merchant families responded at once to the discovery that the route to the Caribbean islands was the fastest way to riches. To Barbados and Hispaniola and the islands beyond, they shipped a variety of goods, including second-class fish for the slaves working the plantations. And from those islands they brought back sugar and molasses, basic ingredients for the New England distilleries. When to this pattern they added trading voyages to Europe (raw materials to England; first-class fish to Spain) and Africa, the outlines of the famous Triangle Trade were established. As Benjamin W. Labaree pointed out in the stirring book *New England and the Sea*, the vessels sailing forth from Boston often had several owners who shared the risks and the profits. Merchants generally gave shipmasters wide discretion in the sale of their cargoes; even when a bit of smuggling or illegal dealing with outlawed islands was involved, the merchants shared knowingly with the skippers in returns from the ventures.

New England boomed as a result of its seafaring daring; Boston was on its way to becoming the richest city in the New World, with as many as five hundred vessels clearing the port each year. The so-called lords of trade in England smiled benignly on their prospering colony, disinclined to interfere with its somewhat independent-minded practices. Although Parliament passed successive Acts of Trade and Navigation during the 1600s—acts that generally restricted American traders, commanding them to operate only between British-controlled ports—the regulations were enforced with notable laxity. This was because English merchants were benefiting from the Triangle Trade, too. The fact that some of the cargoes contained forbidden materials and involved forbidden ports seemed a forgettable detail. Fortunes were being made, the face of Boston was changing as more wharves were thrust eagerly seaward, as ships grew ever larger, and as stylish merchants' mansions replaced run-down seamen's shanties.

Along with the new wealth went both an increased willingness to take any risks to augment family fortunes and an aggressive intention to protect the port of Boston at all costs. In 1662, at the time of

Cromwell's downfall and the restoration of the Stuart monarchy, the General Court of Massachusetts felt that it must make that intention clear to all, even to the Crown itself. It issued a remarkable statement, declaring that Massachusetts would defend itself by force of arms against "any who should attempt destruction, invasion, detriment, or annoyance" of the Bay Colony's government. Although this was not at all a declaration of independence, it certainly demonstrated an autonomous turn of mind; it might be likened to a manifesto issued by the rulership of Taiwan at the time of a regime change in Beijing.

Yet despite its posture of confident defiance, Massachusetts was by no means secure. A tectonic economic shift would soon shake Boston more powerfully than any hurricane could. Just as in other parts of the Western world, where centuries-old agricultural economies were about to be challenged and superseded by industrial economies (including mercantilism), so here on Massachusetts Bay the local business of fishing was gradually overpowered by the predominance of transatlantic trade. As cosmopolitan Boston boomed, fishing, which had sustained the old ethos of the town, went elsewhere, to smaller and more older-fashioned ports like Marblehead and Beverly. And with the departure of fishing went the oligarchal assumptions and social prescriptions that had kept Boston so tightly controlled for so many decades.

Whereas fishing was based, as previously noted, on the tradition of "lay"* payments, with each fisherman getting his own proportionate share of the total income, merchant shipping and all of its accrued wealth were based on the work of seamen earning weekly or monthly wages per contract. Seventeenth-century commercial shipping was therefore, as Marxist and other historians have pointed out, the first of the industrial systems to assert itself on coastal populations. Seamen—that is, those of them who had to give up their fishing positions for posts aboard merchantmen—were supposed to become mere cogs in wheels, following orders without question, rather than contributing to an onboard consensus. That was particularly true as the merchant

---

*The men's take was part of the master's, which was one-third of the total, the shipowner claiming two-thirds.

vessels grew larger, their crews increasing to twenty or thirty from an old fishing vessel's five or six hands. Yet the fact remained that seamen and their extraordinary ability to carry out high-risk tasks under the stormiest of circumstances were of fundamental importance to the shipping enterprise.

By 1690, seamen involved in merchant shipping constituted a growing portion of Boston's male population (increasing from 5 to 10 percent), a notable fraternity among the town's then total population of seven thousand. Theirs was, always had been, and always would be an incomparably dangerous calling, even more deadly than that of the fishermen. More than half of New England mariners died between the ages of twenty and thirty-nine years. Only a small number survived their youthful years, to die, on average, in their forties—as opposed to artisans and gentlemen, who lived into their fifties and sixties. No wonder that Benjamin Franklin's father beat him when he expressed the desire to go to sea.

Yet there was that strange and eternal appeal of the sea—the chance to get away from grinding poverty ashore and take a chance beyond the blue horizon. This existed despite knowledge that service on board a merchant or a naval vessel was often likened to slavery or imprisonment. In writings of the day, whalers were singled out particularly as "refuges" for runaway servants and escaped slaves. Indentured servants and black slaves existed on the lowest step of the long ladder leading up to Boston's merchant mansions. Benjamin Labaree wrote that "Historians of early New England have been slow to recognize how much of the region's prosperity depended upon the institution of slavery. Black servants were employed as carpenters in shipyards, as longshoremen and truckmen along the waterfront, and as mariners aboard vessels."

When the number of slaves and freed blacks then engaged in maritime occupations (about eight hundred) is added to the variety of indentured European immigrants then landing in Boston, one begins to gain a vision of a much more racially mixed, economically and socially repressed dockside populace and to lose sight of the conventional social profile. Unfortunately, demographers have had difficulty identifying the precise number of African American and immigrant families in Boston at this time, for the simple reason that most of them had to live in nonregistered boardinghouses or in the homes of established whites.

Even so, this new diversity hardly made for a social scene of harmonious heterogeneity. Regrettably, Puritans had always had difficulty accepting people unlike themselves and their (most often) male leaders into their society. With extraordinary passion they persecuted whatever Quakers, Roman Catholics, and freethinkers happened to land on their shores. Independent-minded women, particularly those who expressed themselves unguardedly, were a special problem. The cases of the hanging of the witches of Salem and the banishment of the antinomian Anne Hutchinson (an ancestor of Lieutenant Governor Hutchinson) are too well known to need repeating here. Less well known or remembered are the uncalled-for murder of female and male Native Americans by Plymouth's militaristic Myles Standish at Wessagussett (Weymouth) in 1622 or the Puritans' ardent warfare against the Pequot Indians in 1637. That continuing, unsaintly bellicosity against Native Americans not only nearly cost the Massachusetts Bay Colony its life in the so-called King Philip's War of 1675 but also, even more grievously, set the tone for American discrimination and warfare in future generations.

Although almshouses, schools, and work programs for the poor existed in early Boston, these were for the Puritans' own people—and their purpose was not purely charitable. In 1657, the Bay Colony government issued a series of orders designed to protect the working people from unfair dismissal from their jobs. This and various attempts to control wages and prices can be seen either as evidence of the Puritans' noble "commonwealth" concept or as artifices to keep everyone at work, thereby preventing the town from having to pay for the support of the poor and the unemployed. However it may have been applied or interpreted, a central doctrine of Puritan government had always been that each community was required to grant subsistence to its own indigent folk.

Many of these possibly altruistic measures began to fall by the wayside as Boston's population grew and as the character of its employment changed. In the old days of fishing, shipyards were small enterprises with five or six workers. As orders for larger and larger merchant ships came in, yards grew, too, employing upward of two dozen carpenters, caulkers, shipwrights, and other trained personnel. The associated ropewalks were even larger, with teams of fifty to do the tricky "rope dance" and handle other phases of that very stressful, very necessary work. Boston, having displaced the old fisher economy with the new merchant economy and having committed itself and its workers to this grand task of creating America's busiest, most creative port, was unfortunately unprepared to address socially or politically the forthcoming, consequential periods of depression and deprivation.

Large numbers of unemployed people—a problem that would soon be visited upon Boston—have caused disruption in many historic cities over eons and have been seen as the origin of many social upheavals. In this port, even before the problem became acute, the maritime laborers and the servants assigned to shipyard work (along with the transient population of seamen, fishermen, and unskilled workers) lived a chancy existence and posed an unsuspected danger. Although they were vitally present and numerically strong among other, more accepted groups in the cramped streets and the public houses of the town, they were to some extent alienated, often resentful, and generally disregarded.

John Adams, in looking back at these early times, made the point that the poor man was simply not visible, adding, "he is not disapproved or reproached, *he is only not seen*" (Adams's italics). They were viewed, if at all, as non-Bostonians. Many of them either had been "warned out" of villages in the interior (because they, as charity cases, represented a drain on that place's resources) or belonged to the "strolling poor" of some other race or origin. They had but a minimal stake in the status of Boston; when driven to desperate extremes by poverty and repression—in short, with very little to lose—they had little reason to withhold their fury. With a certain turn of events, they might indeed become Hawthorne's garish rider with a sword.

## Politics on the Waterfront

Just as Boston's maritime workers—those men who risked their lives to bring ships home with profitable cargoes—were not present in the

social consideration of their "betters," so were they excluded from
the political process. Although Boston was truly notable among
other colonial ports for having at its political heart the town meeting, a uniquely Puritan institution, that gathering of franchised citizens was open only to white men of property. Indeed, to think that
Boston's original town meeting was a yeasty matrix for an emergent
political structure that would one day express the democratic will of
the people would be to grant it something more than it deserves.
Treasured though it might have been in local hearts, the town meeting of colonial times was designed as, and functioned essentially as,
an institution for the election of traditional and expected delegates
to the lower house (the Assembly).

That house, in which sat representatives from the province's
towns, had the particular duty of nominating higher-ranked gentlemen to the upper house, or Council. Those gentlemen, however,
were actually approved or disapproved by the governor. Massachusetts, way back in the time of Winthrop, had chosen to give a rather
confusing collective name to the two houses, the General Court. In
the time to come, when riots were getting out of hand and some
gentlemen were siding with, if not directing, the rioters, John Hancock, a member of the General Court, had the distinction of being
nominated to the Council. It gave Governor Francis Bernard pleasure to ignore the nomination and choose a more dependable loyalist. Unintentionally, he thereby made a "martyr" of Hancock,
making Boston's political situation all the more tense.

Yet the Town Meeting of Boston, in a way quite unanticipated by
either the Puritan fathers or the later royalists, did serve increasingly
as a forum in which people of the "middling sort" presumed to
express their opinions. When the seventeenth century merged into
the eighteenth and as the spirit of that enlightened century encouraged the liberalizing of tongues, these town meeting members—artisans and tavern owners, small merchants and retailers—even
organized themselves into pressure groups or "caucuses." Deacon
Samuel Adams, and later his son Samuel Jr., would take lead roles
in that development. But, of course, only white males possessing
some property could serve as or vote for representatives. In 1690,
for example, from the entire population of seven thousand, only six

hundred "freemen" actually cast ballots. Even as the role of the town meeting increased and its influence on the General Court grew stronger—an influence that the successive governors deplored—the propertyless people of the waterfront remained without a political voice. Except for their riots, that is.

Yet, notably, there were *no* "tumults and alarums" in all the years from the founding of the city until near the end of the seventeenth century. And this was definitely not the result of a heavy-handed police force or a military presence. Not at all; those elements were entirely lacking. Only seven constables, the night watch, and the governor's guard were on deck to keep the peace. For the community remained extraordinarily united, even as merchant wealth made for a widening gap between rich and poor and as bonded foreigners arrived by the shipload. Although the whipping post and public stocks had long since lost their power, the very real power of public demonstrations to shame malefactors and to correct those who strayed from the accepted norm remained in effect. Woe unto ladies who kept houses of ill repute or to storekeepers who charged excessively or hoarded food in hard times. They would receive visits from "the body of the people," enforcing the communal conscience. As the years would demonstrate, this popular moral force had the might to topple kings. For the moment, however, it expressed itself in such pesky ways as boys throwing mud at the passing carriages of the ostentatiously wealthy or fishwives insulting some wandering Indians.

Given this generally peaceful, self-controlled scene, one must ask, what went astray? Was it the shift from old cultural ways to a more capitalistic system that caused the unease? In fact, the explanation of why Boston's maritime laborers went from a condition of disregarded servitude to a pattern of successful rebellion is far more complex than the mere sum of this community's commercialization and religious decline. It had to do with the habits, the mores of these maritime people themselves.

It also had much to do with a cataclysm brought down on the people of Massachusetts and Plymouth by their own aggressive actions, the previously mentioned King Philip's War (1675–1678). As this war between land-grabbing settlers and aggrieved tribesmen exploded across southern New England, burned-out farmers and townspeople streamed across the Neck into Boston, reduced to the role of hapless refugees. Wives now widows and children now orphans sought public shelter, of which there was precious little to be found in the cramped capital. These pathetic wards of the state were, however, among the more fortunate victims of the war. Others who had not escaped were led off into Indian slavery—a condition that matched in horror the slavery imposed by the English settlers on their captives. The death toll on both sides reached nearly nine thousand, the greatest loss of life, proportionately, in all of America's wars.

One-third of those killed were English; two-thirds were Native Americans. Of New England's ninety-two towns, fifty-two had been attacked, twenty-five overcome and pillaged, and seventeen razed to the ground. Massachusetts's war debt exceeded £1,000; Plymouth's share was larger than that colony's total property valuation. As the days of March 1676 turned into April, and Boston quailed in the face of further expected attacks, it was evident that the bold light in the Cittie on the Hill might be blown out. A deep economic and spiritual depression gripped the town, particularly severe for the stricken and starving families of the unemployed maritime workers. Their overcrowded shacks nurtured a rampage of smallpox and intestinal diseases.

Riding onto the scene as yet another fury, royal inspectors and imperial officials arrived to give special treatment to the impotent, no longer autonomous town. The destiny of Bostonians of high rank and low would no longer be completely in their own hands; they had let it escape them. From this time forward into the next century, the Puritans' shattered experiment in independent colonial living would be overhauled and reshaped by British administrative and mercantile policies. It was only when the mobs burst forth and when the descendants of the original Puritans learned to work with the strengths of those violent waterfront personalities through inventive, homemade political systems that the bonds of British control would be broken.

# 2

# The Seaport's First Revolt

Among Great Britain's American colonies, Massachusetts won early notoriety for unseating its royal governors by mob action. Governor Francis Bernard, introduced in the last chapter as being forced out of office after Boston's Stamp Act riots of 1765, was but one of several governors pitched overboard by the Bay Colony's fractious citizens. Their disrespectful practice of nudging royal officials over the rail, which would have Revolutionary consequences in the late eighteenth century, actually began at the end of the seventeenth century.

The governor who came to Boston at the time immediately following King Philip's War was a briskly efficient administrator named Sir Edmund Andros, appointed in 1686 by the Duke of York (soon to become King James II). In his preceding assignment, when he had been commissioned by the duke to seize power from the Dutch in the newly won province of New York, Andros had demonstrated his effectiveness but also several other characteristics that would make him particularly unacceptable in Massachusetts. The first of these was a contemptuous disregard for the charters and the boundaries of the New England colonies.

Soon after arriving in New York and near the beginning of King Philip's War, Andros concluded that the crisis on that front gave him a grand opportunity to exercise his authority to the full. On July 7, 1675, having raised a troop of foot soldiers and horsemen, he set sail in a two-boat expedition for the mouth of the Connecticut River. His objective: to seize the territory to the west of that river, which had been promised to the Duke of York by his brother, King Charles II, in a grant that ignored Connecticut's charter of 1662. Andros had few doubts about his ability to prevail amid the rusticities of the New World. Having proved himself an all-purpose professional officer when serving in the Low Countries as a major of Prince Rupert's dragoons, he assumed that no provincial force in New England would presume to stop him.

When he arrived at Fort Saybrook on July 8, though, he was warned by the local militia that on the orders of the colony's governor, a sizable detachment was coming down from Hartford. The legislators of Connecticut were totally opposed to the duke's claim of precedence; they would defend their charter and their land, even amid the perils of the Indian war that was breaking out around them. Andros, realizing that he was outgunned and possibly out-chartered, withdrew in considerable humiliation. Indeed, Andros's poorly considered invasion had the result of persuading Connecticut's leaders that they had as much to fear from the British militarists to their west as they did from the restless Native Americans to their east.

Andros did succeed, however, in securing the Duke of York's claims to the islands of Martha's Vineyard and Nantucket by sending a brisk barrage of authoritative messages to the confounded magistrates of Massachusetts Bay Colony. Also, soon after the Saybrook folly, he succeeded in the more important endeavor of taking over from the departing Dutch their "Chain of Covenant" with the Five Nations of the Iroquois. He accomplished this by sailing up the Hudson River to Fort Orange in August 1675, where he invited the chiefs to attend him in council. His military bearing, ample handouts, and eloquent promises convinced the gathered Iroquois that he would be their protector and confederate in whatever crises might occur on the northern frontier. They hailed him as their new

"Corlear," a significant title coined by the Dutch in the early years of their fur-trading empire.

Yet by making this unbreakable alliance with the dominant Native American league in northeastern America, Andros revealed a strategy and a philosophy that further alienated him from the New England colonists. That is, he indicated a willingness to take the Native Americans' position into account whenever there might be a contest involving their interests. And such a contest there definitely was throughout the northeast in the spring and summer of 1676. By that time, the nearly victorious King Philip had begun to feel the lack of surviving warriors. Although his cause of liberation had found adherents and champions along the coast of Maine—thus presenting beleaguered Bay Colony forces with a two-front war—he had suffered depleting losses in central Massachusetts. In urgent need of men and arms, Philip had retired for the winter of 1675–1676 to the northwest, seeking allies along today's border of Massachusetts and New York.

Edmund Andros had virtually no sympathy for the Puritan and the Pilgrim leaders who had instigated this war, probably for their own land-grabbing purposes and surely as a result of their repressive treatment of the Native Americans. On the other hand, he saw Philip and his Algonquian allies as nothing but unneeded trouble. Boston, he learned, was in a desperate condition, jammed with panicky refugees, and the capital's leaders had limited reinforcements as the war swung northeast. With the approach of a second summer of hostilities and the continuing resistance of many tribesmen even after Philip's diplomatic and military failures, Andros realized that he would have to act. At the beginning of July, he ordered a force of three hundred Mohawk rangers, among the fiercest of the Iroquois' military warriors, to sweep down upon the Algonquians. From Philip's force of four hundred men, only forty survived. This, along with the chief's own subsequent death, hastened the end of the disastrous conflict.

Yet Andros would not give the exhausted New Englanders the victory that they craved. He made it clear to the Puritans, eager for vengeance as well as for slaves, that in the interests of peace on the frontier, he would offer safe haven in his province of New York to the once-hostile Indian warriors then streaming west in defeat. This gesture, in the eyes of the Bay Colony leaders, was tantamount to favoring the cause of the Native Americans over that of the colonists. It would be remembered far longer and with greater aversion than would the memory of any positive action on Andros's part to defeat Philip's allies in the west. Nor did Andros win any friends in Boston when he moved to end the war on the northern frontier by establishing a royal fortress on the Pemaquid Peninsula in Maine and by convening what became the Treaty of Casco (1678). Those moves were viewed as further efforts by the government of New York to interfere with New England affairs.

The third factor that might have warned Boston's leaders that Governor Andros would threaten them and their commonwealth at its very heart was his enmity toward the local Lutheran and Calvinist churches when he took over rulership of New York as the Duke of York's appointee. Though that colony's theological controversies were notably different from the denominational issues in New England, they bore a cogent similarity. The historic persecution of Protestants in Catholic lands was still a burning memory; the archenemy of all Protestant lands was believed to be the Pope or any king pledged to him. And Andros's master, the Duke of York, was reported to have swung to Rome. Also, the established Church of England (which the duke's kingly brother now headed) seemed offensively hierarchical and conspicuously anticolonial in the eyes of both Boston's Puritans and New York's Reformed Church members. Paying little heed to those sensitivities, supporting Anglicanism at the expense of other churches, and declaring that he detested the whiffs of republicanism that emanated from Calvinism, Andros exercised his gubernatorial powers over the churches with maximum arrogance.

His disdain for colonial traditions could be seen in its most naked form in a contest with New Jersey. Philip Carteret, the governor of that province, was reported to have been collecting customs duties from shipping within New York Harbor, an action that Andros interpreted as an intrusion on his territory. Striking swiftly, his men seized Carteret and bound and jailed him, releasing him only after the intervention of the duke himself. As a result of that presumptive strike and other diligent service, Edmund Andros won a magnificent title when the duke became king on his brother's death. He was named governor-general of a new administrative entity: the Dominion of New England.

King James II's plan to bring all of America's northeastern provinces—including both New Jersey and New York, as well as New England—into tighter control had certain merits as part of a grand imperial design. It does seem curious, however, that the king specified Boston as the capital for this strategy. Had the Puritan emigrants not made their abomination of the Stuarts and their concepts of church and state perfectly plain? But perhaps that was the point. Boston needed a lesson in empire, and Andros, armed with rod and whip, seemed the proper schoolmaster.

## "This People Are Rivited in Their Way"

The governor-general (or vice regent, as he preferred to be called) was scheduled to arrive in Boston on December 19, 1686, along with a military entourage that included sixty redcoats. But before that, indeed while King Charles II still reigned, an agent was sent by the Crown to assess and bring charges against the people of Massachusetts Bay. Charles had a number of issues to resolve with these independently inclined colonists, the most bothersome of which was their constant evasion of the terms of the Navigation Acts. By smuggling, by dealing with prohibited territories, and by maltreating the king's customs officers, they had manifested their characteristic will to steer clear of any laws that would restrict shipping and to keep all profits to themselves.

Another more personal affront to the Crown that the Boston Puritans had committed was their harboring of two of the ten judges who had condemned the king's father to death in 1649 and who had escaped punishment after the Stuarts had been restored to the throne. These two regicidal judges, William Goffe and Edward Whalley, had slipped out of England and fled to Boston. It was rumored that from that welcoming town, they had moved on from one friendly Puritan household to another, until they had finally hidden themselves somewhere in Connecticut. Then, in addition to that crime of personal disloyalty, there were the two issues of the Puritans' dangerous mismanagement of relations with Native Americans and their implacable hostility toward territorial claims in today's Maine and New Hampshire made by heirs of two early royal grantees (John Mason and Sir Ferdinando Gorges). Reasons abounded why they should be examined and judged; hence the agent dispatched to Boston by the king and the Lords of Trade.

To this assignment, Edward Randolph brought unlimited enthusiasm, an eye that missed very little, and a scurrilous pen. He arrived in Boston in 1676, just when King Philip's War was entering its most painful phase. With his own critical eyes he then saw, along with the war's starving and disease-wracked refugees, what he believed to be government-gone-wrong at the hands of the locally elected Governor John Leverett and religion-gone-wrong in the practices of Puritan orthodoxy. All of this he related at the time and recapitulated in a report of 1685, just before Andros's arrival. Accurately but one-sidedly, he described King Philip's oppressed tribesmen as "these poor people," mentioning how the Puritans had whipped and cheated them. He then went on to make fun of the local theologians' seeking out explanations for God's displeasure with their own sinfulness.

One can hear the Restoration dandies in the Stuarts' court snickering as they read Randolph's words about the Puritans' fulminations about transgressions that they believed they had committed themselves. As an example, they referred to certain disgusting behaviors among the Indians for which they had mistakenly extended tolerance, ". . . which is a sin highly provoking to the Lord: [i.e., tolerance] For men wearing long hair and perewigs made of women's hair; for women wearing borders of hair and for cutting, curling, and laying out the hair, and disguising themselves by following strange fashions in their apparell."

Randolph also quoted the Puritans as flagellating themselves "for profaneness in the people not frequenting their meetings, and others going away before the blessings be pronounced; for suffering the Quakers to live amongst them and to set up their thresholds by God's thresholds, contrary to the old lawes [sic] and resolutions."

What strange people. But it was not all to be laughed at. Randolph observed the huge debt of the colony, the crops not planted, the fishermen not able to put out to sea. He also saw that the people had learned little from their miserable war with the Native Americans: "[They] are rivited in their way, and I fear nothing but necessity or force will otherwise dispose them." That force would be supplied in the person of Edmund Andros.

Having landed in Boston just before Christmas 1686, the new governor-general took joy from the number of townspeople who seemed glad to welcome him. Their cheers truly did represent a new spirit in Boston. The merchants whose businesses had survived the war or who were attempting to get something started now were grateful for a regime that would be free of the old moralisms and fair-trade-isms. They looked forward to entering into the broader mercantilism of the day, under the protection of the British flag. Even so, Boston, this quaint capital of Puritanism, seemed crude and alien to Andros. He noted with displeasure that on Christ's birthday, which was not recognized as a holiday, shops stayed open, business was carried out with unceasing clamor, and the meeting houses, rather than offering praises, were shut.

Answering that apparent irreverence with his own view of the proper relationship between God and man, Andros plotted to take away power from the Puritan clergy. In an early step he decreed that Boston's ministers would no longer be allowed to perform marriages; that ceremony would be carried out only by his newly appointed magistrates. Then, having requested the use of Old South Meeting House for his own Episcopal services, and that proposal having been denied, he responded as would many another royal military commander: he "borrowed" the church for that purpose on desired occasions (most notably on Good Friday).

Andros also decreed that no citizen would be obliged to pay any part of a minister's salary, and he revoked long-existing laws for the support of the established clergy. This seemingly liberal provision was not liberal in any real sense; it was but another power move in the attempted reduction of the importance of the traditional aristocracy. It also had the inflammatory effect of confirming the worst fears of the town's pastors. As they put their heads together to mutter against the governor, they knew they had obedient parishioners on their side, and that those parishioners would not be gentle in their wrath.

In an even more dictatorial move, Andros curbed the liberty of the press: all publications had to be cleared through his office. Such unilateral regulations and such total mastery of the government were possible only because the Stuart monarchy, as part of its plan to tighten control of the colonies, had annulled Massachusetts's historic (1629) charter in 1684. The intention of the Crown, as carried out by Andros in the Dominion of New England, was to turn the old pattern of government upside down—authority would no longer flow up from the people (or from the elite who spoke for them) but down from the vice regent. Accordingly, the long-established Assembly having already been abolished, Andros ruled solely with the assistance of his councilors. When he banned Boston's town meeting, which for all its ineffectiveness as a democratic institution had been to the people the most precious of all governmental bodies, it became evident to the community and to the province at large that their ancient privileges had become dust.

Not content with reshaping the political structure of Massachusetts Bay, Andros went on to address its neighbors, determined to turn them, too, into subservient royal colonies. As a first step, he demanded through representatives that Rhode Island surrender its charter. Although the legislators succeeded in keeping that document out of the governor-general's reach, they saw that there was no choice but to renounce dreams of autonomy and to accept the change in their colony's status. Connecticut, however, proved to be a more difficult target.

Riding down to Hartford in company with his troop of sixty guardsmen, Andros appeared before the colony's assembly and demanded that it hand over the colony's charter at once. The session droned on into the night, however, with the legislators showing few signs of concluding their deliberations. Suddenly, as the famous story goes, all lamps and candles were extinguished and darkness gripped the hall. The Connecticut charter of 1662, which had been lying in all its grandness on the table, was spirited away by the bold Captain Samuel Wadsworth. Riding off into the night, he concealed the precious parchment in the hollow of an oak tree, giving birth to the undying legend of the Charter Oak. Though frustrated by the escape of the charter, Andros eventually got his way, bringing that colony, too, under his royal administration.

On a working level well below the restructuring of his fiefdom, the operations of Boston's free-wheeling merchants, smugglers, and fishermen were a source of constant irritation to Andros. He repeatedly told all mariners that the Acts of Navigation must be obeyed; he specifically ordered the Royal Navy to stop New England vessels at sea for inspection. He also imposed additional taxes on the impoverished town of Boston, while increasing fees for the services of public offices. In all this, he enlisted the aid of the ever-diligent Edward Randolph, making him the secretary and the register for the Dominion.

Randolph, for his part, continued to enumerate the townsmen's violations of the maritime laws and their insults to the royal purpose. The annulment of the Massachusetts charter had been his work; the Parliamentary verdict against the Bay Colony was based on his advice. He had charged that the people of Boston's waterfront "obstruct [the king's] officers in the discharge of their duty." Instead of obeying the Acts of Trade and Navigation, they "have invaded the rights of the . . . Lord High Admiral by erecting an Admiralty Court of their own." What disturbed the suspicious Randolph most, however, was the way Bostonians went about their subversion in an organized and united way. He wrote that they "continue to exact an oath of fidelity to themselves, notwithstanding the King's orders to the contrary, and make such an oath essential to the tenure of [public] office."

If there was any such conspiracy in Boston, as he surmised, it was certainly centered in the discontented waterfront community. Seamen were unable to find berths as the Andros government cracked down on illegal operations, particularly piracy. The heavily armed frigate HMS *Rose* patrolled the harbor, appointed to catch any illegal traders and demanding salutes from all passing vessels. Ships sailing home with rich cargoes after a raid here or a bit of freebooting there were impounded, with their crews flung into jail and branded as pirates—unheard-of treatment! Merchants also faced ruination as their cargoes were seized and condemned for violations of the Acts.

As the town's fundamental way of life suffered shock after shock under Andros's restrictions, a mood of united outrage spread. It eventually embraced both ends of the social spectrum, from the sailors' underworld of taverns and brothels to the gentry's world of church and school. Although Andros had prohibited the townspeople from communicating with the Lords of Trade or other branches of the British government, Boston's inventive minds considered other means by which an effective protest to the king's court against such tyranny might be made. Increase Mather, the pastor of North Church and a particular opponent of Randolph, took upon himself the risk of fashioning a vibrant protest on behalf of the community. Disguised as a seaman, he boarded a friend's ship by night and sailed off to England.

## The People "Should Do Well to Stand for Their Priviledges"

As Boston reeled under the weight of oppressive taxes and imperial regulations, other nearby communities also felt the slowdown in the economy and the buildup of anger at the Andros administration. The community of Chebacco, part of the larger town of Ipswich, was one of several formerly prosperous fishing ports along the coast reaching out from Boston to Cape Ann. Its shipyards would, in better times, be famed for having created and produced the "pinkie" fishing ketches whose peaked sterns and deep, narrow hulls could be seen across Massachusetts Bay. The town's Puritan character was rugged, orthodox, and vocal; its pastor, John Wise, epitomized those strengths. A man large in physical properties and gifted in salient language, Wise considered Andros's tax policies both a cruel imposition on his impoverished parishioners and a hateful abrogation of their rights as Englishmen, transplanted though they were.

In March of 1687, Andros had signed into law "an Act for the continuing and establishing of several Rates, Duties, and Imposts." These required all male adults to pay a poll tax of twenty pence and a tax of a penny a pound on all property, real or personal. Though not a large increase over former taxes, the point that angered Pastor Wise was that this one was laid on not by the people's accountable representatives but by the central government, without consultation. He chose to speak up in protest at the Ipswich town meeting of August 23, 1687. In the words of the warrant sworn out against him soon thereafter, he "did particularly Excite and Stur up his Majesties subjects to Refractoryness and Disobedience—contrary to and in high contempt of his Majesties Laws and Government here Established." By so doing, John Wise gave and continues to give Ipswich some justification for its claim to be the "Birthplace of American Independence."

Just how revolutionary his words were may be difficult for people of today to understand. He had told his listeners that they "had a good God, & a good King, and Should Do Well to Stand for . . . [their] priviledges." It was reported that he "spoak agt. Raising mony without an Assembly." Although mild to modern ears, that language was definitely too radical for Governor-General Andros; he focused his wrath on Ipswich generally and on Wise in particular. Summoned before Andros's council, Wise reportedly asserted "the priviledges of Englishmen according to Magna Charta." But in reply, he and his group of accused Ipswich townsmen were told that "wee had no further priviledges reserved saveing to be exempted from being Sold for Slaves, to like Effect."

Andros's council had delivered his message: these New Englanders were only Englishmen of a second and lesser class; they would be judged accordingly. John Wise and his fellow townsmen understood and bowed their heads to the inevitable. Wise was jailed and tried, his writ of habeas corpus (meaning, in this case, his request not to be hauled into court) having been denied. By the court's judgment, Wise was fined and prohibited from preaching. But the prohibition was lifted within a month, and he recovered most of his fine money from a grateful town. His words in definition of their rights and their identity would not be forgotten.

Yet the most recent biographer of Edmund Andros, Mary Lou Lustig, urges readers to take a longer view. Although the governor-general was surely a martinet and possibly a tyrant as charged by

New Englanders of high and low degree, he did have a rational plan for reform. This reform plan called for not only the reduction of the Puritan aristocracy but also the economic upgrading and the sensible administration of the Dominion of New England. Indeed, as Andros's next steps would indicate, he put as much energy behind plans for the stimulation of trade as he did for those behind construction of a viable (if punishing) tax and financial program.

For example, Andros and Randolph demanded that the franchise in Massachusetts not be limited to church members; they even reduced the property requirements for voters. This reform, to be sure, was offered at a time when the province's Assembly had been obliterated and the town meeting limited to but one session a year for the purpose of confirming town officers—at a time when, in fact, representative government had been done away with. Yet the attempted integration of the Bay Colony and the rest of northeastern America into the wider British world of mercantilism and imperialism did represent a credible vision of the future. Andros strove to be that policy's flag bearer. Had he succeeded in turning New England around in that direction (which would have involved turning all New Englanders inside out), the red-and-black face of revolution might never have been seen in Boston's streets.

Andros had a specific kind of overseas trade in mind: carefully monitored ships sailing dutifully back and forth to British harbors with approved goods. This was supposed to revive the moribund shipyards and bring grateful, right-thinking merchants more strongly to support the Crown's policies. But that was not at all the kind of trade Boston's shipping families preferred; they regarded the tightly enforced Navigation Acts as murder by strangulation. No longer could they range freely among the West Indies, trading whatever goods might be profitable to whoever might pay the most. No longer could the merchants' skippers bring in tax-free barrels of rum for the New England distilleries or pipes of French wine for the finer tastes. All these lifeblood activities Andros monitored closely. He did, however, recognize the one traditional area of profit making to which New England turned when all else failed: the fisheries. And these he chose to support with all the strengths at his command.

Andros agreed with the chagrined leaders of the Codfish Aristocracy that the king had been misguided to have signed a 1686 treaty with the French that excluded New Englanders from the inshore fishing grounds of Acadia. At issue was the precise description of Acadia, a province of French Canada that included Prince Edward Island, Nova Scotia, and some part of the coast leading southwest from what is now New Brunswick toward Maine. But how far into Maine—a territory regarded by the leaders of the Bay Colony as their very own (the opinion of the inhabitants to the contrary notwithstanding)? That was the question. Andros, who had demonstrated in Connecticut back in 1675 that when it came to territorial situations, military action was the way his mind turned, decided to make a fast thrust into Acadia from his established base at Pemaquid.

His target was the highly strategic peninsula of Pentagoet (now Castine, Maine). There, a brilliantly adaptive French nobleman, the Baron de St. Castin, had fashioned a conspicuously successful fiefdom. To his trading post, Penobscots and other Algonquians brought upcountry beaver pelts, and from it St. Castin sold the fur to French marketers. But Andros's interest in capturing Pentagoet arose less from its economic value than from its strategic importance. If he could seize it, he would undergird his claim that Maine, as part of the Dominion of New England, extended northeast along the shore of the Bay of Fundy all the way to the St. Croix River (today's border). And his chief reason for wanting to back up that claim was for the sake of the New England fisheries.

Although the successive King Louises had never supported the concept of New France to the extent that the Tudors and the Stuarts had supported New England, Louis XIV's interest in his American possessions suddenly intensified. The knight whom he appointed as governor of Acadia in 1687, Chevalier de Méneval, realized that if he was to champion his monarch's expansive cause successfully (meaning economically as well as militarily), he should protect Nova Scotia's fisheries by force of arms. He took action by commanding a French frigate, *La Friponne*, to drive New England interlopers from the inshore waters of his province. He also requested and received a company of first-line soldiers to defend the reconstructed fortress at Port Royal, across the Gulf of Maine from Pentagoet.

When, in defiance of Méneval, Andros's attack force sailed into Penobscot Bay in April 1688 and anchored before St. Castin's trading post, the baron himself could not be found. Sensibly, he had disappeared into the surrounding forests. Infuriated at finding the small fort abandoned, Andros stripped it of everything that could be removed, including the baron's personal possessions. Before sailing back southwest, he left a note saying that if the baron wanted any items returned, he must first come and swear an oath of allegiance to the English king at Pemaquid.

By this insult, Andros unleashed against northern New England the full fury of Native Americans allied with St. Castin, tribesmen numbering in the thousands. And by his challenge to Méneval's control of the Acadian fisheries, he ensured that France would back up the forthcoming Native American attacks on English settlements with all its imperial might. In August, a party of Native American allies led by St. Castin captured the fort at Pemaquid and massacred the inhabitants of the adjacent village. In the forthcoming contest (King William's War, 1689–1697), Boston, called to supply men and ships, would suffer its most grievous losses since King Philip's War. Altogether, what Andros accomplished by the end of 1688, as well as the commencement of the costly French and Indian wars, was the destruction of his reputation as defender of the northern frontier and the beginnings of his own downfall.

## "The Rabble Acted and Managed by the Preachers"

At the opening of 1689, discussions grew more vehement in Boston's centers of religious and commercial power about Andros's tyranny and what might be done about it. For his part, the governor-general sought to secure his authority over Boston by tightening information control even more drastically. When Edward Randolph brought word that a messenger from abroad had reported what sounded like a coup d'état to dethrone England's king, Andros had the messenger arrested and locked up out of earshot. But when Andros made moves to arrest the young and meddlesome Cotton Mather (who had taken his father's place as the pastor of Old South Church), the rumbles of discontent could be heard above all other noises of the town.

By March, the truth of the revolution in England could no longer be suppressed. The birth of a son to James II had seemed to his restless subjects a sure sign that they must take action, for this prince of the now openly Catholic king would surely put the Crown under Rome's control. An aroused Parliament would not tolerate that possibility. An invitation to the Protestant ruler, William of Orange, in Holland and to his wife, James's daughter, was extended by a group of Whig and Tory leaders. When William landed at Torbay with an army of twenty-five thousand men, James's forces deserted him; he fled to France, where his queen and his son awaited him. Early in 1789, William and Mary were installed as joint sovereigns. The "Glorious Revolution," which guaranteed the rights of the English people everywhere, had succeeded and could not be reversed, in any part of the realm.

The reaction in distressed New England was swift. Militia units from Roxbury, Charlestown, and other communities surrounding Boston began to move in toward the capital on April 18. Joining as a united force at the Neck, where Boston's own militia declined to oppose them, they surged toward the center of town, seeking Andros, the hated and now discredited officer of the deposed king. At the head of the crowd marched a thousand armed men. Boys ran along with them, bearing sticks and cudgels; as women joined them all, the total exceeded five thousand. Surrounding the Town House, they demanded the governor-general's surrender.

Andros had at his command only fourteen soldiers up on Fort Hill and perhaps a dozen more down at Castle Island. Making the wise decision not to command his gunners on the hill to aim their cannon toward the town and pulverize the huge crowd, he let himself be captured. Seized by the mob's leaders and secured in chains, he was conducted to the fort's prison. Subsequently, he was taken to a single cell at Fort Mary, into whose confines were also hauled some fifty of his councilors (including Randolph), fellow Anglicans, and other Loyalists. Months passed, during which Andros attempted two escapes, one in the disguise of a woman. Finally, in the spring of 1690, he was shipped back to England, along with a set of charges against himself and Councilor Joseph Dudley, who was dispatched with him. The charges had been prepared by Massachusetts Bay's interim governor, eighty-six-year-old Simon Bradstreet, and his "Council of Safety." The royal court was impressed neither by their eloquence nor by their authority; instead, King William absolved Dudley of all the points made against him and, figuratively, clasped Andros to the royal bosom.

Increase Mather and other Puritans in London continued to plead that the movement against Andros had come "from the people," from the Boston townspeople. But the king also learned from a quickly prepared study and an official report that a "violent and bloody zeal was stird up in the Rabble acted and managed by the Preachers." The report made a valid point. Despite the claim of some sentimental historians that the overthrow of Andros constituted a popular revolt, the event is properly seen as an affair managed by the town's commercial-religious elite, an affair in which the people vigorously cooperated. Like the Boston Tea Party almost a century later, it had been conceived and put into effect by the traditional leaders of the town, using the people's rage-become-revenge as their cover. Yet that does not mean the people had no share in the overthrow's execution or import.

Indeed, a close examination of what happened during the riot of April 18, 1689, shows that the people of the waterfront were involved in ways not just physical but also political. On their way to the Town House, the crowd made a point of swinging past the jail, from which they freed a crew of privateers whom Andros had imprisoned for piracy and murder. The crowd wanted it known that in the judgment of the people, such actions were no longer grounds for condemnation. The crowd then surged on to attack a lodging house in the North End where they knew that the captain of the patrol ship *Rose* was ensconced. Hauling him out by the collar, they marched him off to prison. Along with the message that the captain and his kind were to be tolerated no longer in Boston Harbor, they

Congested with naval vessels (foreground), as well as fishing smacks and merchantmen (background, right), Boston Harbor boomed with activity in this 1725 view by
artist William Burgis. At the far left is the narrow Neck, which connected the hilly
peninsula to the mainland; to the right of that rises Fort Hill, where Governor
Andros was imprisoned by the people of the town.

made the subsidiary point that they were responsible citizens, not
about to indulge in killing or property destruction.

The royal court of inquiry in London remained convinced that
the Bay Colony's old guard was solely to blame. The Bostonians'
argument in court that Andros had fallen to a *popular* uprising made
little sense; *the people*, as they were then perceived, could not conceiv-
ably have entered into such a high-stakes political drama. The
judges deemed Increase Mather and his supporters to be representatives of a disloyal, old-fashioned, and somewhat foolish clique.
King William let Andros, the former governor-general, know that
he, by contrast, was regarded as an effective and trustworthy officer—despite the fact that the war on the northern frontier was now
raging quite out of control. Making a final decision in the matter of
the small revolt in Boston, the king appointed Andros the governor
of Virginia. He held that post quite respectably until 1698, when as
an elderly knight he moved on to become the governor of his
beloved island of Jersey.

Andros's overthrow by the Boston leadership and the cooperating crowds was not, it must be said, the first toppling of a British governor in America. That distinction goes to the royal colony of Virginia and to Governor Sir William Berkeley, who had had to run for his life from the capital, Jamestown, back in 1676. To compare these two rebellions and another nearly contemporary one in New York is to gain an understanding that they were all upheavals along the stress and fault lines of the British Empire, where local ambitions went one way and imperial policies another.

The leader of the Virginia settlers who had struck at the Crown was Nathaniel Bacon Jr., a planter from Henrico County. Curiously, young Bacon looked not much like a rebel, being related to the governor and having received several favors from him. But when Sir William imposed upon the colony a new policy that seemed to favor the Indians, Bacon raised a troop of volunteers and stormed into the territory of the Pamunkey tribesmen. The governor struck back, riding out after Bacon with a troop of three hundred "well armed" gentlemen. Bacon fled into hiding but soon returned to power as a newly elected member of the House of Burgesses. His presence there coincided with the passing of several reform laws, but Bacon himself should not be seen as a reformer. His backwoodsman's focus was entirely on Indians and their rich lands, which he coveted.

When it became clear that the governor was not going to change his policies and would not allow the settlers to persecute Native Americans further, Bacon stormed out of the Burgesses, returning with an armed band to surround the statehouse. The governor was forced to flee to Virginia's eastern shore, leaving Bacon to become the self-appointed ruler of the colony from July through September 1767. Sir William returned with sufficient forces to drive Bacon out of the capital, though Jamestown was burned by Bacon soon thereafter. Ultimately, bad luck was the winner, with Bacon dying of the "Bloodie Flux" in October 1676, thereby evading the noose.

In recognition of that turn of events, Virigina schoolchildren learned to sing this ditty:

Bacon is Dead.
I am sorry at my hart
That lice and flux
Should take the hangman's part.

There was, indeed, little of historic consequence about the so-called Bacon's Rebellion—except that it did show that Englishmen-turned-American settlers tended to have a different view of what part of America they owned than did their English governors, and that they could take violent action to prove their point. Somewhat more closely related to Boston's overturning of Governor-General Andros was the destiny of Lieutenant Governor Francis Nicholson, who had served as Andros's right-hand man in New York.

Opposing Lieutenant Governor Nicholson and his officers, along with their clique of aristocratic patroons and rich fur traders in New York City, was a successful Germany-born merchant named Jacob Leisler. He had become the leader of a rising faction of shopkeepers, small farmers, and artisans. When news of the Glorious Revolution and the imprisonment of Andros reached New York, Leisler and his followers took possession of Fort James at the southern end of Manhattan (May 31, 1689) as a direct challenge to royal authority. When Nicholson capitulated and was allowed to sail off to England, Leisler took charge of the entire province. He and his largely Lutheran and Dutch Reformed middle-class partisans might be described as bourgeois who had caused a collapse of the Anglican upper crust.

Yet Leisler was neither a socially concerned democrat nor a popular leader. He did, however, summon the first intercolonial congress in America (May 1690), a significant attempt to mount a concerted drive against French Canada and the northern Native Americans. This attack, part of the war named for King William that Andros had sparked by his assault on Pentagoet, was doomed to fail. Its chief purpose had been to capture Montreal, but thanks largely to Leisler's inability to raise enough men or to persuade the Iroquois to join in the plan, it went nowhere.

Soon afterward, New York's Fort James came under an expected attack by the Crown's forces. At first, Leisler refused to surrender, forcing a battle in which two soldiers were killed and several wounded. But when Colonel Henry Sloughter arrived on March 19, announcing that he was the king's newly appointed governor, Leisler lowered his flag. He and his main accomplice, his son-in-law Jacob Milborne, were not to be so lucky as Nathaniel Bacon: they were convicted of treason and executed on May 16, 1691. Soon, it was as if nothing like a revolt had ever taken place in New York.

In Boston, however, the results of the crowd's expulsion of Andros were like seeds grown into a mighty forest, a prominent feature on New England's cultural panorama. Here, unlike the oblivion into which Leisler sank or the mocking ditty about Bacon, one heard Andros referred to across the generations as "a tyrant as any New England schoolboy will tell you." He was the evil British tyrant whose dethroning would serve as a paradigm for future rulers. Governor Joseph Dudley, installed in 1702, was hated and hounded to the end of his days for his unforgettable service as one of Andros's council members; Governor James Shute, installed in 1716, was frightened out of the province by threats from mounting opposition. Contributing to the downfall of Governor Francis Bernard at the time of the Tea Party was his failure to heed that well-established tradition.

This peculiar pattern of political action in Boston seemed to bridge the classes, or rather to reflect the homogeneous conviction of the merchants, the mariners, and other townspeople that no outside power should interfere with their businesses. That conviction combined the policies and the desires of the traditional elite in their merchant mansions with the needs and the moods of the maritime laborers in their waterfront underworld. Rooted in the history of Boston—that is to say, in the town's oft-noted bigotry and its risky mercantilism—this throwing overboard of unsympathetic British rulers can hardly be viewed as one of the classical wellsprings of American democracy. But in its early form, it had sufficient authenticity to unseat royal governors and to defeat British admirals (as the next chapter will illustrate). Developed over the decades and through the generations, it had enough dynamism by 1775 to constitute one violent part of the American Revolution.

# 3

# The Rising of the Mobs

Years after a grisly event at sea in the year 1717, Boston parents scared bad children into better behavior by reminding them of what had happened to Captain Samuel Bellamy, master of the pirate ship *Whidah*. After Captain Bellamy had succeeded in capturing a small trading vessel rigged as a snow[*] as she was sailing into Massachusetts Bay, he demanded that the boat's skipper lead him and his black-flagged squadron into the harbor of Provincetown, presumably for bloody purposes. If the skipper complied, he would be freed and would get his snow back. But the skipper, having agreed to the deal, fooled Bellamy by tossing overboard a burning tar barrel that decoyed the pirate ships onto the mud banks of Wellfleet bar.

In the ensuing wreck, more than a hundred pirate crewmen were said to have perished, their bodies claimed by the tidal currents and cast up on the shores of Cape Cod. Only nine of the crewmen survived; of these, six were captured, condemned, and executed.

---

[*]This curiously named vessel was essentially a brig made more maneuverable by the addition of a triangular fore-and-aft sail raised on a short mast aft of the square-rigged mainmast—as if a small mizzen were added to a schooner.

Decades later, broken ship timbers could still be seen. Ghosts of the drowned brigands continued to haunt the coast, their howls heard at night over the crash of the breakers. Essayist Henry David Thoreau reported a man of "very singular and frightful aspect," possibly one of the survivors, wandering the beaches in the off-seasons, searching for coins from the treasure chests of the foundered ships.

No portrait of Boston in the early or mid-eighteenth century could be called accurate that omitted the reality and the specter of piracy. No seaman or fisherman regarded the pirate's life as impossible to consider. A short-term tour of duty under the skull and crossbones might help him and his family through a period of unemployment. Piracy as a prospect and a threat constantly enlivened newsletters and diaries of the time. The execution of pirate captain John Quelch and his five confederates on June 30, 1704–an event sufficiently important to command the presence of forty musketeers and two ministers–was considered by reporters a splendid augury for the new century. Less well reported were other maritime sins in which Bostonians of all ranks participated: illegal trading, customs evading, and ship-wrecking. These were the outlawed and the traditional behaviors that both enlivened and enriched the town and gave it its special, irregular character, dependent on the sea.

In the years between Andros's expulsion in 1689 and the Stamp Act crisis of 1765, Boston's maritime crowds provoked and participated in at least twenty-eight riots and illegal actions. Such "tumults" went beyond the fractiousness that might be expected of seamen and waterfront laborers anywhere. For example, in the comparable ports of New York and Philadelphia there were, respectively, only four and six similar events during these years. No, this tumultuous opposition to authority was something peculiarly Bostonian, an aspect of what Harvard historian Justin Winsor recognized more than a century later as among the town's carefully preserved "local characteristics," cultivated down through time and aided by the "stationary [meaning inbred] character of the population."

Yet during those same years of the eighteenth century preceding the Revolution, not all was piracy, parochialism, and popular unrest in Boston. The town, even with its isolated geographical position and its generally unmixed social character, became once again an international boomtown. Indeed, it stood forth as the American colonies' busiest and most aggressive port. As townsmen repeatedly boasted, more than five hundred vessels sailed out of its island-protected harbor to distant lands each year. A nearly equal number sailed home, passing through the well-protected narrow passage ("not above 160 foot wide . . . at high water") that led to the inner harbor. Having been sighted by the lookout at Castle William, each of the incoming ships and lesser vessels was hailed with a welcoming signal. Whether they berthed at the Long Wharf, the official point of entry, which had room for upward of thirty trading vessels, or at one of the fifty other wharves, they functioned as essential components of the town's commercial calculus.

To its financial detriment, the port of Boston could never benefit from a hinterland yielding a great wealth of products for export. By 1735, however, upcountry farmers had begun to produce enough surplus goods so that local merchants' vessels carried abroad a variety of homegrown beef and pork, as well as the long-standing exports of lumber, fish, and whale oil. Incoming vessels brought rice, pitch, and spices from the West Indies, in addition to vast quantities of cane sugar, both for Boston's eight rum-producing "still-houses" and for distilleries in other New England towns.

Since Boston-built ships carried the bulk of coastal trading at this time, as well as a good share of the British Empire's ocean-borne cargo, the number of shipyards in the town had grown to sixteen, the number of ropewalks to eight. The population doubled between 1690 and 1740, from seven thousand to more than fifteen thousand. Despite strict observance of the Lord's Day and even with tribal memories of Puritan ways, Boston could no longer be viewed as the aloof Cittie on the Hill. Quite properly, it was regarded as the "Mart Town of the Indies" and, as such, was subject to all the external stresses of Great Britain's imperial system.

## "Take the First Wind, and If You Think It Safe . . ."

It was precisely because of all the town's busy traffic in trade that the pirate ships existed, hovering in offshore waters. They resembled the bluefish that swam in the same waters and that, on catching a glimpse of silvery masses, swooped in to devour schools of mackerel. And it was precisely because of the cutthroat aspect of its overseas trade that Boston struck foreign visitors as a cruel contradiction between the adventurously rich and the desperately deprived. Proud merchant families, their ships having failed to return, collapsed, joining other destitute men and women at the almshouse door. Boston's population was heavily overbalanced with women, many of them having been widowed by sailors lost at sea or by seamen killed in battle. So severe was the toll in the recently completed King William's War that preacher Cotton Mather estimated in 1715 that a fifth of his congregation were war widows.

More important, as certain merchants of Boston prospered magnificently by raising their sails to the new winds of commerce, so the bulk of the population suffered from the destruction of the ancient Puritan welfare state and the basic instability of the emerging economy. Crime and burglary by night became, for the first time, communal issues. There were, to be sure, the previously mentioned public institutions to take care of the poor—the almshouses and the make-work programs like spinning houses for women who might not have excessive pride. But the numbers of the poor kept increasing as more and more job-seeking families moved to town in the wake of disappointing harvests and denominational disruptions in the surrounding communities. As a result, the number of poor in Boston rose 14 percent in the years after the ousting of Andros and before the Revolution. In other words, by 1757, one out of every eight townspeople was on poor relief.

There was one chief cause for this distress: the port of Boston had been replaced by more seaward locations (particularly, Marblehead) as New England's fishing headquarters. As a secondary cause, the labor of seamen and carpenters was not so much in demand in overbuilt and overpopulated Boston as it had been in earlier times. Yet despite disappointments and depressions, the dream of wealth to be won by going to sea continued to have a seductive appeal for Bostonians of all types and classes. Women, who once had seen their men go off fishing while they themselves went out to seek jobs washing the clothes or polishing the silver of

This may Certify all whom it may Concern; *that the Bearer hereof is an Inlisted* MONTROSS *at his* MAJESTY'S NORTH-BATTERY, *in* Boston *under my Command. Given under my Hand this In the Year of his Majesty's reign*

This may Certify all whom it may Concern. *Tho. M. is an Inlisted Montross, at his* MAJESTY'S *South Battery, in* Boston, *under my Command, Given under my Hand this In the Year of his Majesty's reign.*

*Located at the ends of Boston Harbor's curving shoreline, the stone-fronted North and South Batteries, as depicted on these certificates, served as the port's prime defenses against marauders and also sheltered naval repair yards. Such certificates were granted to waterfront laborers who had been conscripted as "montrosses" (actually, matrosses, or gunnery apprentices).*
Courtesy of the Bostonian Society

the rich, now, as successive wars broke out (Queen Anne's War of 1701–1713 and King George's War of 1745–1748), saw their men go off privateering or for a bit of smuggling. Or even for smuggling's first cousin, piracy.

Before one of these high-seas adventures, the seaman was generally offered a berth in hoarse whispers from a skipper across a tavern table. The rewards sounded worth the risk, even though these were not set up as wage-earning jobs, unlike the berths won by crewmen on merchant ships. Demanding of life and limb, these on-the-sly operations called for many months at sea, as well as the chance of being captured by an enemy or, more often, returning home with no gold or silver to show for it. Only occasionally were the profits for ordinary seamen notable, even if a stunning prize was captured. In 1746, the French *Soleil* was captured after a dramatic chase and was brought into Boston Harbor with a cargo estimated at a value of £30,000. After courts and officers had helped themselves to the bulk of it, the lucky seamen each claimed £78, considered a fortune.

Another much-heralded capture at sea was scored by the ship *Bethel*, owned by the Quincy family. She carried twenty-four guns and a crew of 110 men; a "letter of marque" authorized her captain to seize perceived enemies as prizes and to divide the spoils among officers and men. In 1748, the *Bethel*, cruising southern waters, came upon a Spanish treasure ship bound for home in Cadiz. After a bloody contest of crashing masts and splintered wood, the Americans triumphed, bringing back to Boston a reputed hundred thousand pounds of bullion. It is not recorded how large the seaman's share was that would have been granted by the Quincys, but it is known that the Quincys themselves became rich enough to gain admission to the town's merchant oligarchy.

For Boston's highest-rolling merchants and shipowners, those who might be lucky in times of both war and peace, the chances of their captains' bringing home fortune-making cargoes were imperiled not just by French privateers and Spanish men-of-war but also by British regulations. That had not always been the case. Until the middle of the eighteenth century, the great landowners of Britain who had the ears of Parliament and the king had remained content to see the American colonies prosper. Whatever illegalities at sea and customs irregularities in port might be involved, customs officials winked and governors looked the other way. For everyone benefited: the famous triangular—actually, quadrilateral—trade pattern allowed Americans to pay off debts incurred for receipt of British goods with letters of credit won by their shipping of fish to Iberia and to the West Indies and by their return of molasses. Prosperous Boston merchants and their wives made English tradesmen additionally rich by ordering a steady stream of luxury items. Portraits of the period by the precocious Bostonian John Singleton Copley, who won first fame at age sixteen, glow with the magnificence of these imported clothes and hangings, furniture and glassware.

An advertisement in the *News-Letter* of August 27, 1716 (cited by Winsor), gives an idea of the variety of these luxuries and the height of that style:

This is to give notice, That at the House of Mr. George Brownell, late School Master in Hanover Street, Boston, are all sorts of Millinary Works done; making up Dresses and flowers of Muslin, making of furbelow'd Scarffs, and Quilting and cutting of Gentlewomen's Hair in the newest Fashion; and also young Gentlewomen and Children taught all sorts of fine works, as Feather-work, Filigre, and Painting on Glass, Embroidering a new way, Turkey-work for Handkerchiefs two ways, fine new Fashion Purses, flourishing and plain Work, and Dancing cheaper than was ever taught in Boston. Brocaded work for Handkerchiefs and short Apron upon Muslin; artificial flowers worked with a needle.

Along with the newfound sense of luxury went a growing perception of rank. Whereas in Boston of Puritan times, black or gray was the color of everyone's clothes, and only the clergy existed on a plane above anyone else, now there were the governor's councilmen, the royal magistrates, the honorable this and that. Deference had to paid by workaday men and women to the ladies and the gentlemen, for whom they had to make way on the sidewalk. Whereas the top 10 percent of Boston society had owned less than half the town's assets in earlier times, now they commanded nearly

80 percent. And along with that property went control of the town's politics: they were given the government's contracts, and they supported the governor.

It was a society of merchant aristocrats and indentured servants, with a small middle class of artisans and tradesmen. Something like a fifth of the population, representing the upper and the middle classes, owned slaves and thought that absolutely proper. Whereas, in the country towns, church seating for families was still assigned by the long-accepted social rank system, now in Boston seats were assigned by who paid the most—a clear recognition that even on Sundays, wealth spoke and was the dominant criterion.

Yet when British plantations in the Indies began to decline in the 1720s—largely as a result of the intransigencies and the horrors of the slave labor (including suicide, abortion, and harshly repressed uprisings)—the great capitalists in England changed their let-live-and-let-prosper attitude toward the North American colonies. They demanded of the king's administrators that they enact revenue-producing laws that would benefit the plantations and thereby strengthen the king's entire imperialist-mercantilist system. The Molasses Act of 1733 was the result, followed in 1747 by another similar act, one that involved lower fees but called for an extremely strict examination of ships' holds.

Among the prudent and typically sly merchants of Boston in these pre-Revolutionary years, Thomas Hancock played an increasingly important role. For many reasons beyond having been the uncle of the better-known John Hancock, Thomas deserves recognition as a man who helped build his town into a successful commercial entrepot—and helped keep the money flowing even in difficult times. He had risen from impoverished clergy family beginnings, lucky to have found a job as a bookseller and a wealthy widow as a wife. These he translated into the greatest fortune in Boston, including ownership of one of the largest wharves and an investment in at least two privateers. Yet his was a highly competitive, incredibly risky business, with ships that never returned and financial procedures that demanded constant attention. It is instructive for us today to read the letter he penned to his captain Simon Gross in December 1743 and to keep an eye on how he ordered the

captain to be evasive here, not altogether honest there. The first part
of the letter reads,

> You having the Command of the *Charming Lydia* Brigantine,
> and She in all Respects fit for the Sea, My Order to you is that
> you take the first wind & weather for Sailing and proceed to
> the West Indies. You have Liberty to go to any of the English
> Islands, & if you think it Safe, to any of the French Islands.
> But I advise you to proceed direct to St. Eustatia where you
> will learn how the Marketts Govern, & advise with Mr. Godet
> on your affairs, after which you will be able to form a better
> Judgement where will be the best place to make a voyage, &
> so proceed accordingly. You have Invoice & Bill of Lading
> Inclosed Consigned to yourself, you are to procure a Load of
> Molasses & proceed back to Boston & if you have more Cargo
> than loads you, then Ship it on the best Terms you Can in
> Molasses or bring it in Indigo. I'd have you unload at Nantas-
> ket [Boston's outer harbor] if no man of War there. You are
> Interested in One eighth in the Cargo & are to have one
> eighth of the neat proceeds of Returns; I doubt not of your
> making the best Sale of everything. . . .

The letter ends,

> . . . a load of Molasses will be the best Cargo you can bring
> here; write me all Opportunitys. The Good Lord protect you
> & our Interests, From all Dangers & Enemies & Give you
> Conduct & prudence in all things to act for the Best. I wish
> you a Good Voyage & am your Owner.

His owner, indeed. His nervous owner, in fact, for the letter
shows how after the great expansion that preceded the Molasses
Act, Boston merchants were feeling the squeeze from enemy and
king alike. There followed the punishing depression of 1740, an
event that might be understood now as one of the inevitable consequences of a capitalistic economy. But then—with merchants' families like the ostentatious Olivers careering around in their handsome

carriages and with ladies like Mrs. Hutchinson vying to show off the latest fashions—it seemed oppressively cruel to those who were affected most by the hard times, the unemployed and impoverished people of the waterfront. They appeared to have been abandoned by their own city, the ideal of the commonwealth having been nearly forgotten. They seemed to have but one recourse: to rise up and claim some fish heads and maybe more for themselves.

## Merchants, Masters, and Mariners: Alliance on the Waterfront

As history has often demonstrated, a lack of bread can make desperate the minds of urban populations. This is particularly true when the people are isolated from natural supply systems and dependent on civil authorities for fair marketing arrangements. In Boston, the first of a great series of riots was caused by this lack of bread at a decent price. The dreadful bread riots, to Boston's cumulative distress, occurred coincidentally with the tremendously destructive fire of 1711, the smallpox plague of 1721*, and the inflation accompanying the end of King William's War. Historian Paul Gilje has marked the bread riots of 1710, 1713, and 1729 as being of special note for their violence and mounting impact. They must also be understood as part of the perhaps predictable behavior of hungry men and women in this parochial port during a stressful time when its old, fish-prosperous days gave way to the new preindustrial times and as its free-swinging maritime laborers became an often unemployed underclass lacking other opportunities.

Riots against monopolistic and overcharging butchers also disturbed the Boston scene during these years, with some of the actions severe enough to resemble mass uprisings. The basic issue in these contentions between the nearly starving people and the

---

*On the well-known 1722 map of Boston by John Bonner (page 2), the cartographer, feeling impelled to chronicle the town's formative incidents as well as its topography, listed the eight "Great Fires" and the six smallpox outbreaks that occurred between the time of founding and 1721.

conservative and rich authorities was that the once-Puritan town had not solved the problem of establishing a regulated and equitable market. A public granary had been set up as a rather passive experiment in 1714, but the mistrusting people had torn it apart. They believed more in their own skills at finding a bargain here or a special deal there than in any scheme of regulations engineered by the town's elite. That freedom of choice had always been a part of local waterfront tradition. The people seethed in their neighborhoods and considered taking action not just in the interest of bread and meat but in the defense of traditonal ways.

Led by such newly popular figures as Dr. Elisha Cooke Sr. and attracting great numbers of women and children, the mobs rose up in 1736 and destroyed the market in North Square as a public insult—a "threat to Englishmen." Some of the men who cut down the market house's posts disguised themselves as clergymen in order to make the point more clearly that they were acting as agents of communal morality (and, of course, to disguise themselves). They announced in a public letter that they were "five hundred men [who had vowed] in solemn League and Covenant to stand by one another, and [who could] secure Seven hundred more of the same mind." Having wrought their damage by night, they became known as the Midnight Mob.

Governor Jonathan Belcher, the scion of one of Boston's largest shipping fortunes, answered them, using the word *seditious* to describe those who continued to oppose his official plan. His colleague the Reverend Benjamin Colman helped the matter not at all by urging "inferior" people not to mutiny against their ordained subservient position. Jack Tager, the historian who has distinguished himself by analyzing, most tellingly, the phenomenon of Boston's perennial mobs, quotes Colman as preaching contemptuously against the lower-class sorts who were inclined to take "rash and very sinful steps . . . in open defiance of that Government which God has set over them." Yet Tager points out that Belcher and other upper-class Bostonians were impotent in the face of the mob's fury. The people had succeeded in punishing the butchers, in destroying the markets, and in making the climactic point that they were powerful enough to fear no reprisals.

This may seem a puzzlingly easy victory for a time when heads were supposed to bow at the name of the king and when magistrates were revered as parts of a natural, divinely sanctioned order. At the very least, it seems a strange nonfunctioning of police power. But, in the words of Professor Alfred Young, "law enforcement was not yet invested" in New England's authorities. In fact, Boston had only twelve constables (called "officers"), amounting to only one of them for every 1,250 inhabitants of Boston, hardly enough to hold down a rebellion. The governor also had but a handful of soldiers at his disposal, and he realized the dangers of using them. It was the support of the public, their readiness to act in the cause of justice and good order, that he normally counted on to keep the town under control. It was also this sense of good order that had brought the people forth to tear down certain showy brothels in the North End in 1734 and 1737. And it was this sense, allied to New Englanders' willingness to aid a neighbor in putting up his barn, that brought out firefighters with cries of "Town born! Turn out!" whenever that dread bell rang.

But as the 1730s advanced, that same type of communal action, spontaneous or planned, threatened Governor Belcher's authority. The vulgar mob—so called from the Latin, *vulgus mobilis*—had become such an impudent force that, as Pastor Colman observed, its members seemed to be shaking their fists at the king himself. In addition to the inadequate constabulary, Belcher had at his right hand a dozen councilmen who naturally supported his concept that power should flow from the top down. He and his magistrates could also summon a posse (referring to selected individuals who were specially empowered) to assist in times of trouble. There was, as well, the militia, but its members seemed to swing too frequently in the direction of the mob. Indeed, there were troubling signs of a curious alliance being made between the mobbish underworld and certain members of the newly prominent merchant class.

This alliance was becoming more and more obvious as the eighteenth century progressed. Back in 1701, by contrast, a tip from a sailor not sensitive to the way Boston worked alerted customs officials to an illegal cargo on the ship *Bean and Cole*. She was seized under the terms of the hated Acts of Trade, and the owners were judged guilty and fined. But after the trial, the presiding judge, a proper Bostonian, caught up with the tipster in the street and subjected the turncoat sailor to a brutal cudgeling.

A similar event occurred in 1723, when two sailors reported that their ship, the *William and Mary*, had secretly landed a cargo of untaxed goods. In this case, Tager's research gives us an account that is even more graphic. After the tipsters had presented their evidence in court, "some merchants and masters of ships with a great number of other persons in a violent and mobbish manner assaulted the said evidences [informers], Kicked and pushed them downstairs and beat one of them so unmercifully dragging him thro' the streets that it is not yet known what may be the consequence."

So concerned was the then governor Samuel Shute about these unified activities on and off the waterfront that he committed an almost unforgivable act of local betrayal: he wrote to the treasury in England asking for troops "so that our Officers and their assistants may be protected in the execution of their duty." But still the attacks went on, attacks that involved Bostonians from the judge-and-merchant rank to the dockside laborers and the underground toughs. Given that nearly a quarter of Boston's male population was involved in maritime activities (meaning, in many cases, handling smuggled goods), small wonder that this large diversity of people resisted any heavy-handed judicial threats to their community of interests.

Yet it should be remembered that the sailor was always perceived as existing on the edge, the salty and stinky edge, of society. Although the seaman was an essential ingredient in the creation of the merchants' wealth, and although his shanty may have stood beside the merchant's mansion in the North End (where 61 percent of Boston lived), he did not really have a share of, or much of a chance in, the merchants' world. Because he most often had no property, he was excluded from the political process. He functioned as part of a separate, inferior community—the crew.

The maritime scholar Marcus Rediker points out that as the business of shipping became an international industry in the mid-eighteenth century, wage-earning seamen became the world's first collective laborers. Along with that, as mentioned earlier, the seamen became associated less with the rising apprentices and the

striving citizens of the port and more with the passing-through out-
siders and the racially mixed laborers on the cosmopolitan waterfront. In those years, when the population was booming as never
before as a result of immigration (from seven thousand in 1690 to
more than fifteen thousand in 1740), the look of Boston's waterfront
was definitely not Anglo-Saxon: African Americans, many of them
assigned to work as carters and stevedores for the wharfingers, constituted 8 percent of the town's total population. White seamen also
functioned as a part of this underworld of escaped slaves, runaway
indentured servants, and deserters from warship crews. And here a
special danger lurked: in that dockside company, the New England
sailor was a ripe candidate for capture and impressment in the
Royal Navy. Particularly in times of war, the harbor front of Boston,
even more than those of other American ports, was a kind of battle-
ground. A running war raged between impressment crews from
anchored warships and terrified seamen seeking to escape a shipboard life that they perceived as near-certain death. Rediker esti-
mates that easily half of those impressed died at sea; if the men did
survive, with all their limbs, it was to describe their life as a brutal-
ization as severe as slavery. The impressment teams and the hunted
men hated each other with a mutual passion. The officers who dispatched the teams, those tough-minded captains and admirals dedicated to defending England's overseas colonies, regarded the
seamen as near-criminals and viewed the Boston merchants who
sided with them as near-traitors. Indeed, the merchants challenged
the navy's priorities by wooing incoming sailors with offers of rich-
sounding posts aboard ships of marque. They also joined the seamen in fighting impressment, daring on occasion to oppose the
authority of the king's officers.

When matters came to trial, and when a contest developed
between His Majesty's navy and civil authority, defenders of the
seamen cited a law called the Sixth of Anne. This liberal piece of legislation had been passed by Parliament in 1708 during the reign of
Queen Anne "for the Encouragement of Trade to America." It had
supposedly freed all American seamen, aboard ship or on shore,
from impressment, stating that only naval deserters could be
grabbed. But naval commanders, under the stresses of war, went

ahead with impressment anyway, winning the royal wink for their actions, and in 1746 they succeeded in having the law repealed. Nonetheless, American seamen and their backers all through this period continued to protest that they, as English citizens, should be free from such oppression.

They gave as a hideous example of injustice a case from the preceding century when, in 1693, a press gang had pulled two of the colony's legislators from their very beds, their unjustifiable action forcing the governor to seize the offending captain and send him back to England in irons. Tager also reports an incident in 1741 when Lieutenant Governor Thomas Povey had had to order a cannon barrage fired against a man-of-war that had been pressing Bostonians without a legal warrant. One important rule that was established stated that after obtaining a warrant, the captain was pledged not to take men from any outward-bound vessel. Such a practice, it was agreed, would interfere excessively with the port's trade.

But still the warships patrolled the harbor menacingly. In 1741, merchants complained of the ready-to-pounce posture of the HMS *Portland,* which "greatly Terrifies the Coasters and other Vessels bringing Grain, Wood, &C [sic] to this Town." Since Bostonians had long ago stripped their peninsula of its natural resources, just as they and others had depleted Massachusetts Bay of many of its fish, the citizens were indeed dependent on coasters to bring in vitally needed supplies. In that same year, after a crowd had resisted two officials bent on seizing native sailors, the town meeting issued a paper pleading the case against impressment. The authors of the paper referred sadly to "the once cherished now depressed, once flourishing, now sinking Town of Boston." Thus they gave polite, even poetic expression to a fact that the jeopardized mariners had long recognized and would emphasize again and again with their violence: His Majesty's impressment of crews could not be tolerated in Boston.

## The Continuing Perils of Impressment

In addition to riots and "tumults" for bread and meat and against customs officials and impressment, Boston's waterfront mobs had another favorite target for their violence: foreigners of the Catholic persuasion, particularly Irishmen. That ingrained, spooky fear of papist devils had by no means disappeared after the hangings and the burnings of the seventeenth century gave way to the more enlightened eighteenth. In July 1729, an aroused crowd prevented the landing of an Irish ship on the Boston wharves. In 1736, the town's selectmen forbade a packet from Ireland to land any of its passengers. Here again, the merchants and the mariners exercised communal, even official, action that evidenced their common purpose, however strained their homogeneity might be. It demonstrated that what Pastor Jonathan Mayhew had called the "sensitivity" of the Boston mind knew no class boundaries.

The religious element in the town's character intensified, rather than leached out, in the 1730s. This was the time of the so-called Great Awakening, when such "New Light" preachers as Jonathan Edwards and Gilbert Tennet hurled bolts of Old Testament fire from their pulpits. In the process, they inveighed against earthly riches and called on individual men and women to seek repentance before it was too late. When the English evangelist George Whitefield came to Boston in 1739, it was with the intention of bringing the unfettered gospel to working people in that essentially urban, authoritarian environment. Appalled at the ostentation and the rank-consciousness he found among the town's merchant elite, he was determined to help the poor seek their own salvation, not by violence but through his brand of evangelical Christianity. Eventually, Whitefield's emotional sermons against the merchant life and the secular way of looking at things turned Harvard's initially supportive faculty against him.

Yet George Whitefield did join Bostonians of all classes in seeing Catholics, including the French Canadians, as a dangerous threat to the Cittie on the Hill. The concept of a devil lurking in Canada had become increasingly popular among members of the Codfish Aristocracy as their fishing ketches and schooners in the Gulf of Maine were threatened by privateers operating out of Acadian ports. Governor Dudley had been fond of referring to Nova Scotia's ports as "those nests of robbers." That sentiment was heightened during Europe's War of the Austrian Succession (linked to the strangely named War of Jenkins's Ear), which began in 1740 and gradually spread to the South and North American colonies. The war had a devastating effect on the economy of Massachusetts, causing further depression and higher taxes. With the province's regular overseas trade jeopardized and its offshore fisheries at risk, the treasury could issue only paper money on the basis of zero assets and minimal expectations. Simultaneously, menacing rumors blew in on the east winds about Louis XV's immense expenditures to strengthen and equip the Gibraltar-like fortress of Louisbourg on the easternmost crag of Nova Scotia's Cape Breton Island.

In the eyes of the Bay Colony's shrewd governor, William Shirley (whose term lasted from 1741 to 1757), the idea of a campaign against the French Canadians appeared to be both godly and financially advantageous. It also looked like a good bet to the band of enterprising merchants who supported Shirley's regime. Thomas Hancock, for one, was pleased to be granted a generous goods-supplying contract for the grand expedition. Shirley enlisted the aid of Preacher George Whitefield in convincing the best available leader, Maine's militia colonel William Pepperrell, that he should take charge of an armada and should set forth in the spring of 1745.

For the difficult task of rounding up the necessary numbers of soldiers and sailors, Pepperrell had several attractive ideas: he would offer a decent wage (25 shillings a month) plus a blanket, and he would see that any debt charges against a volunteer would be suspended during his service time. Most important, in an arrangement made with British authorities, he would guarantee to all who served that they would be exempt from navy impressment on return. There was also the implication that plunder would be available. Men rallied from all the New England colonies; those from America's southern colonies declined, considering the affair just another typical Yankee bit of risky adventurism. The Reverend John Barnard of Marblehead, regarded as the fishermen's saint, gave the blessing to the fleet and it sailed off, three thousand strong. The campaign, for all its religious dressings, bore a closer resemblance to a Viking raid than to a crusade.

After establishing a secure base at Canso on the tip of mainland Nova Scotia just southwest of Louisbourg, Pepperrell and Commodore Peter Warren (the commander in chief of Great Britain's naval forces) landed an expeditionary force of nearly two thousand men at Louisbourg at the end of April 1745. By mid-May, that force's cannons were bombarding the outworks, its soldiers surrounding the fort, and its camp followers plundering the nearby villages. When the fort fell in June, Pepperrell—who had at first irritated, then impressed Warren with his unflappable deliberateness—ordered that the plunderers be restrained. Although he lost some of his popularity with that decision, he gained it back when he increased the soldiers' pay upon learning that their occupation time in Louisbourg would have to be extended.

On returning to Boston, Pepperrell was hailed as a hero and was knighted by the king. His special virtue, in the eyes of Massachusetts Bay authorities, was that his conquest of Louisbourg had liberated sufficient treasure for the colony to restore the value of the province's dangerously depreciated currency. The other participating New England colonies also benefited from the victory, because it reestablished briefly and to some small degree the economic health of the region. J. S. McLennan, the author of the definitive *Louisbourg*, finds, specifically, that the following amounts in pounds sterling went into these provincial treasuries: Massachusetts, £183,649; New Hampshire, £16,355; Connecticut, £28,863; and Rhode Island, £547. Pepperrell had indeed earned his baronetcy.

Warren received his share of rewards as well: he was saluted at court and made Admiral of the Blue. Moving on to mightier imperial posts, he left behind him his second in command, the irascible but influential Captain Charles Knowles. Knowles's daunting assignment was not only to maintain order at Louisbourg but also to establish British rule throughout Acadia. Yet within little more than a year, to Knowles's joy (and undoubtedly because of his connections), he was relieved of that chilly duty, promoted to commodore, and invited to take command of Great Britain's squadron in the West Indies. War had broken out again, King George's War (1745–1748), and Knowles intended to shine in it. The fact that his ships' crews were diminished by the plagues that had hit land and sea forces during the Louisbourg siege meant simply that he would have to acquire more sailors when stopping in Boston to replenish stores on his way south. The guarantees of freedom from impressment issued to veterans of the siege bothered him not at all.

Back in November 1745, a few months after the fall of Louisbourg and exactly two years before Commodore Knowles's squadron dropped its anchors in Boston Harbor, an incident had occurred that alerted the waterfront once again to the perils of wartime impressment. The officers on the HMS *Wager* had set about that fell business by first obtaining a warrant from Massachusetts Lieutenant Governor Spenser Phips and pledging thereby that they would not take either men from the province or "any of the men that had been in the Late Expedition" (meaning Louisbourg). They then led a press gang into the North End for what turned out to be a bloody free-for-all. At a captain's house where seamen were lodged, a tremendous battle ensued, in the course of which two local sailors, while fighting back, were "stab'd and hack'd" to death. To make the outrage worse, the murdered men had both been veterans of Louisbourg. Though comrades of the slain men managed to restrain and hold two of the impressment team, most of them escaped, sailing away the next day.

The official arrest order for the restrained navy men, issued by Lieutenant Governor Phips, rings with what might be called Bostonian high dudgeon. It demands justice so that "the Guilt of Blood shall not ly upon this Land." The town meeting, for its part, charged the arrested men with breach of the Magna Carta, the Province Charter, and an Act of Parliament (presumably the Sixth of Anne). When Admiral Warren was later asked to testify about this violent event, he spoke of Boston's maritime population with some sympathy. On the other hand, in what must have sounded like a warning note in Great Britain, he added that New England's seamen "have the highest notion of the rights and liberties of Englishmen and indeed are almost levelers." His reference to Cromwell's violent, communistic supporters of the 1640s may have sent a small shudder through the admiralty.

Generally, the British naval command regarded Boston as, to use a phrase from subsequent years, a "metropolis of sedition." Its combination of elusive seamen and officials who seemed not to understand that England was still carrying on a demanding and costly war infuriated visiting commanders. Worst of all, the merchants of the port, pushed to even riskier endeavors than usual because of high wartime taxes and the restrictions of the new (1747) Sugar Act, sought to lure seamen from navy vessels so that they might join privateers at sea. Deserters, if they managed to get ashore, could almost surely find an attractive berth with a willing skipper. Hearing of Commodore Knowles's approach two years later (by which time judgment had still not been rendered on the arrested naval officers), the waterfront was prepared to resist whatever impressment teams he might send out.

## The Knowles Affair: An Impressment Riot That Became a Political Cause

While Commodore Knowles's ships were still assembling in Nantasket Roads outside Boston Harbor in preparation for heading south on his West Indies campaign, some thirty of his sailors were able to slip over the side and escape to the mainland. Then, on November 17, five more men deserted in what was described as "a large canoe belonging to his majesty's ship *Lark*." Beside himself with rage, Knowles ordered his squadron's boats to sweep the harbor that very morning and to bring back sufficient men, of whatever description and nationality, to allow him to sail to the Indies adequately crewed. His men complied, bringing in a harvest of forty-six victims, thereby setting off the most violent eruption of Boston's mobs before the Stamp Act uprising.

Thomas Hutchinson, the aristocratic Massachusetts native who would loom large in American history as a royalist official before the Revolution, was then serving as Speaker of the House. Like all other townsmen, he was appalled at Knowles's careless assault on Boston's populace. He wrote in indignation that the commodore's crews had "surprised not only as many seamen as could be found on board any of the ships, outward bound as well as others, but swept the wharfs also, taking some ship carpenters, apprentices, and laboring land men." Particularly poignant was the deposition of one of those impressed, a Jonathan Tarbox. As his testimony is reproduced in Tager's pages, Tarbox and "two or three persons all inhabitants of Boston going in a Boat to Mistick (having their tools with them) to Caulk a Vessel there—[had been] chaced by three Boats belonging to Commander Knowles Squadron." When Tarbox objected to the seizure, saying that he and the others were residents, the press officer "in a very rough manner answered that they did not care for that, for the Commodore had ordered them to impress all they could meet without distinction."

Immediately, a mob of angry protesters began to assemble, with the clear purpose of capturing and bringing to account whatever officers and men might have been involved in the impressment. Hutchinson first glimpsed the mob sometime before ten o'clock on that morning of November 17. He said that it "consisted of about three hundred Seamen and Strangers (the greatest part Scotch) with Cutlasses and Clubs," and that "they had seiz'd and detain'd in their Custody a Lieutenant of the *Lark*" as well as another officer. Tager and other historians caution readers of today to beware of the self-serving aspects of reports by Hutchinson and his contemporaries, advising that the officials' objectives were to make themselves look valorous and loyal and to make disturbers of the peace look foreign and rebellious. For example, were men in this mob really "Strangers" and/or "Scotch" and not really Bostonians? The answer seems to be that some were and some were not.

Whatever the composition of the initial gathering, by the time the crowd reached the town center, it was a huge, howling mass of people. Governor Shirley called out the militia to restrain them, but neither the militia nor any other supporting force came to his aid. The governor's immediate problem was that the mob had dragged along with them three officers of the impressment team, as well as Knowles's personal servant, all of whom they had captured and were holding as hostages. Fearing what might happen to them if he did not intervene, Shirley was somehow able to interpose himself between the prisoners and the mob and to get the men safely inside his house. Frustrated, the crowd then took out its anger on the sheriff and the deputies who had been aiding the impressors, beating them and hauling them along to the center of town. There they put the sheriff in the public stocks—about the most shameful punishment that could be imposed on a public official, though certainly preferable to death.

By the afternoon's end, the crowd had swollen almost beyond belief: of the town's sixteen thousand people, nearly a quarter were now engaged in the tumult. They surged in the direction of the Town House, which stood at the corner of King (now State) and Cornhill (now Washington) streets. Governor Shirley had arrived at his offices there earlier and had urged the consideration of an emergency bill to disperse the mob and apprehend its leaders. But soon after the passage of the bill, the crowd appeared, surrounding the building and demanding entry. According to Hutchinson, this occurred "just after candlelight." He and Shirley both recognized that by then, the mob had changed not only in size but also in character. Laboring-class Bostonians from many employments had joined its ranks. If ever it had been simply a rude group of "seamen and strangers," now it had the look of an enraged citizenry—Boston's common people on the march.

Hurling a barrage of stones and brickbats at the closed Town House, the crowd succeeded in breaking all windows on the lower floor. Its leaders then battered down the door and charged in, forcing the few militia officers defending the place to withdraw up the stairs. But there the charge stalled, giving time for the governor to come forth and attempt to impose calm. Remarkably, Shirley succeeded, even though this involved a kind of bantering with the people that was then regarded as beneath a royal official's dignity. Among the questions he had to parry was, what had happened to those men from the HMS *Wager* who had never been punished for their murderous action in the North End? (Answer: the court was still awaiting the Crown's judgment.) Shirley also had to promise to do everything possible to get the impressed men back from Commodore Knowles's grasp.

Somewhat cooled by the governor's words but its rage not spent, the crowd then went on to look for other targets, including, if possible, more British officers or a vulnerable British vessel. It found one such vessel, a handsome, presumably official, launch; this the men dragged to the Common, where they burned it in yet another symbolic demonstration of communal judgment. Ironically, the barge belonged not to Knowles's squadron at all but rather to the master of a Scottish ship in the harbor, possibly one of the men in the first gathering. The riot's leaders also made a point of closing the town gates at the Neck, determined to prevent the escape of any of the impressment team. And, in an interesting move that paralleled the Andros uprising of fifty years earlier, they went to the naval hospital to free sailors held there, as well as to search for more officers.

Governor Shirley, having perceived that no additional militia men would come to his assistance, decided that his only course was to flee to the well-armed Castle William and from there to attempt a consolidation of forces. His withdrawal and the implicit surrender of control to the people from both the governor and the town's power center altered the nature of this riot and elevated its importance. Here was the largest community in Great Britain's North

*When Governor Shirley fled to Castle William, he sought the safety of a fort removed from rebellious Boston by three miles of water. The fort is shown above later in that century, guarded by warships. Today, Fort Independence stands on renamed Castle Island (now connected to the mainland), boasting the oldest granite base of any fortification in once-British North America.*

Courtesy of the Bostonian Society

American colonies, the seat of Massachusetts's proud and ancient regime, totally bereft of any operational government. For three days, from the violence of November 17 to the restoration of order on November 20, 1745, no one ruled the people, nor did the people quite rule themselves. Yet claims that anarchy then reigned unchecked in Boston must be modified: anarchy could never totally claim the people's hearts in this self-monitored town.

Back to the event. From the sanctuary of Castle William during those lawless days, Shirley wrote a bombardment of letters, both to the General Court and to Commodore Knowles. To the Court, he said that he blamed the "Insurrection" on "some ill-minded Inhabitants and Persons of Influence in the Town . . . [Who had secretly] Countenanc'd and encourag'd it." He thereby revealed that he, for the moment, had ceased ascribing it to foreigners and drifters-through. To Knowles, he wrote, as he had promised to do, that the commodore must release the impressed Bostonians. Indeed, Shirley seems to have rowed out to confer with Knowles on his flagship, HMS *Canterbury*. The commodore's outrage at Boston for having taken his officers as hostages was initially white hot; at one point, he threatened to turn the cannons of his ships upon the town so as to strike at the heart of the rioting. And he apparently knew where to aim, for he stated to a horrified local carpenter that "the North End people were the Rebels." But Shirley was finally able to reason with him, leading him to the conclusion that the release of most of the impressed men had become mandatory.

Gradually, the power dealers at Town House were able to get themselves back together and to develop a rationale and a policy for action. The General Court officially condemned the riot, instructing the militia to repress such actions in the future. The town meeting, picking up the beat, totally disavowed "such illegal proceedings" as they had just witnessed and insisted again that the crowd had consisted mostly of foreigners. The militia leadership, on hearing Shirley's tactful request that they organize themselves and come out to assist him, decided that it would indeed be best if they went to Castle William and formally escorted the governor back to Province House. Thus, by the twentieth, all official parties seemed to have recovered a certain commanding stance, and the people who had constituted the mob had dispersed.

Indeed, the ceremony with which the governor was conducted home turned the uprising into something like a celebratory event, particularly because Commander Knowles's squadron, as Hutchinson reported, "sailed [off], to the joy of the town." But there remained the very difficult matter of fixing the formal blame for this disruption of British order on some individuals' shoulders. Hutchinson, one of the most astute minds on the colonial scene, recognized that there was but one convenient way to go. Certainly, the government should not fix the blame on the vitally important merchants who, when angered at Parliament for having passed the new Sugar Act, had disrupted naval affairs by offering berths to deserting sailors. Nor should it put the blame on the magistrates who had quaked and quailed in the threatened Governor's Council or even on the representatives in the attacked General Assembly. No, the best thing to do was to emphasize that it was the "Unanimous Opinion of the Town" that the mob had been "a tumultous, riotous assembling of armed Seamen, Servants, Negroes, and other People of Mean and Vile Condition"—the sort one might expect to find in a onetime pirates' port. Then, having made that point, a few men of the previous description had to be found who would face a captured pirate's fate.

Governor Shirley, also working in support of Boston's reputation, kept another part of his bargain with the town administration and wrote to the Duke of Newcastle, then in charge of colonial affairs, that Boston had suffered unusual hardships in recent memory, what with the strains of war and the economic turndown. Yet he also admitted there was a villain in the town's tradition of participatory government, pointing to the province's constitution and to its provision for a representative assembly, as well as to Boston's open town meeting (which was, to state it again, unique in the colonies). Those latter remarks may, of course, have been to tell the king's councilors exactly what they wanted to hear, rather than to reflect his own true feelings.

Eventually, the reassembled authorities of Boston were able to discover and arrest a group of "ringleaders" whose backgrounds might reveal the riot's true origins. The men numbered eleven, and their names deserve to be noted and considered: Stephen Parkinson, mariner; Richard Hughes, bookkeeper; Moses Witcher, laborer; Henry Kenyon, laborer; Thomas Patrick, mariner; William Harris, laborer; Edmund Sheay, laborer; Jacobus Dukenyrin, mariner; Patrick Dowley, mariner; Henry Fitspatrick, mariner; and Samuel Gyles, housewright. These were, by measure of their employments, Bostonians from a wide range of occupations along the waterfront. They certainly did not seem to be the exotic personalities whom the officials represented as having been at the root of the riot—an embarrassment that went unmentioned.

The men were nevertheless charged and convicted of terrifying the town, abusing the sheriff, and causing costly property damage. From their prison, they were brought before the superior court to be sentenced. Perhaps because very little harm had actually been done—no deaths, only a limited amount of destruction of public property—the condemned eleven received fairly light judgments. Three were fined £60, £30, and £20, respectively; the rest were acquitted. Yet it seemed to some, particularly to a certain columnist named Amicus Patriae (Friend of the Country), that the court, however lenient its conclusion, had missed the point. These common laborers and mariners were not the ones who had caused the riot; that crime had been committed by the navy and its practice of impressment. The colony's legislators should make it their business to place the blame on those shoulders.

Amicus also had a good deal of journalistic fun mocking the way Governor Shirley had been so carefully safeguarded by the people on his way back from Castle William, "to which he [had] thought fit to retire." But the major point made in his article, entitled "Address to the Inhabitants of the Province of the Massachusetts-Bay in New-England; more Especially, To the Inhabitants of Boston; Occasioned by the late Illegal and Unwarrantable Attack Upon their Liberties, And the unhappy Confusion and Disorders consequent thereon," was that those inhabitants deserved better from their leadership. After stating that the people "have natural Rights to treat their Oppressors as under such Circumstances," he went on to present a strongly favorable view of those citizens "of the lowest Rank (though I think full as useful as their Neighbors, who live at Ease upon the Produce of their Labor)" and to characterize their rage as justifiable.

Amicus painted a particularly grim picture of the sins of impressment, saying that "scarcely One in a Hundred [of those taken] ever returns," and went on to write of the general hardships that the colony had endured. Finally, he leveled his guns at the authorities of the province and the town for not emphasizing those truths to the Crown. "I am sure," he concluded, "there are Gentlemen to be found in England who want neither Abilities, nor Inclination to undertake . . . such an Application to the Throne." And he warned that the people's "Eyes are upon the Conduct of the General Court." By that warning, he made of the Knowles Riot a political cause. This climactic event of 1747, in which the realities of an imperial war and the brutalities of His Majesty's navy had disturbed the populace of the no-longer-isolated province, thus became a trumpet call for the people to be on their guard and to watch over their own government and its relationship with Great Britain.

The real name of Amicus, it must be added, was Deacon Samuel Adams—not a pirate of yesteryear but a politician for the forthcoming revolutionary era.

# 4

# The South End Gang
# and the Stamp Act

Deacon Samuel Adams, dutiful son of a successful ship captain and devoted father of the radical politician Samuel Adams, owned both a wharf on the waterfront near Purchase Street and a successful brewing establishment in the North End. Located purposefully between land and sea, he was seen as a typical upper-class Bostonian. As a leading Congregationalist and a businessman, he also stood betwixt the town's dying theocracy and its new plutocracy. This amphibious, civic orientation allowed him to be as congenial with the excitable maritime laborers of the early 1700s as with the staid merchants and selectmen who struggled to keep the town in order. He was, in this sense, a pivotal figure of the pre-Revolutionary era, contributing not only a son who would become the leading rebel of his time but also a system of communication across classes and across land-sea interests that would become the precedent for later political structures.

Deacon Adams (1689–1748) dealt regularly and adroitly with the power brokers of the royal government, winning election to the colony's General Court in 1736. As a minor participant in the province's governmental system, he witnessed, on the one hand, the growing caste consciousness and the restrictive stances of the local elite (his later election to the Governor's Council was killed by a veto from on high) and, on the other hand, the emergence of a new breed of enlightened intellectuals who professed a great love of humanity and natural law. These humanists, who mostly called themselves Whigs and were, like him, graduates of Harvard, believed in the economic theories of John Locke and in the capabilities of Sir Robert Walpole to reform king and Parliament. Deacon Adams, in contrast to those English-oriented Whigs, trusted in his own Puritanical god and in his town's moral traditions; in later years, he was referred to as "a true New England man, an honest *Patriot* [author's italics]"—one of the earliest to be identified by that word.

At the lower end of the social scale, even further down the scale from the waterfront tipplers who bought the deacon's ale, stood (sometimes, yes; sometimes, no) a roisterer named Ebenezer Mackintosh. He, too, should be counted among the American Revolution's precedent patriots, despite the fact that neither he nor the deacon had anything like an independent nation in mind. What they did have in mind may be called, for the moment, simply "liberty." From different social strata and different generations, they both smote vigorously at the existing establishment's roots. Heedless of concepts of republicanism or democracy, they nevertheless helped bring down the tree of privilege and position; loyal to their respective codes and pressed by their own needs, they pushed fellow Bostonians toward greater liberty.

Ebenezer Mackintosh (1737–1816) was called by Thomas Hutchinson "the consummate rioter"; at a later point in his career, he earned the title "Captain General of the Liberty Tree." Though that sounds rather glorious, Mackintosh spent time confined in various jails, was deemed a drunkard, and ended his Boston days by departing into exile. Born in the shadow of the gallows on Boston's Neck and undisputably a member of Boston's maritime underworld, he tried to work as a cordwainer—that is, someone who could shape leather, or cord, into prescribed patterns for shoes and boots. But he never seems to have acquired his own shop, lodging mostly in the attics of friends and acquaintances, for whose families he made shoes as requested. Far greater than his talent for fabricating footwear was his ability to find and lead men—men originally from the South End but eventually from across the entire town—who would join him in nighttime revelry and in riots both spontaneous and planned. Outstanding in that role, he would hold the power of Boston in his raised fist for three wild days in 1765.

Sadly, Mackintosh spent his final days in poverty and died in a Vermont poorhouse, forgotten by other patriots. This hints at the complexity of Boston's radical politics in the generation after Deacon Samuel Adams had helped lay their foundation. There was indeed something else developing in Boston concurrently with the crowds' brutal rioting and the intellectuals' theorizing. There was a conscious attempt by a few activists (not the majority) to alter the flow of authority. In their revised system, power would no longer be imposed from above by the gilded elite (as Andros had wished) but would spring up from groups of regular citizens, men such as artisans, carpenters, and mechanics. That radical ideal, which did not, of course, embrace apprentices and seamen or slaves and indentured servants or Native Americans and men without any property, was one with which the deacon's famous son, Samuel Adams Jr., was strongly identified. He wrote, "I glory in being what the world calls, a poor Man. If my Mind has ever been tinctured with Envy, the Rich and the Great have not been its objects."

## We Shall Not Be "Slaves and Vassals of the Rich!"

The crisis that prompted Deacon Adams to commence his decades-long campaign against the colony's hierarchy stemmed directly from the depression of 1740, mentioned in the last chapter. This economic downturn occurred in the wake of early wars that had left the town financially devastated and overpopulated with widows and unemployed seamen. It dragged on for five painful years before the coffers of Massachusetts were partially refilled by the Crown from the capture of Louisbourg. In this time of peace and consequent economic distress, the deacon and other concerned citizens established a Land Bank whose assets consisted of little more than the dreams of land sales in the West and the visions of certain soft money–minded investors. It had no government backing. The deacon himself put into the bank not only the major part of his family fortune but also all of his political capital. He was determined that although the commonwealth's original program of support for needy citizens may have been proved impracticable, its philosophy of assistance to the willing-to-work should be supported.

The Land Bank and the paper money that it issued proved wildly popular with those hard-pressed Bostonians who feared they had no chance to get a leg up in a business world ruled by old-line merchants. At the vanguard of this enthusiastic group were the artisans and the storekeepers, the taverners and the chandlers of the waterfront. But to the merchants, who could pay off their personal and trade debts to factors in Europe only through bills of exchange based on London's pound sterling, the bank and its soft money constituted a threat of alarming proportions. The very idea that the ordinary people could compete equally in business affairs or could be relieved of their hard-money indebtedness by some local currency arrangements caused Boston's gentility to demand of the governor and his councilors that immediate action be taken.

The situation became even less tenable while the General Court debated the issue, as an irreparable rupture developed between the merchant elite and the rest of the populace. Strengthening the elite's determination to maintain a firm hand on financial affairs was the grim fact that the number of would-be merchants in town was increasing even as the effects of the 1733 Molasses Act and of other mercantilist restrictions decreased revenues. Competition was intense among such high-risk plutocrats and sometime smugglers as Thomas Hancock and Peter Faneuil; they could secure their fortunes only by gaining more control of the mechanisms of power. Their aggressions squeezed the town: the rich (representing 5 percent of the total population) were increasing their share to nearly half of Boston's property holdings in the face of the impotent poor. Even as word came of victory at Louisbourg and as the prospect of financial relief from London sailed into town, the debate intensified about what this ameliorative turn of events would mean to the Land Bank issue.

The representative in the General Court who thought he knew best how to handle the issue was the rich, young, previously introduced Thomas Hutchinson (1711–1780). Legend has it that this born and bred Boston aristocrat—who would win a measure of fame by the crowd's destruction of his mansion during the Stamp Act crisis—had first demonstrated his ability to make money when he was a youth, when he successfully sold a cargo of fish given him by his father as a trial. Young Tom parlayed those three or four quintals of cod into a quick profit and translated that return into an eventual capital of more than £4,000. Now he stood forth in the legislature, proposing that the funds London had provided as Massachusetts's share of the wartime booty from Louisbourg be used to redeem the colony's depreciated currency. He believed that this move would boost the merchants and their hard-money policy, doing away with the need for anything like the Land Bank, which he considered an ill-conceived idea.

Backed by the governor and, of course, by the merchant elite, Hutchinson's proposal won the day. It also won Hutchinson a definite place as the brightest star of the conservatives' Court Party in the legislature, as well as earning the adamant hatred of Deacon Adams and his so-called Popular Party. But because the subsequent judgments against the Land Bank* resulted in the ruination of that very popular institution, it also cost Hutchinson the election of 1749 and caused a mounting panic in the streets of Boston. And word that Great Britain's 1748 Treaty of Aix-la-Chapelle had returned Louisbourg to France added heat to the angry mood of the mob, for they could not forget that four hundred New Englanders, 8 percent of Boston's male population, had died in the fortress's capture. When news broke of those two distressing events, they rebelled. Again, onrushing rioters surged against the gates of Town House, the crowd swollen to more than a thousand by men and women from all the town's neighborhoods. Again, the governor of the province found himself facing a threat that resembled a civil war. But unlike Governor Shirley three years earlier, Governor Belcher moved decisively to quell the uprising, imprisoning the leaders and

---

*The judgments included the outlawing of the bank by Parliament, brought about by an ardent request from Governor Jonathan Belcher that had been enthusiastically endorsed by British merchants.

using all the forces at his command to keep the royal government in power.

The consequences of the firmly suppressed rebellion were dire. John Adams later commented that the Land Bank riot had been a "greater ferment" than even the Stamp Act uprising. As for Deacon Adams, who had lost all of his official appointments in the course of the disputes over the Land Bank, which he had supported against the ruling elite, he was now financially destroyed as well. His son, initially a proud and privileged undergraduate at Harvard, was forced to wait on tables in order to finish his studies. It was from that moment on, from the time of the Land Bank's collapse, that this branch of the Adams family identified itself with the working people of the town and did everything possible to invest them with more political power.

The deacon's cause was, as already indicated, not a new one in Boston. The crowd had always been able to find its leaders, whether from within or without, whether against impressment and customs tippers on the waterfront or for more equitable markets and more discreet whorehouses within the town. Of particularly fond memory was Dr. Elisha Cooke Sr., a wealthy physician, who, though definitely a gentleman of the seventeenth century, had left a legacy for future generations by emphasizing the liberties of the people at every turn. Because he proclaimed, rather than hid, that political turn of mind, he was vetoed as a councilman by the colony's then-ruling governor, Sir William Phips, after having been elected to that position in 1693. Although he finally advanced into the ranks of councilors, he was later rejected under the next governor (Dudley).

His fight on behalf of the people was carried on into the early 1700s by his similarly inclined son, Elisha Cooke Jr., to whom Governor Belcher gave the contemptuous name "Idol of the Mob." Young Dr. Cooke returned the compliment by calling the mob actions the "Belcher Riots." He was quite right to do so. The people's destructive attempts in those years to get good bread and to oppose crooked butchers had all been provoked by the governor; it truly was the governor and his policies, rather than the destitute and their actions, that had caused the violent disruptions of the people's peace. However, Elisha Cooke Jr.'s greatest gift to the people of

Boston and to the much-later concept of American democracy was not just recognizing where the fault lay but in doing something about it. In 1718, he founded the first Boston caucus.

Previously, political clubs, such as they were, existed for gentlemen—well-to-do merchants and lawyers who had the leisure to discuss the news from Parliament and the theories of the French *philosophes*. By contrast, Cooke's wide-open caucus, which provided free liquor and inflammatory handouts for a mixture of artisans, shopkeepers, and other middle-class citizens, dealt with local issues and real needs. Participation by captains, wharfingers, and denizens of the waterfront was noticeably heavy. That is, Cooke's attempt to awaken a response within the populace to political issues was particularly successful on the waterfront.

One of the first reliable historians of Boston, in his 1873 description of the town and its nautically influenced caucus system, reported that "Joseph Field, master of a vessel," was a prominent member. Also, very tellingly, he told of a certain Captain Cunningham who had been invited, but who apparently was somewhat resistant, until Cooke and other leaders "assured him [there would be] benefit in his business." He then commenced attendance. Certainly, there was an effort from the organizers to pull the chiefs of the waterfront into the political system. These were the well-recognized captains who, in keeping with Boston's maritime traditions, would be obeyed when they ordered their men to march.

This connection between caucus and waterfront was so tight that some commentators (including Winsor in his 1880 *Memorial History*) have speculated that the very word *caucus* was invented for these meetings on the basis of the great number of caulkers and ship carpenters who attended. The theory, though possibly fanciful, is yet to be disproved. Another apt word for these gatherings was *raucous*. Located in locked tavern rooms and in the attics of rooming houses, the caucus club meetings boomed with the sound of rum-based arguments and rang with the debates of people who had never before been invited to voice their opinions. There were three such clubs, one each, in the north, the south, and the central districts of the town. They magnetized the neighborhoods.

Yet there was nothing subversive about their political purpose.

Elisha Cooke and Deacon Adams, in steering the discussions about such matters as paper money and public works, genuinely believed that all Bostonians, even the upper-class merchants, would benefit from a more broadly based polity, as well as from the more practical and progressive policies that would result. At the same time, it must be said that for all their populist spirit, there was not much democracy in these sessions; they were managed by an inner circle of idealistic and relatively wealthy men. Indeed, the foremost purpose of the caucus clubs was to build up a popular head of steam behind certain desired improvements, including pothole-free roads and noncollapsing bridges. The deacon, Elisha Cooke, or another member of the inner circle would be empowered by the caucus to advise Assembly representatives that this needed to be built or that needed to be fixed, to which the pressured representatives could only nod in agreement.

By catching the port town's attention, caucus-backed candidates drubbed those of the Court Party in the election of 1763. Conservatives howled in protest, seeing the clubs as "juntos" and surmising that the motives of their activists were "selfish." But, as explained by historian Edward Gault of the Paul Revere House staff, "The majority of Boston voters did not perceive the [coercive] activities of the caucus to be counter to the . . . open politics of the town meeting [if only] because the caucus system delivered the best results for them, which at the time mattered more than how the elected officials were chosen." Here, interestingly, one sees organized and popular pressure groups revealed as one of the true (if slightly embarrassing) fathers of what is called modern representative democracy, with its often objectionable, strong-armed, nondemocratic party leadership.

From the caucus clubs streamed a steady flow of pamphlets against the high-handed actions of the elite. Many of these publications were charged with the single-minded passion of Elisha Cooke to defend Boston's Town Meeting against the provincial governors' attempts to diminish it; others rang with the eloquent language of the deacon as he praised the virtues of paper money and lower taxes. Through the pamphlets and in the caucus debates, he proclaimed his defiant gospel, "We shall not be 'slaves and vassals of the rich!'" And so the Boston caucus clubs developed, becoming the voice of those not previously heard and an alternative to regular, static governmental procedures. In the generation before the American Revolution, the clubs grew to be so powerful that they served as young Samuel Adams's sturdiest tool for arousing popular protest. They were the greatest gift from his now impecunious father, whose financial debts Samuel had to struggle to pay off.

Many other formative events and developments out of human hands needed to occur, however, before Massachusetts and the rest of America would be seized by the heretofore-incredible concept of independence. And surely the most world-changing of those events was the Seven Years' War, called by contemporaries the New French and Indian War and by some modern historians the First World War, which burst forth in 1754. That was not quite the date when the pauperized and jobless Ebenezer Mackintosh enlisted—he waited until 1758, the last day before an advertised bonus ran out—but it was the date when impoverished Boston perked up once again, at the thoughts of military contracts and pelf-yielding adventures in the air. Almost immediately after the outbreak of war, a surreptitious fleet sailed out from Boston to Louisbourg, from which reports had come that before the serious shooting began, supplies might be welcomed from allies and foes alike, no questions asked.

Seven years later, with the recapture of that northern fortress by colonial and British forces and with the total victory over the French in North America as codified in the Treaty of Paris, a new world seemed to open to Bostonians and other mercantile Americans. This was the world in which the new governor, Francis Bernard, hoped to capitalize when he moved to Boston, as forecast in chapter 1. In some respects, it was a hopeful and prosperous-sounding world, featuring a new and more attentive king on the British throne (George III) and powered by British trade lords whose interests sailed, as it were, on ships built in New England. But because those trade lords sought to regularize transatlantic commerce and had the ear of Parliament, it was also a perilous world, particularly for those Yankee smugglers and traders who sought to profit either from sugar cane grown on non–British West Indies islands or from goods manufactured on the European continent.

Clearly, they had to develop extraordinary methods to survive, for the downturn of commerce at war's end brought about a horrific 50 percent shrinkage of revenues in Boston. Hearing of the death of the former king and the installation of George III at Whitehall (an event attended by young John Hancock), these quite proper Bostonian smugglers dared to hope that something might be done to bend the rules in the new empire and let them sail on as they would.

They pinned their hopes on the new regime's termination of the so-called Writs of Assistance. On these damnable Writs, the customs officials had based all their authority to obtain search warrants that allowed them to clamber onboard a newly arrived vessel and inspect it for any forbidden sugar products or European machinery or tea. The traders sought out the best lawyers they could find to help them plead their case against the issuance of any new writs. And they found the brilliant, only slightly eccentric James Otis Jr., whose piercing wit and golden tongue might just succeed in defeating the Writs' constitutionality in a case brought before the colony's supreme court.

What made young Otis (1725–1783) a particularly appealing advocate in the eyes of Boston's merchants and captains was that he was a member of a caucus club. He knew what was on their minds, how vital their interests (illicit or otherwise) were to the entire community. Also, he had a personal score to settle.

## James Otis, the Flickering "Flame of Fire"

A member of a Massachusetts Bay mercantile family, James Otis Jr. resembled Samuel Adams Jr. in only certain ways. Chief of those similarities was that he felt his father had been deprived of high public office by the corrupt reigning government of the colony. In the family's native Barnstable County on Cape Cod, the senior James Otis had served for decades as a distinguished judge. Appointment to the Massachusetts Superior Court, long promised to him, had been viewed as certain as the rising of the next tide. Instead, the newly arrived governor, Francis Bernard, had elevated the young lion of the Court Party, Thomas Hutchinson, to that post. Family honor having been tarnished, young Otis vowed to "set the Province afire." This he soon did by leading a lifelong campaign against Hutchinson (whom he called "Sir Thomas Graspall") and by accepting the merchants' invitation to help defeat the Writs of Assistance.

The merchants had first come to the unified conclusion that they must rise in militant resistance after a cooperative port customs officer, Benjamin Barnes, had been removed from his post and replaced by the legalistic Charles Paxton. Governor Bernard thought that this move represented a positive reform, saying somewhat sardonically, "If conniving at foreign sugars and molasses and Portugal wines and fruits is to be reckoned corruption, there never was, I believe, an uncorrupt customs officer in America." His new appointee, Paxton, justified a dramatic increase in ship seizures by stating that new Writs of Assistance would soon be forthcoming.

James Otis, having accepted the case against the Writs and having carried out his research with customary thoroughness, came to believe that if these documents were issued again and if the customs officers were given renewed authority thereby, a "fraud" against the commonwealth would be committed. His mind brimming with principles of natural law learned at Harvard and his eyes ablaze with New England indignation, he demanded that the province, through its treasurer, sue the royal customs office for having taken an illegal portion of the port's fees. He asserted that the customs officials and the governor had connived to pay informers from goods seized from local ships; this could only be seen as a violation of the law's intent. Such a violation not only amounted to a criminal act but also proved that the Writs themselves had been the bases for fraud and should not be reissued.

Otis lacked for neither specific facts nor grandiloquent language. He had been well briefed on the malpractice of customs officials by his caucus club associates, including the powerful William Molineux, as well as by his own family's Barnstable neighbor Meletia Bourne (or Bourn). Together, Molineux and Bourne led the smugglers' cause in the Massachusetts Bay area and expounded it to the people of the waterfront as the cause of all. Commenting on the cozy association between the young Harvard graduate and his underground contacts, the sharp-eyed Loyalist Peter Oliver wrote that "Otis engrafted himself into the Body of Smugglers and they embraced him so close as a lawyer and useful Pleader that he soon incorporated with them."

When he appeared in the Council Chamber of the Town House on November 18, 1761, Otis announced that he was speaking on behalf of the "inhabitants of Boston." He also claimed that, as a gentleman of the court, his only interest was that of "British Liberty." Having established that perspective, he reviewed English history and found that Writs had been issued there only when such "tyrants" as Charles Stuart were at the "zenith of arbitrary power." The Writs, he claimed, had absolutely no precedents in Massachusetts law or tradition. Raising his voice to deliver the speech's climax, Otis declared that the Navigation Acts (issued by Charles II in 1660), coupled with the Writs, were "instruments of slavery on the one hand or villainy on the other." To his "dying day," Otis would oppose these laws as "opposition to a kind of power . . . which in former periods of English history cost one King of England his head and another his throne." He concluded that it was "the business of this court to demolish this monster of oppression, & tear into shreds this remnant of Star Chamber Tyranny."

John Adams, one of those in attendance, reported that "Otis was a flame of fire," and that he successfully persuaded everyone there to "take up arms against the Writs of Assistance." Later, having considered more deeply what Otis had said and what he had ignited on that November day, Adams referred to it as "the day the child of Independence was born."

Yet the judges hemmed and hawed. Chief Justice Hutchinson suggested that they delay their decision until word came from England about the legality of the Writs. When that message finally sailed into Boston, it was exactly what the merchants did not want to hear: the Writs were still valid in the British Isles and were regarded as applicable throughout the Empire. Nonetheless, Otis had made his point, and it would not be forgotten—by the spring of 1762, there was a marked relaxation in the enforcement of customs procedures.

Despite being hailed throughout Boston as the patriot of the hour—"the God-like Otis" he was called in young Samuel Adams's propaganda pieces—the final years of the brilliant orator were tragic.

He initiated a tavern brawl with a customs official who gave him a quite justified knock on the head with his cane. That seemed to accelerate the number of Otis's already alarming episodes of insanity; eventually, he was retired to the country for "recuperation." That left Samuel Adams and his smuggler colleagues in the position of not having a ready champion for their cause. Amid the dense smoke and dim candlelight of the caucus clubs, there must have been fervent discussion of who then, out in the streets if not in the courts, could be the people's visible hero; perhaps a more active, less legalistic champion was required.

One name came quickly to mind, that of Ebenezer Mackintosh. He had caught the town's eye a year earlier, during the terrifying fire of March 1760. Raging through the wooden structures of the waterfront, seemingly unstoppable, the fire had destroyed the homes of some 225 families, driving the people out into the night. Nor did it spare the commercial interests of the town, wiping out 176 warehouses, as well as numerous shops and taverns. It was only when certain fire crews, manned by veterans of the war working together as teams, brought their "engines" into play in a coherent way that the fire was finally doused. Mackintosh, an outstandingly energetic member of one of those teams, came to the attention of the authorities whose job it was to restore order on that night of alarm and confusion.

Specifically, he came to the favorable attention of Sheriff Stephen Greenleaf, a hard-nosed, bull-headed official who would later throw Mackintosh, the maritime roisterer, into jail on a number of occasions. At this point in 1760 and 1761, however, when the sheriff and others in town were trying to build a volunteer fire-fighting corps that would be better prepared for the next conflagration, Greenleaf tapped Mackintosh, described as "slight of build, of sandy complexion and a nervous temperament," to head one of the units—engine number nine. If the stubby, newly nominated fire sergeant can be said to have had any training to equip him for his new post, it would certainly have been his wartime service, for which, as noted previously, he had signed up just in time to qualify for an enlistment bonus. His pay: one pound, sixteen shillings a month—not bad for an unemployed twenty-one-year-old.

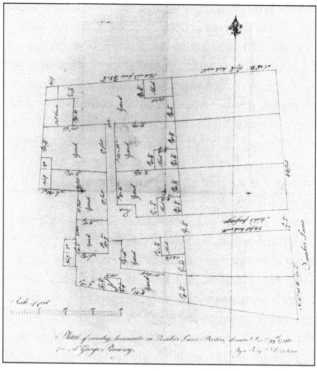

*Boston's North End, where Governor Hutchinson and Deacon Adams dwelled, was also the home of one of the town's pre-Revolutionary mobs. The area was swept by many fires; the brick home shown above, the Tremere House on North Street, was built in 1674 and survived them all. At bottom is a plan for a typical tenement of the day, with one alleyway pump for all units.*

Courtesy of Historic New England/SPNEA

But that tour of military duty had been punishing. His company had been part of the brigade led by the hapless Scotland-born general James Abercromby against the French at Fort Ticonderoga. They never reached the fort, in fact, but were ambushed and nearly destroyed between Fort Edward and Lake George by a force of French-led Algonquians. Mackintosh was lucky to survive; twenty of the men fell around him in the attack. After seven months and nineteen days of service, he returned to Boston with a very low opinion of Abercromby in particular and British military leadership in general. Henceforth, whenever the urge to go adventuring struck him, he would instead ship out on a friend's fishing boat or with whoever else might offer a sea berth. Nonetheless, he had developed certain skills in the army—the ability to lead other men and the knack of survival—and these would stand him in good stead.

His father, Moses Mackintosh, had not been so fortunate. It is worth noting the manner in which Moses had existed at the lowest level of Boston society, for that was the unhappy image before ambitious young Ebenezer's eyes as he struggled to make his way in the years before the Revolution. Back in 1753, Moses had in fact been "warned out" of Boston as a nonself-supporting individual, having failed to find a living for himself and his son (his wife having died) in the town's South End. Although Moses, too, had spent some time in army uniform during the 1730s, he seems to have been blocked from the possibility of learning a trade or of locating himself in Boston society by his humble origins and by the harsh character of his times.

Moses's earliest forebear to come to American shores had been among the Scottish clansmen captured by Cromwell in the battle at Dunbar in 1651, then shipped to the New World as bonded servants—white slaves, in effect. Men in that category had been forced to work at such backbreaking sites as Saugus's unsuccessful ironworks. Although the Mackintosh family attained its freedom in subsequent generations, the burden of being a Scot in the midst of Boston's rigid caste system remained a heavy one. When Moses left town as an outcast, his son stayed behind, a teenager short of stature and hot of temper.

# The Captain of Revels for a Divided Community

To anyone looking for a controversy, Boston at this time offered many opportunities—at all levels of society. In the wealthy world of the town's rival merchants, where their spokesman James Otis had not begun his descent into madness and still raised his voice against tyranny, there were fearful new intimations of economic disaster. These fears had been triggered by the maneuvers of Prime Minister George Grenville to diminish the Empire's war-induced indebtedness (which exceeded £137,000,000) by laying fresh taxes on colonial trade. The Crown's relatively hands-off attitude of benign neglect would be a thing of the past for the American colonies. When word came of Parliament's Sugar Act of 1764, Otis prepared his ringing *Statement of the Rights of the Colonies*. In the Assembly, frantic legislators struggled with one another to write and dispatch a carefully worded objection to the king. Governor Bernard prorogued the Assembly, however, allowing it to meet only in October of that year for the issuance of a much-boiled-down protest.

Otis and his colleagues also set up a committee to communicate with other colonies in hopes of formulating some kind of "united assistance." The conservatives found themselves severely split between the Loyalists and those increasingly determined to resist the new restraints on their free-and-easy shipping practices. Thomas Hutchinson, always sensitive to the moods of his native province, felt the balance of opinion shifting away from its traditional allegiance to the Parliament. Governor Bernard, particularly worried by the attempt to bring the colonies together against Grenville's increasingly stringent enforcement of Crown policies, wrote home of his concerns. He saw the malcontents as seizing this opportunity "to lay a foundation for connecting the demagogues of several Governments in America to join together in opposition to all orders from Great Britain which do not square with their notions of the rights of the people."

Undoubtedly, one of the demagogues on Bernard's mind was Samuel Adams Jr., whose pen seemed to acquire a sharper edge with each of his precocious pamphlets. Although he turned out to be a failure as both the manager of his father's brewery and as a first-term tax collector, he demonstrated his sympathy for the distressed citizens of Boston and his ability to annoy their enemies by his craftily written columns. Even John Adams, who had regarded young Samuel and his failures with cousinly concern, was pleased to praise his "artful pen." The emergent propagandist was determined to stay in the background, however, paying for others' drinks in smoke-filled caucus meetings (where he earned the nickname "Sam the Publican") and trying to persuade even the haughtiest of the Whigs that it was in everyone's interest to bring more of the working people into the political process. Yet the gap in Boston society between the high and mighty and the low and humble was not easy to span.

At the lowest level of all, where Ebenezer Mackintosh attempted to make a living for himself as a cordwainer and to stay out of jail, there were other divisions, exacerbating the plight of the poorest people. There had always been a split between the North End and the South End inhabitants—the latter resenting the former, believing that those living in the more established and seaward part of town had better connections and more pull when it came to getting good jobs in the yards. The laborers in the less densely populated South End, where there were more ropewalks than shipyards and where unsettled folk from the countryside like the Mackintoshes tended to congregate, were particularly infuriated by the superior attitudes of the North Enders. Obviously, the only way to straighten out that attitude was by man-to-man fisticuffs, followed by gang action. Mill Creek, the border line between the two districts, became the conventional place for these moonlit battles of Boston's angry and disconnected seamen and landsmen.

In 1763, at the end of the wars with France, the British Navy discharged some twenty thousand sailors, contributing greatly to the number of men drifting through Boston looking for employment or for a fight. They added their peculiarly salty nature to the interneighborhood combats. The historian Marcus Rediker, a chronicler of seamen in this era, comments that "mariners were among the more radical and obstreperous element in the early American working class"; they added a "particularly violent element" to the disharmony and to the disputes that were already taking place.

In many ports within the British colonies but most notably in Boston, the traditional time for lower-class folk of all stripes to come boisterously together was on so-called Pope's Day. This celebration occurred on November 5 and recalled the plot against Parliament staged by Guy Fawkes and others on behalf of Spain, which was foiled on that date in 1605. As members of the crowd broached the casks of beer and rum and raised their voices in memory of that historic victory, an ages-old chant could often be heard: "The Powder Plot is not forgot; 'twill be observed by many a sot!"

This was indeed a time for Boston's lower classes to act out certain ancient rituals in masks and mummery against the Pope, the Devil, and the Stuart pretender to the Protestant throne. It was also a chance to make fun of whatever politicians and public figures were disfavored at the time. The occasion had grown in importance and in violence as the eighteenth century progressed, reaching a particularly high level of viciousness in 1755. Shocked and dismayed at that rowdiness (despite the fact that their own sons and servants may have been involved), the town fathers passed the Riot Act of 1755, for the following purpose:

> to prevent riotous tumultuous and disorderly assemblies of more than three person, all or any of them armed with Sticks, Clubs, or any kind of weapons, or disguised with vizards, or painted or discolored faces, or in any manner disguised, having any kind of imagery or pageantry, in any street, lane, or place in Boston.

The legislation had little effect, however. And as the tensions and the divisions of the town grew more intense, the Pope's Day celebrations grew into increasingly wild, sectional, nighttime brawls. In typically Bostonian manner, the elite chose to blame these always scary and sometimes brutal events on anybody but respectable citizens. One contemporary account describes a Pope's Day in the 1750s: thousands of lower-class Bostonians, most noticeably "servants, sailors, workingmen, apprentices and Negroes of the North and South Ends" became extraordinarily violent, with the effect that "people were killed and maimed for life."

These tumultuous, occasionally deadly celebrations, which usually began with two competitive parades marching at each other from the rival ends of Boston, reached a climax with a massive bonfire and a brawl at the town's center. There, the North End and the South End gangs each sought to topple and make away with the effigy of the Pope that the other had prepared. And before the evening's events culminated in the final battle, the participants seized on the anything-goes occasion to terrorize patricians in the surrounding houses, banging on doors and making the inhabitants give them food and drink or pay them money lest a window be broken or a fence pushed down.

Jack Tager discovered the following account of the Pope's Day celebration of 1745 in the *Boston Evening Post*:

[The] Popes were made and carried thro the Streets in the evening, one from the North and another from the South End of the town, attended by a vast Number of Negroes and white Servants, armed with Clubs, Staves, and Cutlasses, who were very abusive to the Inhabitants insulting the persons and breaking the Windows, etc. of such as did not give them Money to their Satisfaction, and even many of those who had given liberally, and the two Popes meeting in Cornhill, their followers were so infatuated, as to fall upon each other with the utmost Rage and fury; Several were sorely wounded and bruised, and some left for Dead, and rendered incapable of any Business for a long Time, to the great loss and Damage of their respective masters.

Ideally, the activities were intended to be amusing for all, particularly the downing of the devils and the dramatic performances with lanterns. The performances usually featured one or two heavy carriages with a lantern at the front and with a Pope's or a devil's head on poles. Masked children either rode on the carriage or concealed themselves beneath it so as to manipulate the effigies on the poles. Indeed, some scholars in the liberal 1960s, finding themes that linked the student demonstrations of their own riotous days to historic Boston, saw that town as a traditional "play space" for acting out yearnings for freedom and as a theater for carrying on ancient folk rituals. Certainly, the Pope's Day revels and shows were opportunities for the lower classes to have fun, yet they also provided a chance for them to make a declarative statement about their undismissable presence—to assert themselves as a public force that demanded attention. They were confronting the rest of the town, not quite as a minority party might declare itself in the halls of government but, in the words of the day, as "the people out of doors."

For the upper classes, however, Pope's Day was neither entertaining nor balanced; it was the world turned upside down. For staid people hiding behind locked shutters and doors, this was truly terrifying, revealing a depth of hatred and a desire for payback that no kind of puppet play or symbolism could disguise. Nor could a constabulary force of two dozen men be expected to restrain the crowds. In the advancing 1750s and 1760s, as the property holders were threatened with more telling damage and as the insults against them became more and more direct, they feared not only for themselves but also for their community. Yet as Tager points out, "no official condemnation could thwart the lower classes in this endeavor."

With the town socially and politically divided and in economic peril, the Pope's Day celebrations of 1764 loomed as particularly menacing. For Ebenezer Mackintosh, however, the day promised to be grand: an opportunity to lead his South End gang to long-sought victory over their opponents and for him to demonstrate his hard-won leadership. It all worked out more wonderfully and more bloodily than he could have imagined. By midday, enough alcohol had been consumed to ensure that the normal acceptance of their world of stagnation and oppression was forgotten and left behind. Matters got out of hand in the North End when, early in the afternoon, that gang's carriage—the cart that was bearing its effigy of the Pope toward the town center—ran over the head of one of the lads who accompanied it. The boy died instantly, bringing forth such horrified shrieks from the crowd that the sheriffs were ordered to close things down. The officers were to begin by destroying the effigies of the Popes from both the North and the South End.

But, of course, that could not be allowed by the people. Although the officials succeeded in grabbing the North End effigy and pulling it to pieces, the South Enders, led by Mackintosh, fought back ferociously and preserved their effigy. Winning that battle and demonstrating that power in Boston no longer belonged to the constabulary but to them, they surged northward and encountered their rivals, ready for them, at Mill Bridge. Here the battle became so intense that, as it was reported in one account, "many were hurt & bruised." Although his gang won—for the first time in its history—Mackintosh himself was arrested. But soon, with the weight of the crowd pressing upon the authorities, he was released. His men seized what was left of the North End's dummy and swept it along to a bonfire at the gallows on the Neck, where they burned it along with their own effigy. The crowd of "several thousand" went wild, "hallowing" and hailing the victors. Mackintosh, surviving his first public ordeal and savoring the salutes near the place of his birth and his father's disgrace, must have felt a special triumph.

Yet more was to come. As a result of his acknowledged victory, the red-faced, diminutive cordwainer Ebenezer Mackintosh was referred to henceforth as "Captain." In subsequent revels, he would lead his gang under that sobriquet. Furthermore, in a move that bespoke recognition at much higher levels of Boston society, he was appointed a "sealer of leather"—one of the officials who inspect and approve the quality of that material on behalf of the town. While not exactly the same as being given Athens's golden wreath or as replacing Otis as the undisputed champion of their cause, this award meant that the town's radical leaders saw in him something that might be useful, a force that might possibly help unify the divided town. Before he was betrayed, he would give them all they asked for.

# 5

# The Sailors' Liberty Tree

When news of the so-called Stamp Act came to Boston in the spring of 1765, John Hancock felt that the town had been hit by "a most prodigious shock, like an Earthquake." The radically inclined *Boston Gazette* reported a few months later that as a result of the infamous act, 1765 was a "time of more general distress and calamity" than had occurred since the founding of the colony. The British Crown, by the Act, imposed excise fees ranging up to £10 on American ship clearances, land deeds, and similar transactions of business and law. In the eyes of many Bostonians, the Act looked exactly like the "lurking serpent," which Samuel Adams's articles in the *Gazette* had warned would crush Massachusetts and all the other English colonies in North America. And with the cleverness of all such beasts of prey, it would strike Boston where the town was most tender and vulnerable. That place was the waterfront.

The waterfront had already suffered grievously from Lord Grenville's Sugar Act of 1764, which demanded that merchants pay not one penny but an intolerable threepence per barrel on the molasses their ships brought home from the Indies. It had also suffered from the zeal of Governor Francis Bernard's newly appointed inspectors, whose shipboard snooping made smuggling too risky a business for even the most intrepid skippers. Capping the severity of the Sugar and the Stamp Acts was the cruel stipulation that all arrested smugglers and accused merchants were to be tried in the admiralty court at Halifax, far from sympathetic Boston. In November, when the Stamp Act was to go into full effect, the cost of clearing outward-bound goods from Boston would increase prohibitively. As a result of these prospects, only one-fifth of the usual number of ships cleared for Europe or the southern islands in this key year of 1765. The few mariners fortunate enough to obtain berths on those ships found that their rates of pay had been reduced by more than 50 percent.

While the whip of the Stamp Act had lashed all of Boston's waterfront sectors, the town's fisheries, already diminished and depleted, were hit hardest of all by Grenville's venomous laws. Even in the most stringent of times gone by, a fisherman without a boat could get a berth on a friend's or a relative's vessel. And even when international tensions were at their most severe and the markets most stingy, skippers of those boats had been able to sell their leftover fish to lesser merchants willing to ship them down to the French West Indies, where they were bought by masters of the slave plantations. Now the British Navy made sure that even this modestly illegal traffic was halted. The wrathful reaction in the North and the South Ends, where Mackintosh's mates and other unemployed mariners vented their anger not only in riots but also in criminal rampages, was to raise the alarm of anarchy.

It seemed that each day newspapers reported new and bloody deeds by "disorderly Negroes and more disorderly sailors." Watchmen were hired to supplement the town's constabulary in hopes of controlling the waterfront fights. Boston, gaining renown for its "mobbish spirit," lost its once-proud reputation among other colonial capitals as a bastion of piety and security. Historian Marcus Rediker identifies the "militant presence" of troublemaking seamen as one of the essential elements not only in these mounting disruptions but also in the character of the pre-Revolutionary explosions that would soon follow.

# Sons of Neptune, Sons of Liberty

Even in those landlubber sectors of Boston not involved in shipping or fishing, there was a general sense that economic catastrophe was at hand, intensified by the Stamp Act. At the highest level, the social world in which Thomas Hutchinson moved, news of the people's increasing "tumults" seemed to bring about a counterreaction, a concurrent and mounting disdain for the communal culture of New Englanders, along with a commitment to England's Georgian order. Given his solid position in the camp of the Loyalists—that is, his double assignment of lieutenant governor and chief justice under Governor Bernard—Hutchinson may well have recalled the persecution that his own antinomian ancestor Anne Hutchinson had endured when she departed from the narrow-minded mores of the town. Although he still maintained his membership in the Congregational Church for form's sake, he now favored the Anglican Church. He vigorously endorsed the royalist attitude that Boston's Town Meeting was excessively troublesome (he referred to its "anarchic democracy") and should be done away with. In this opinion, he allied himself with such patrician predecessors as Governor William Shirley, who had said that the meeting, that near-sacred organ of the populace, was "spoiled by too many working Artificers, seafaring men, and the lowest sort of people."

At Hutchinson's official and courtly level, there was the (presumably enlightened) conviction that steps must be taken to strengthen and thereby to rationalize the process of running a colonial government in North America. Boston, as a leading example, must reverse itself and, denying its peculiar, autonomous past, must become an obedient, contributing part of the imperial mercantilist system. The Stamp Act seemed to those at the top of the heap an understandable, if perhaps overly severe, part of that process.

Hutchinson, though he respected Parliament's right to lay the Act on the colonies, did have doubts about the wisdom of such a nakedly obvious tax. Bernard, who had had to pay one fee for his gubernatorial commission under King George II and then another for his commission from George III, was personally hopeful that some new system of taxation could be created, for the benefit of one and all, including himself. He had gained a quick understanding of the way Bostonians flaunted their indifference to customs duties. He wrote to London about the "carts and carriages . . . in the dead of night, which can be for no other purpose than smuggling," and sought consent for taking corrective measures. As for the Stamp Act, like Hutchinson, he had doubts about its timing and methodology but thoroughly approved of Lord Grenville's basic theme—that the American colonies should produce more revenue in recompense for the protection of Empire and its stressed colonial officials.

Although the well-educated merchants and the reform-minded councilors who surrounded Bernard could see that their port had been outstripped in recent years by booming New York and Philadelphia and also recognized the need to curtail the corrosive unrest on the waterfront, they could not believe that along with Boston's primacy, their own day had passed. By 1760, the so-called golden years of American colonial life had in fact become a phase gone by, an era recalled in Copley's paintings but no longer a reality. Yet, as the port diminished and as danger signals abounded, Boston's aristocracy flaunted an opulent lifestyle and exaggerated the social distinctions. By their actions and attitudes, they called down upon their heads the full fury of Boston's still forceful Puritan preachers. "An evil and adulterous generation!" was but one of the clergy's condemnations. Such doom-filled words recalled the times before King Philip's War when Cotton Mather had blamed all imminent disasters on the laxity of the newly rich.

Nor was the clergy alone in its denunciations. From the next-lower level of society, Boston's uneasy assemblage of powerful lawyers, successful smugglers, and ambitious artisans, came cries (words often written by Samuel Adams) against the privileged. They blamed the increasingly snobbish, hierarchical governing class and its royal connections for the town's distress. James Otis, who was at this time serving as an assemblyman, claimed that privileged merchants and British officials were "forging shackles for the country." He went on to charge that unless checked, the royal officials would "grind the faces of the poor without remorse, eat the bread of repression without fear, and wax fat upon the spoils of the people." He also preached (erroneously but effectively) that the Stamp Act was essentially a maneuver specially designed by Governor Bernard and his yes-man Thomas Hutchinson to crush the people and strip them of their rights and property.

Such well-regarded Boston smugglers as Peter Faneuil, who had once satisfied himself that the old Molasses Act was a "dead letter" and that the heyday of the free-wheeling entrepreneurs would last forever, would have been surprised to see that merchants in this new era had to fight for their means of livelihood, even as their rivals collapsed around them. John Hancock, his whale oil business faltering and his English agents clamoring for immediate paybacks for their advanced fees, also felt threatened. He listened to the increasingly radical words of Otis, as did other heedful merchants, and considered how the town's electorate was being split between entrenched royalists and fulminating Whigs. Which would prevail?

Hancock would meet some of those Whiggish gentlemen at Mason meetings, he having become a member of both the Lodge of St. Andrew and Saint John's Lodge. He also attended the sub rosa caucus club gatherings where people not of the elite but craftsmen and lesser merchants were encouraged to express their views. These half-social, half-political meetings, predecessors of party rallies, were reported to Governor Bernard, who viewed them as the "clubb of scandal." That label also applied to a new organization, the Sons of Neptune, designed to transform the variegated waterfront segments into a cohesive action unit. Based on what he heard, Hancock concluded that he and indeed all of the town's leading families being squeezed by the Stamp Act and other economic restrictions could no longer ignore the populace and their rising voices. As the largest stakeholder in the enterprise of Boston, he chose to become involved in political action. Pulling the right strings in 1765, he was elected, presto, a selectman of the town.

In the Massachusetts General Court, matters were coming to a head on the issue of how the province should respond to the Stamp Act. Even with the outcries of distress from the Boston waterfront, Otis and Samuel Adams had failed to transform anxiety into action, either at home or among other colonies; their idea of calling an unauthorized pancolonial congress had met with a shocked and negative response. In the General Court's summertime debates of 1765, the radicals also failed to counter Hutchinson's argument that any petition to the king or Parliament about the Act must be couched in the most respectful and deferential language. Despite Otis's masterful guidance of the Country Party, he could not secure control of the House; Hutchinson won enough votes from the conservatives and others to be named as the delegate who would carry a petition from Massachusetts to London. Adams's strident opinion—that the Stamp Act violated every Englishman's constitutional right to be taxed only by his consent and not by a distant monarch—was reflected on not a single page of the colony's lengthy plea.

Although the strategy of stirring up an intercolonial protest had not proved feasible, Massachusetts had company in its various efforts to fight back against the Stamp Act. Even in England, one member of Parliament, an eloquent veteran of Great Britain's campaign in Canada named Isaac Barré, spoke out against the Act with resonant passion. Scornful of England's high-level snobberies, he expressed admiration for the Americans' self-reliant attitude. In both the early (1764) and the later debates on the wisdom of imposing taxes on the colonies, Barré sought to disparage the proposals of the Grenville administration. At one point, rising to his feet to refute the argument that England had nurtured the colonies and now deserved some economic reward, Barré referred to Americans as noble "Sons of Liberty." The expression soon leaped across the intervening ocean and appeared in newspapers throughout the American colonies. At a time of great transatlantic tension and confusion, Barré's fighting spirit and apt words gave radical protesters the unifying name needed for themselves and their mission.

From Virginia, too, came highflown sentiments. At the time in 1764 when Massachusetts waterfront toughs were knocking heads in Pope's Day brawls and Massachusetts Whigs were conjuring up plots in dockside taverns, Tidewater intellectuals debated the principles of freedom, sometimes effectively. In the opinion of James Otis's Boston colleague Oxenbridge Thacher, the Virginians preceded other Americans in asserting "their Rights with decent Firmness." He was referring most pointedly to Patrick Henry, who had given Americans the explicit theme of "freedom endangered." His famous *Virginia Resolves* stated, among other points, that only the General Assembly of a colony could rightfully lay taxes on its citizens; any other authority's attempt to impose such taxes would result in the destruction of "British as well as American freedom."

Henry's speeches and proposals, as re-created and exaggerated in Boston's radical press, stimulated further disruptions throughout New England. Governor Bernard, understandably alarmed, remarked that the *Virginia Resolves* "have roused up the Boston Politicians & have been the Occasion of a fresh inundation of factious & insolent pieces in the popular Newspapers." Encouraged, even challenged, by the Virginians, Samuel Adams did indeed dip more deeply into caustic ink; the *Gazette*'s readership relished his vitriolic columns.

Besides Adams's "insolence" in print, his tavern-table talents enabled him to galvanize men of diverse callings. He organized the Loyal Nine, a secret league of well-to-do Bostonians willing to risk taking subversive action against the Stamp Act. Although they may not have shared Adams's religious belief in a "Christian Sparta," they felt passionately (Hutchinson said "hysterically") about the need to subvert Great Britain's designs. Several of the Loyal Nine had links to the waterfront. They included Captain Joseph Field (encountered in chapter 4) and housepainter Thomas Crafts, distillers Thomas Chase and John Avery, publisher Benjamin Edes of the *Boston Gazette*, and jeweler George Trott, as well as John Smith, Stephen Cleverly, and Henry Bass. As cautious citizens and basically social conservatives, they epitomized the middle-class people of Boston who were severely threatened by the Stamp Act. Though they were eager to oppose the Act and its agents, their intention was to stay in the background, to direct the energies of the mob, and to keep whatever violence might erupt within civil bounds.

As a further boost to the resistance in Massachusetts, Samuel Adams Jr.—who, though born to an aristocratic family, had earned a positive reputation among the populace for the inefficiency with which he carried out his job as tax collector—was elected to the General Court. There he served as a trusted representative from the town of Boston. In the legislature, he helped Otis stimulate the

Country Party and was also able to obtain a seat on committees that produced resolutions critical of the royal government. But the time for careful resolutions and Patrick Henry–style words had passed; the time to link patriotic sentiments with rough action had arrived, and the radicals were prepared to make that happen. To stand forth in the exposed positions as the active leaders of the multitudes, young Samuel Adams and the Loyal Nine had two well-known fire-brands as nominees. The first, as might be expected, was the increasingly popular Ebenezer Mackintosh.

Victor of the Pope's Day riots nine months earlier and captain of a fire battalion in the South End's Ward Eleven, as described in chapter 4, Mackintosh was said to have some 150 men at his personal command. Although Hutchinson and Bernard chose to portray him, after the cataclysmic events of that August, as an alarmingly dangerous and often drunk roisterer, he had in fact been recognized by many as an acceptable member of society. He relished his official, albeit low-level, post as a leather sealer. Though poorly schooled, he could read, write, and recite popular poetry of the day; an avid reader of the *Chronicle*, he was fully aware of what the radical press had to say about those uneasy and changing times. In keeping with that spirit, he named the older of his two children Paschal Paoli, after the famous Corsican revolutionary. His hot-tempered actions were quite expectable reactions to his perennial lack of funds and to the difficulty of opening his own shop to provide a reasonable living. As the Stamp Act made conditions even more crushing, he must have walked with clenched fists among Boston's unemployed.

Mackintosh might have remained simply a minor, noisome representative of the repressed laboring class, removed from the merchants' and mechanics' protestations about the Stamp Act, but he happened to fall badly into debt once again, this time in company with his fellow shoemaker Benjamin Bass. He and Bass, according to scholar Dirk Hoerder, were in the tight squeeze of having received citations (warrants) from tax collector Samuel Adams. But Adams, the ever-flexible official and the political leader who recognized potential crowd leaders when he saw them, provided the accused men with an alternative to going to jail: they could join as active members in a plan that would provide everyone with a bit of fun and excitement. It would go into effect on the morning of August 14.

Another firebrand identified and approached by Boston's radical leadership was the ringleader "Captain" Henry Swift. He had been chief of the North End gang in the Pope's Day riots of the preceding autumn. Like his father before him, Swift was a shipwright from the motley and crowded North End. Now, as he was informed by spokesmen for the Loyal Nine, he had a chance to find new prominence. By combining forces with Mackintosh, his former antagonist from the South End, he could gain more power. He could, in fact, help to liberate the town from the Stamp Act and break its hold on Boston's shipping. The celebration of that potential triumph would be even more boisterous than a Pope's Day revel; the gentlemen would pay for ample drinks and costumes for all.

## "Liberty, Property, and No Stamps!"

After a frantic night of secret work, all under the command of Ebenezer Mackintosh—who had accepted the extravagant title "First Captain General of the Liberty Tree"—the dawn of Wednesday, August 14, broke on an astonishing scene. Hanging from a grand old elm in the South End across from Chase and Speakman's distillery (at the corner of what are now Washington and Essex streets) were two objects: an effigy of a man and some sort of a boot. Closer inspection of this display at the designated Liberty Tree revealed that the man was labeled "AO"—Andrew Oliver, the official appointed by Grenville to distribute the stamps that would soon arrive from England. Even closer inspection revealed an appended verse, which read, "A godlier sight who e'er did see/ A Stamp-Man hanging on a tree!"

The boot, out of whose top peeped a hideous figure that could only be the Devil himself, represented a more complex theme. It was a pun on Lord Bute's name, for Bute was the king's friend who was widely, if incorrectly, believed to have dreamed up the Stamp Act. Here was his image in the form of "Jack Boot" himself, a figure traditionally associated with the Devil. And here were the townspeople of Boston, gathering in ever greater numbers to mock him and the oppression that he had brought upon them. Thus, at first, the demonstration had all the marks of an old-fashioned English crowd action, with parodied figures and slogans and naughty kids making fun of their elders, and with all the troubles of the day pinned on hateful effigies. But then something fundamentally different was seen and heard, something that in its unambiguous directness revealed the evolved American character of this event.

It was not merely the novel fact that as the crowds swelled—with everyone invited to join (everyone, that is, except the Negroes, who were still considered too risky)—the expected mob unruliness was replaced by a definite, uniting discipline. More than that, it became evident that the North End delegation, led by Henry Swift, had been specifically appointed to keep everyone, even the law itself, from removing the effigies. Sheriff Greenleaf, acting on a directive from Hutchinson, attempted to haul down the insulting images but was prevented from doing so by this well-prepared group of men. Some of them were clearly the usual suspects, that is, the Pope's Day rioters; others could be recognized as gentlemen dressed up as workers.

Clearly, this was neither a traditional protest of symbols and ritual nor a spontaneous uprising; a new kind of predetermination gave the crowd program and purpose. As directed by Mackintosh with the support of Swift, the people, now numbering in the thousands, directed themselves toward Kilby Street, their assigned task being to demolish the nearly completed office building of Andrew Oliver. Charging through the streets, they shouted, along with their usual huzzahs, a new chant: "Liberty, property, and no stamps!"

This linking of "property" and "liberty" with a mob action might seem unlikely or even contradictory. But, as may be recalled, riots in Boston had long been carried out for communal objectives, with the town itself regarded as a common holding for which all had responsibility. The word *property* acquires a new, less private meaning in this context. Indeed, Boston's Stamp Act riot, the first of many nearly simultaneous riots against the governments of American colonies, was not, despite all its appearances, an act of anarchy or destruction but of construction and reclamation. Other attempted actions or interventions by superior powers having failed to protect the townspeople

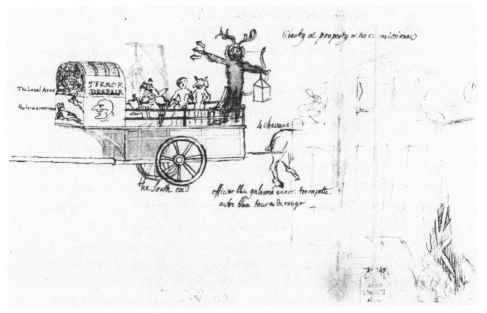

*Elaborate wagons became a major feature of Boston's nocturnal Pope's Day celebrations, particularly during the anti–Stamp Act actions staged by the town's obstreperous youths and antiauthoritarian crowds. Sketched by a Swiss artist in 1767, this wagon, featuring a devil with a lantern and an official hanged in effigy, proclaimed, "Liberty & Property & No Commissioners."*
The Library Company of Philadelphia

from economic disaster, this planned reaction carried out by the working or the unemployed poor against the grasping elite and the oppressive royal government was a remarkable event. It was, in fact, a reaction to protect the people's perceived property. However small, or even just imagined, their lot may have been—a fishing boat, a marginal distillery, or a humble shop like the one Mackintosh wanted—in that humble share of the community lay the people's basic hope.

Boston's united, willful opinion on that point was demonstrated soon after noon when, Oliver's house having been reached and ransacked and the plundered planks having been removed to Fort Hill for a massive bonfire staged by the people, Governor Bernard saw not one person move to defend him against a potential attack. As with Governor Shirley in the previous generation, Bernard chose to read the unwillingness of the militia or other citizens to gather

around him as a sign that he no longer ruled this land and its popular base. Wisely, he fled to Castle William.

Another key aspect of the onrushing events of that August day
was that the crowds, though at first directed by the Loyal Nine in
the persons of Mackintosh and Swift, soon took off on their own ini-
tiative, which was when they charged on to Andrew Oliver's house.
As night came on and as the bonfires' flames mounted, the
marchers were described as an "amazingly inflamed people," looking perhaps like the grotesques described by Hawthorne. They
were, in fact, acting in this attack contrary to the strict wishes of
their supposed leaders; it was as if they had grown to realize that
they could rule the town. They beheaded the effigy of Oliver as a
clear statement that that would be his manner of death, too, if he
disobeyed their wishes. Polite mocking and resonant words had
been replaced by volitional, popular violence.

Although the usually courageous Lieutenant Governor Hutchinson and the more or less faithful Sheriff Greenleaf had pursued the
mob, hoping to disperse it, they were soon chased away by men
hurling rocks and brandishing brickbats. Thereafter, while some
members of the crowd rooted through Oliver's ornate house searching for its owner (who had fled), others demolished "his Looking
Glasses, Tea Geer and Other China." The specificity with which the
press indicated these items indicated the hatred that the people lavished on such symbols of what they viewed as undue wealth. Now
quite on their own, they seemed to be distinguishing between
invalid property (the aristocracy's), which could be smashed in
response to the demands of the crowd, and real property (theirs),
which was to be respected and not taxed. They also felt free to con-
sume a great deal of Oliver's wine.

The next evening, when Boston protesters again besieged
Oliver's house and threatened to level it, Oliver, then at home,
understood what he must do. He requested "the Liberty of being
excused from his new office." That was precisely what the crowd
sought. His besiegers, after raising "three Cheers . . . took their
Departure with Damage."

A new order of things appeared to be at hand. Sensing this, the
men of the Loyal Nine (which had been set up with the specific and

limited purpose of fighting the Stamp Act) began to identify themselves more openly as Sons of Liberty. They now seemed to have not much to fear, the governor having offered to resign. For his part, Governor Bernard stated, "I am entirely at the Mercy of the Mob." Rejoicing in their power, the people convened the following night atop Fort Hill and resolved to get at the one official who had tried to stop their revels of the preceding day: Thomas Hutchinson. But on arriving at his house and after banging on his doors, they were persuaded by a courageous neighbor that the lieutenant governor had left for his house in suburban Milton. They withdrew—for a while.

Eleven days later, they came back with a vengeance. In this case, vengeance was powered by a peculiarly New England ingredient: the righteous word from a powerful pulpit. The Reverend Jonathan Mayhew, mentioned in chapter 1 as the outspoken voice of liberty in Boston's North End, had recently lectured that "The purpose of the divine mission of Jesus Christ is the happiness of man: but that happiness can only result from Virtue, and virtue is inseparable from Civil Liberty."

Mayhew must surely have been aware of the heady mood of the crowd as a result of its Stamp Act demonstrations in those heated days of August 1765. Yet into that inflammable atmosphere, he tossed a sermon based on this red-hot text: "I would they were even cut off which trouble you; for, brethren, ye have been called to liberty." It was all that was needed to ignite the crowds of Boston to their next deed of corrective destruction. This violent deed, the tearing apart of Hutchinson's house in Boston, occurred on Monday the twenty-sixth, the very next day after the sermon. But Mayhew held himself blameless. Indeed, he spent many of the following days explaining himself to Hutchinson and protesting to the Hutchinson family from "the bottom of my heart" that he had no intention of initiating "these proceedings."

After igniting bonfires, the crowd divided itself in two parts in order to tend, separately, to the ripping apart of the homes of Loyalist William Story and customs official Benjamin Hallowell. Regrouped, the two bands of men—some of them fueled by the cases of Madeira wine found in Hallowell's cellar—arrived at the Hutchinson mansion at dinnertime. They beat on the great doors with bars and axes, demanding to be heard. Mackintosh, reportedly quite drunk, raised his voice again as the undisputed leader: the family must leave. Though Hutchinson at first chose to stand his ground and defy the mob, his daughter finally persuaded him to flee with the rest of the family.

The crowd immediately set to work. In Hutchinson's words, "The hellish crew fell upon my house with the rage of devils & in a moment with axes split down the door. . . . Not content with tearing off all the wainscot & hangings & splitting the doors to pieces they beat down the Partition[s]." In a manner that was actually more orderly than frenzied, they labored until three or four o'clock in the morning to reduce one of New England's grandest houses to a naked shell, bereft of cupola, of walls, of floors, and certainly of contents. Scattered across the lawns, wine bottles and business documents told the evening's tale.

As another reminder of what had provoked them, Mackintosh's followers destroyed Hutchinson's formal gardens—symbols (like Oliver's coach) of the British-style opulence that they despised. Furthermore, in addition to the objects of value that they had liberated and taken home with them, they stole coins valued at £900. This theft, a measure far beyond the bounds of any normally accepted English-style crowd actions or any actions the Boston elite might have countenanced, demonstrated that a kind of rebelliousness quite apart from the Stamp Act issue was also at large that night. The people now, at this intoxicating moment, far more than during the Knowles impressment riot, seemed really to be opening up the prospect of anarchy. As crowds of them flocked to the site in the days that followed—Hutchinson's destroyed mansion having become (in the words of historian R. B. St. George) a "tourist attraction"—they demonstrated that joy in liberation from arrogant mercantilism was the mood of the day.

## Anarchy and Order at the Union Feast

The technical word for rule by the mob is *ochlocracy*, a locution that Governor Bernard used in panicky letters to London that sought to describe the local scene. "The real authority of the government is at an end" was the letters' most repeated theme. At the same time, the governor tried to come to grips with the strange civil contest in whose midst he found himself, little knowing that it was the first stirring of the American Revolution. As he analyzed it, it was a contest between, on the one hand, the royal rulership and its enlightened supporters and, on the other hand, the liberal Whigs and their "trained mob" of common people. Andrew Oliver's Tory brother Peter Oliver described the second group as "vicious and wildly ambitious rebels" whose unruliness had turned Boston into the "Metropolis of Sedition" and whose purpose could only be the overturn of the whole social order. Far more than a conventional riot of the sort Boston had grown used to over the years, this was, in Bernard's terms, "a War of Plunder, general levelling, and taking away the Distinction of rich and poor."

Hutchinson viewed the matter similarly, though with more sorrow than rage. He described the terrible moment in which he realized that his beloved old world of privilege had come to an end, saying that the "Mob was so general and so supported that all Power ceased in an instant." Yet he saw this cessation of established power not primarily as a move by levelers or anarchists but as a deft maneuver by certain rival politicians, the ploy of extremists whose names and characters he knew all too well. For months, he had watched the supposedly secret Loyal Nine and their operations with a mixture of concern and contempt. He viewed these troublemakers as "generally tradesmen" who commanded the lower orders to do their dirty work.

Bernard and Hutchinson joined in regarding Mackintosh as an important but not necessarily central figure. The former described him as "an expert in hanging and burning effigies and pulling down houses . . . without doubt a mad man [who] with his mobbish eloquence prevails in every motion." Hutchinson went so far as to conclude that the pint-sized, red-haired fireman, in league with radical Whigs, might now command sufficient influence to control the Boston Town Meeting and the Massachusetts House. So uncharacteristically panicked was he about the deterioration of authority and the threat of additional violence brought on by Mackintosh and his backers that he seemed almost to abandon hope. He broke down and wept in his own court the day after his house's destruction; he even chose not to press charges against Mackintosh as the leader of that destruction for fear of his family's safety. A few days later, he resigned his judgeship.

For Bernard, no such surrender and stepping down from office was possible. He must somehow reestablish authority—though he saw no clear sign that the citizens would support his return to power. He wailed that "Some of the principle ringleaders of the late riots walk the streets with impunity. No officer dares attack them, no witnesses appear against them, and no judge acts upon them." And so the governor bided his time.

Through these days of terror, the Bernard-Oliver-Hutchinson clique retained some faith in Boston's ancient civility, its desire not for anarchy but for order. Just as Preacher Jonathan Mayhew had expressed horror at what his impassioned words about freedom had generated, so did most of Boston's leadership, radicals and conservatives alike, hurry to denounce the actions of the people, which seemed in the cold light of day not reformist but provocative. Although there had been reports (from John Adams, among others) that gentlemen in disguise had been seen mixed in with Mackintosh's men, those same gentlemen were now quick to disassociate themselves from the affair. Even Samuel Adams, in genuine-sounding words of shock and disapproval, deplored the "mobbish nature" of the Stamp Act riots. He opined, possibly with tongue in cheek, that they must have been the acts not of organized gangs but "the diversion of a few boys in the streets"; the destruction of Hutchinson's house must have been caused not by Bostonians but by "vagabond strangers." In biographer Benjamin Irvin's opinion, Adams had never meant for the violence to get so far out of hand; in the days that followed, he even feared that this excess might cause Bostonians, by way of reaction, to sympathize with Hutchinson and his party.

In the taverns and through the streets, Adams spread the word that there should be no further violence: it might hurt "our cause." A town meeting was called, whose purpose was to reassert order and to calm the public. Seeing the way matters were tending, the governor emerged from retirement and summoned the militia in hopes that it would now muster properly (as it had not on the fourteenth) and would secure the town. Heeding the call, a number of "gentlemen volunteers" took charge and reestablished a night watch.

From his recently attained position in the House of Representatives, Samuel Adams renewed James Otis's original call for a pan-American congress. There had been significant riots in other colonies as well, and he shared with patriots elsewhere the vision of a combined colonial protest against the Stamp Act.* But Governor Bernard, fearing that Massachusetts would take the lead in writing such a protest, thus fomenting an even wider rebellion, used all of his skill and regained popularity to ensure that the chief delegate to the Congress from his province would not be a radical but one of his supporters. When the historic Congress finally met in New York on October 7, with representatives from the nine northern colonies in attendance, it honored the Bay Colony by electing as its chairman Massachusetts's Timothy Ruggles. But he happened to be Bernard's man. He did his work well, joining with John Dickinson of Pennsylvania and other mild-voiced patriots to see that the "Declarations of our humble Opinion" sent to the king and to Parliament was the opposite of rebellious.

In the months preceding the issuance of the Congress's statement of the "Rights and Privileges of the British American Colonies," New York City had, itself, been ripped apart by waterfront riots that echoed in some respects those of Boston. The significant fact is that like Boston's, these disruptions had been powered by the energies and the fury of unemployed seamen and that they had been led by maritime personalities—notably, Captain Isaac Sears and Privateer Alexander McDougall. Alarmed by the nature and the activity of these local forces, as well as by reports from New England, General Thomas Gage, the commander in chief of British forces in North America stationed in New York, worried that the illicit Congress might succeed in seducing the sentiments of colonial

---

*Scholars now concur that it was the New York Sons of Liberty, meeting with the well-organized Connecticut Sons of Liberty at a tavern in New London, Connecticut, who succeeded in conceiving and bringing about the Stamp Act Congress of October 1765.

participants away from loyalty to the Crown. Seeing that there was a wide range of opinion among the colonies, he wrote home that "There are various characters and Opinions, but it's to be feared in general, that the Spirit of Democracy,* is strong amongst them." Yet the Congress's final document, while being a precedent-setting declaration of the fundamental rights of the American colonists, was also a courteous bow to the overarching authority of British rule.

The Congress's obeisance gave some further encouragement to Boston's regrouping conservatives. In the days immediately following the attacks on Hallowell's and Hutchinson's houses, these unswayed loyalists had pondered how to move against the seeming chief of the mobs: Ebenezer Mackintosh. To curb him might be the fastest way to quell the rebellion. The generally agreeable sheriff, Stephen Greenleaf, was therefore ordered to arrest his firefighting colleague.

Spotted on the corner of Green Street, Mackintosh gave himself up without the slightest struggle, seemingly confident that his stay behind bars would be short. And he was quite right: at day's end, a number of gentlemen, some of them from the customs house (which had been threatened with destruction), arrived at the jail and instructed Greenleaf to hand over his keys so they could free the prisoner. The sheriff, caught in a contest of powers beyond his comprehension, could only agree with those who seemed currently in charge. When he reported the release to the Governor's Council, he received an official rebuke but was not charged; the horse had left the barn.

Historians tend to regard this somewhat farcical incident as evidence that the once-bold liberals of Boston, far from being confidently in charge, were now in retreat, terrified about what further damage Mackintosh might cause when questioned in prison by authorities. But there is also the interpretation that the citizens had so much regard for Mackintosh and his potential that they chose to rescue their hero. It was obvious to many that this mere cordwainer from the waterfront had won power, had an unswerving conviction, and had the public with him.

---

*By which he did not necessarily mean democracy as a mode of popular and representative government, but democracy as any way of ruling other than by dint of the British Parliament.

At this point, Boston's craftsmen and urban artisans, the middle-class strivers called "mechanics," were the most consolidated of Boston's social and professional groups, given the divisions among the upper classes. Though the acceptance of Mackintosh within this group also allowed him to consort with merchants and legislators, it by no means meant that he would make the grade as a gentleman. Yet at all levels of society, he had a certain romantic persona. In the Governor's Council, Mackintosh was spoken of as "Masaniello"— the barefooted fisherman who had staged a partially successful uprising against unjust taxes in seventeenth-century Naples and had achieved legendary status thereafter as the model for revolutionary upstarts.

In the most down-to-earth circles, Mackintosh was seen simply as the boss, not only the paramount leader of the town's violent waterfront gangs but also a force whose political power extended far beyond its South End base. He had sufficient contacts to summon supporters from beyond the Neck, even from Massachusetts's interior towns. One of those off-Neck supporters, a former ship's captain then living in Woburn named Laommi Baldwin, heard the call and rushed in with others to join in the fray of August 14. His willingness to bring his muscle and his musket to the fight on behalf of the distressed capital, though no one could see it at the time, hinted at the generous assistance from outlying towns that would produce patriot forces for the Battle of Bunker Hill. Mackintosh's attractive leadership, a reputation broadcast not by noble words but by recognized actions, demonstrated that from the people themselves could come a leader. Though Mackintosh had no intention of heading a government or of becoming the kingpin of anarchy, his rather comical title, First Captain General of the Liberty Tree, seemed not so laughable after all.

## The Union Feast and the Liberty Tree

When November 1765 arrived and, with it, the official commencement of the waterfront-crippling Stamp Act, Bostonians of all sorts and conditions braced for new demonstrations of mob power.

Hoping to regain control of the popular base, Samuel Adams made the rounds of the caucuses and Masonic meetings where Whig associates, mechanics, and ship masters joined him. They now seemed quite willing to become active parts of his carefully plotted moves. John Adams, on observing those maneuvers, referred to his cousin Samuel disapprovingly as "a designing person . . . [there is] no man more ambitious." At the same time, John Hancock, who had been meeting with Samuel Adams in the Green Dragon Tavern, made up his mind definitively that official attempts to thwart the Stamp Act having failed, he would throw in his lot and his fortune with those who would raise resistance to the next level of protest.*

With November and the season of demonstrations upon them, the townspeople begged the Assembly to convene and protect them against the expected assault. But even as homeowners on the Common boarded their windows and double-bolted their doors, busy workers set the stage for the Pope's Day revels. Then on the morning of the fifth, effigies appeared hanging once again on the Liberty Tree. A crowd rapidly assembled, and, not long after noon, the people could hear the sound of trumpets and drums. But then, to their wonderment, down the streets leading to the town center came not the rush of a mob unleashed, not two ferocious gangs from the South and the North Ends led by their rival chiefs. Instead, there marched into view two beautifully disciplined teams, led by the old rivals Mackintosh and Swift. Loyalist Peter Oliver was among those to express his amazement. He described how Mackintosh

> paraded the town with a Mob of armed Men in Two Files, and passed by the State House when the General Assembly were sitting to display his Power. If a Whisper was heard among his Followers, the holding up of his Finger hushed it in a Moment; & when he had fully displayed his Authority, he marched his Men to the first Rendezvous, & ordered them

---

*At the end of October 1765, he had persuaded 250 other Boston merchants to join New York and Philadelphia resisters in a contract for the non-importation of British goods.

to retire peacefully to their several Homes: & was punctually obeyed.

"What had happened here?" Oliver and others must have asked themselves.

Unknown to them, the answer lay in the "Union Feast" that many of the marchers had shared the night before. Arranged by Samuel Adams and John Hancock—the former with his ability to bring disparate parts of the town together in a common policy, the latter with his capability to buy however much liquor and victuals were required to make men jolly—the feast had succeeded in uniting many factions of the divided town. This rolling event, actually a series of dinners at Boston's most popular taverns, allowed merchants and politicians, along with representatives of the waterfront laborers, to come together with, as it was said, "Heart and Hand in flowing Bowls and bumping Glasses." The largest of the dinners was held at the Royal Exchange Tavern, where two hundred carefully screened guests were feted. Indeed, the conjoining of forces and the planning of the next day's march were by no means invitations or opportunities for anarchy to triumph. The Whig leaders made a point of dividing the people into five ranks by their classes, having again excluded Negroes (who were considered violence-prone) and having admitted only those they deemed respectable.

The uniforms that the leaders handed out also varied according to the social position of the marcher in Boston society—proper infantry for Samuel Adams's Christian Sparta. The most elaborate outfit went to General Mackintosh: blue-and-red trimmed, topped by a gold-laced hat. He was also awarded a gilt gorget to gleam upon his breast. And to show that he was now, at least in some eyes, worthy of a gentleman's airs, he carried a rattan cane. So it happened that when the two files of marchers came together, Ebenezer Mackintosh and the handsomely accoutered Henry Swift bowed to each other with great formality under the Liberty Tree, signaling the commencement of yet another grand celebration.

This staged event of the two gangs' meeting might be viewed as an indication that the mob chiefs had sold out whatever principles they may have possessed and had given themselves regardlessly, a

pair of dupes, into the hands of Hancock and Adams. Other interpretations are possible, though. Mackintosh was, as has been seen,
no fool. He commanded a sizable following and considerable
respect. Even Peter Oliver remarked of him that he appeared to be
"sensible and manly," adding that he dressed genteely. Such personages as militia captain and councilman William Brattle were not
ashamed to be seen in public with him now, even arm in arm.

Such interclass amicability occurred just at this time, to be sure,
at the height of Mackintosh's popularity, when it was useful to be
seen with him and to present him as the man of the hour (or possibly as the goat on whom all would be blamed). Yet he had been the
indispensable agent in bringing the people into the political picture,
and never again could they be totally excluded. In the grand political debates on the Stamp Act and subsequent issues, his symbolic
voice—and the roar of the mob behind him—had to be heard. As
Peter Oliver ruefully put it, "The People, even to the lowest Ranks,
have become more attentive to their liberties."

In fact, the last dramatic act in the working out of the Stamp Act
belonged to Mackintosh, with Peter Oliver's brother Andrew playing a degrading role. Although Oliver had said that he would resign
his post as royal stamp distributor after the crowds had leveled his
shop and office and had threatened his house with destruction back
in August, there had been no official statement of such resignation.
Boston's Whig leaders and waterfront chiefs feared that the town's
merchants, damaged along with everyone else by the close-down of
shipping operations, would finally give in and accept the imposition
of the cursed stamps. To prevent that, it was necessary to take further, even more definitive action against the man who seemed to
epitomize the Stamp Act.

The drama was preceded on the night of December 16 by the
delivery of a sternly worded message to Peter Oliver's house. The
message demanded the official's "public resignation" and went on to
warn that "Your non-Compliance, Sir, will incur the Displeasure of
the True Born Sons of Liberty." Thus on the next day, during a
bone-chilling rainstorm, Oliver was forcibly conducted to the Liberty Tree by none other than General Ebenezer Mackintosh. Before
a throng of more than two thousand soaked but jubilant spectators,

Oliver then swore to take no steps "for enforcing the Stamp Act in America." It seemed that the Liberty Tree had become almost an additional house of the legislature, a place where the "people out-of-doors," in the phrase of the day, could carry out certain governmental procedures. Into that public meeting place, the royal government had been compelled to come, humbly.

As well as a severe blow to royal authority, this performance at the end of 1765 was a thoroughly humiliating personal experience for a once greatly respected gentleman and his entire species. To bend to the will of the crowd, a crowd led by a mere cordwainer, was an unprecedented development in an age of deference to those of higher status and in the social scheme of this tradition-bound town. Even more than the soon-to-follow repeal of the Stamp Act itself—which occurred early the next year, after British merchants complained to the king's new administration that the loss of trade was intolerable—this rain-soaked ceremony at the Liberty Tree seemed to be of profound local importance. It indicated that in company with the attacks on the existing power structure by the people of Boston's waterfront went certain social consequences. The rage of the seamen and the fishermen had been transformed into a push for change in the order of human affairs, a theme for the American Revolution that would follow in the next decade.

Part Two

# WATERFRONT UPRISINGS BEFORE THE REVOLUTION

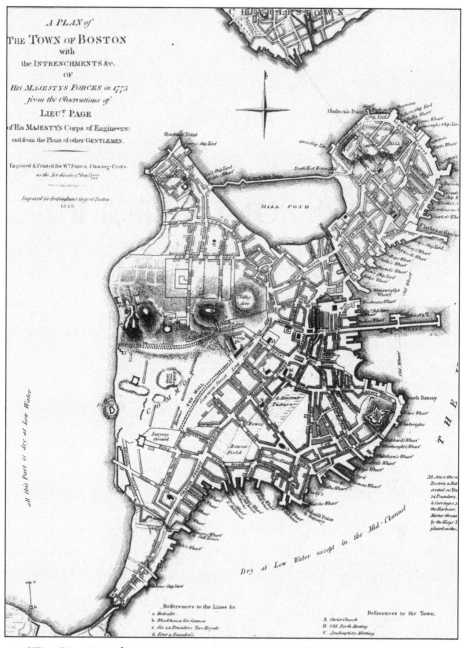

*When Lieutenant Thomas Page of His Majesty's Corps of Engineers composed this map of Boston in 1775, British forces occupied the town. From John Hancock's mansion atop Beacon Hill, the marines' encampment on the Common was all too visible. Page's map also shows the strong fortifications at the Neck, as well as the battery on Copp's Hill across from Charlestown.*

The Boston Public Library/Rare Books Department, Courtesy of the Trustees

# 6

# Tar, Feathers, and Terror

**E**ven before official word came of the repeal of the Stamp Act in May 1766, John Hancock had the crews from his ships at work building a platform for the launching of celebratory fireworks. The event was staged in front of his Beacon Hill mansion, no expenses spared, spreading across the night sky for all to see the explosive message that Americans had overturned what they considered to be an unjust Act of Parliament. In all the feasting and saluting of that evening, a subsidiary message could be read: Hancock, the richest merchant in town, intended to stay in charge of Boston's politics, if not of its government, and to turn aside the efforts of radical Whigs to run the town. He had the money, the will, and the muscle to do it.

There remained the question whether entertainments like those of this evening could placate or even moderate those muscular mobs. They had played such a significant part in the Stamp Act crisis, taking over the government in the process, that they had made of violence a political tool. Many of Boston's gentlefolk had been forced to leave town by the fear of what John Adams disdainfully called "private mobs" and of the Mackintoshes who headed them. Many others of the controlling elite, including Hancock, saw the elevation of crowd leaders from the laboring and the artisan classes as dangerous and counterproductive. In writing retrospectively about Boston's and New York's ambitious Whigs, General Thomas Gage observed that "They began to be terrified of the spirit that they had raised." A growing majority of those in charge agreed that something must be done to get the port's ships sailing again, to restore the merchants to their proper place in the political system, and to disassociate provincial and local politics from waterfront violence.

The brilliance of Hancock's fireworks, if not their effectiveness as a mob-charming device, was remembered for many a year. "Such a day has not been seen in Boston before or since," wrote the first biographer of a diminutive shoemaker who had been in attendance. That shoemaker, who bore the curious name George Robert Twelves Hewes and who has become the subject of a more recent, masterful study of this period by Alfred Young, was one of many from Boston's laboring class who revered Hancock as a particularly obliging patron. Long after the splendid night of the fireworks and indeed after the Stamp Act riots had been forgotten and the Revolution won, Hewes recalled with special zest the fact that on that historic occasion, he had drunk from a pipe of Madeira wine that Hancock had set out on the Common below his mansion.

Yet this free wine, that paternalistic gesture to slake the thirst of the people, did not go so far as to imply any commonality between Boston's four major groups of people—its upper-class merchants and court functionaries, its successful smugglers and "radical" Whigs (meaning the ones who thought they favored social change), its overweeningly ambitious artisans and mechanics, and its lowly shoemakers, seamen, and laborers. During the latter 1760s and early 1770s, these four lots separated themselves from one another in Boston as clearly as do shore birds of different habits. To be sure, these Boston aggregations occasionally merged, reformed, and shifted ground, but most often they competed bitterly with each other for whatever bits of power they could garner. Yet each one, though it stressed its own agenda, existed as a functioning part of Boston's peculiar, overarching homogeneity.

George Robert Twelves Hewes, having come from the same group of frequently failed working people as Ebenezer Mackintosh, would spend time in the same debtors' prison as Mackintosh in 1770. He was a sometime patriot, an activist in the Tea Party that would be staged eight years later, and an excellent observer of many other critical events leading to the Revolution. But, like Mackintosh, he and his opinions were left off the pages of the glory stories when the Revolution became formalized "history" in the first two centuries of the emergent republic—a process that left Americans with a prejudicial picture of who had been involved in the birth of their nation.

That process of keeping the men and the women of the laboring classes off the pages and out of the commanding positions commenced as soon as Boston's merchant elite saw that given the very success of the Stamp Act protests, they had not one problem but two on their hands. First, they had the continuing pressure from above, as British authorities clamped down on the activity that gave the city its life—namely, illegal trading. Then they had the new pressures from below, as both Whigs and artisans sought to claim greater shares of power, occasionally with the incitement of the sailors and the laborers.

Years later, on reviewing the events leading up to the War for Independence, Loyalist Peter Oliver made the comment that "had sailors not been so ignorant, they would have spurned their leaders [of the Whig class] and there would have been no Revolution." The obtuseness of that observation can only be measured by looking directly at the players in these earlier dramas, in 1766–1769, when seamen and other laborers began, of their own volition, to take increasingly important roles. Their actions were frequently carried out in cooperation with their artisan neighbors and sometimes at the direction of the radicalized Whigs and smugglers. But, occasionally, the actions were also out-of-control expressions of the people's own desire to strike hard at authority and to cause some new kind of future to occur.

The merchants at the top of the heap had been gratified that their business associates in England had listened to their complaints and had leaned on Parliament sufficiently to bring about repeal of the Stamp Act. But to their distress, Parliament almost at the same time had passed the notorious Declaratory Act. This hated bit of legislation demonstrated that Samuel Adams and James Otis's cries for no taxation without representation had fallen on deaf ears in imperial circles. It appeared that any hope of colonial autonomy–the hope that characterized such self-identified "patriots" as Deacon Adams–was illusory. The Declaratory Act proclaimed that the Crown could make any law that it considered advisable throughout its colonies "in all Cases Whatsoever," particularly in subjugated Ireland and North America.

Although George III had replaced the Stamp Act's author, Prime Minister Charles Rockingham, with the popular William Pitt, that doughty statesman was soon forced to withdraw because of failing health, his place being taken by Charles Townshend, chancellor of the Exchequer. And for Townshend, there were two clear goals in addition to his own advancement: to restore Great Britain to fiscal health after its many wars, and to pay the Empire's governors and other officials from customs fees levied on goods exported to the colonies. These levies would not, it was thought, be so offensive to the colonials as had been such "internal taxes" as the Stamp Act. They would, nonetheless, be fees levied on trade–in fact, taxes by another name.

One can imagine the fury with which Adams and his colleagues read the list of much-needed British items on which heavy duties would have to be paid. These were such essentials as paper, glass, lead, and tea. But then Adams and his fellow activists realized that in the Townshend Acts was an opportunity to rally the people of Massachusetts and other colonies in a new cause, the cause of "non-importation." The Sons of Liberty, whose ardor had cooled considerably with the news of the Stamp Act's repeal, would now come forth once again in what Adams came to call the "Cause of American Freedom."

All good citizens would be urged to make their own clothes of homespun cloth, to let their houses go unpainted, and to use paper made from local rags. The designers of the non-importation drive added to the list a number of other items–notably, shoes, Mackintosh's product–which should be bought only from local cordwainers. Above all, good citizens should abstain from drinking tea–regarded by Samuel Adams and other latter-day Puritans as a British affectation. To Adams, it seemed that tea, along with a love of the theater and an inclination toward Anglicanism, had helped to corrupt the entire society in which the widely resented Tories moved.

To ensure that the new patriotic standards of non-importation were strictly adhered to, an association was established whose members would keep tabs on their fellow citizens, using the Puritans' old tool of social ostracism—or possibly more violent tools—to keep deviants in line. Crowd actions would also be necessary to ensure that when the customs agents charged with collecting the Townshend Act's fees arrived in town, they would quickly understand the countervailing will of the people. The only greeting they could expect would be consonant with violence lavished on Stamp Act officials and impressment officers in Boston's earlier days.

## For a Time, "No Mobs, No Confusions" but "Rights and Liberties"

To Thomas Hutchinson, still serving as the colony's second in command under the restored Governor Bernard, the year of Hancock's fireworks, 1766, was the "critical year." To him, far more than to Hancock, this was the ultimate opportunity, now or never, to take the extremists out of the picture and to bring the people back from their present condition, which was apparently "verging on hysteria." News of the Stamp Act's repeal gave Hutchinson satisfaction and even pleasure, allowing hope that the "Great Uneasiness and Tumults" might be somewhat alleviated. But his anxiety rose as the old dependables on the Governor's Council were purged, one by one, and replaced by more radical politicians. Then, as the citizenry reacted to news of the Townshend Acts, he had to try to prevent a rash of new actions.

In his own studious, intellectual way, Hutchinson considered any deviations from royal/aristocratic rule (that is, rule from the top down) as steps toward "plebiscitarian tyranny," which he pedantically classified as *dominatio plebis*. That despised form of government seemed to him a total refutation of English constitutional principles. Even the people's efforts to resist the new Townshend Acts by certain essentially peaceful non-importation strategies he regarded as intensely subversive. When Boston's Town Meeting passed what he regarded as the uncalled-for Non-Importation Resolves in the autumn of 1767, and passed them *unanimously*, he interpreted that independent action, that expression of the popular will, as tantamount to rebellion.

At the end of 1767, Hutchinson read with mounting alarm a letter that appeared in the first issue of the new, supposedly conservative *Boston Chronicle*. Written by the preeminent Philadelphia lawyer John Dickinson, it was rather coyly entitled "Letter from a Pennsylvania Farmer." The first of several brilliant essays on the emergent self-awareness of the American people, this letter focused particularly on Parliament's Quartering Act, which had authorized the billeting of British forces in New York City. It praised the New York Assembly for its refusal to comply with the Act and urged united action by all the colonies to resist the imposition of any such authority. Dickinson's *Letters*, when collected in book form, rapidly became the best-selling publication in Massachusetts and all other colonies.

Although their author, like Hutchinson, was basically a conservative,* he had been educated (at London's Middle Temple) to read the British constitution in an entirely different way. To him, it was not a series of laws and customs that prohibited expressions of the popular will but was, rather, a permissive fiat that guaranteed Americans, as overseas Englishmen, certain rights. "A virtual American Bill of Rights," Governor Francis Bernard called it indignantly, when transmitting Dickinson's thesis to London. Hutchinson also wrote wrathful refutations of Dickinson's thesis. Both officials recognized that this voice from Pennsylvania was a powerful new enemy. For his part, John Hancock, Harvard-educated and

---

*During the Second Continental Congress of 1776, when representatives from the various colonies were called upon to vote for independence, American patriot John Dickinson could not bring himself to make that vote; he believed that only the British constitution could provide sufficient guarantees for individual freedom. Later, he fought bravely as a Delaware infantryman in the War of Independence. He is also noteworthy as the author of the Articles of Confederation.

almost equally conservative, agreed with Dickinson's letters and their interpretation of the evolved British constitution. Indeed, he seems to have been inspired by them, finding in them a broader rationale for his locally focused sentiments. At the time of the Stamp Act, Hancock had declared that because of his guaranteed rights, he would refuse to use the stamps by which his ship's papers were supposed to be legalized. Hancock intoned, "I have a right to the Liberty and privileges of the English constitution, and as [an] Englishman will enjoy them." Now he put a more American twist on that constitutional claim. Whatever the lingo or the rationale, his ships *would* sail. In fact, his and many other ships began to sail forth from Boston even before the formal repeal of the Stamp Act. Although the port remained officially closed, the customs house functioned, and shipping was permitted without the affixing of stamps.

Yet a battered port it was. Boston by this point had lost for all time its supremacy over New York and Philadelphia as America's premier entrepot, in part because of the recent riots, in part because of an unfortunate reputation for poor shipbuilding. Consequently, the town's population was shrinking, and the waterfront populace was again suffering. Hancock, as the richest man in town (indeed, Hancock functioned as the town's biggest banking house), vowed that he would build better and bigger oceangoing vessels that would give more employment to the waterfront laborers. He would become the avuncular patron of those at-risk maritime families. In turn, their own leaders, Ebenezer Mackintosh, Henry Swift, and the like, were all requested to curb their passions; their riots and destructions were now viewed as excessive. If any kind of consensus was to be established within Boston and in the Bay Colony, Hancock believed it must be along his conservative (though definitely not British-imposed) lines.

Samuel Adams agreed, for the moment, with this view. While hoping that the new Townshend Acts would stir up the dormant Sons of Liberty again, he had to counsel his tavern cronies to cause "No mobs, no confusions." His own jeopardized status in the town had to be considered. Always careless about matters financial, he found himself facing the official charge of being some £4,000 in arrears in his collection of taxes. Or, if he had collected any such funds as a part of his tax collector's duties, they had not been turned over to the treasury. The charge had been brought by the still-remaining members of the Old Guard who regarded Adams as an unremitting threat to stability, even though the powers of "Sam the Maltster" had weakened noticeably with the resolution of the Stamp Act crisis. Columns in the *Boston Chronicle* called for the zealot to be brought to justice, but Adams still had his wealthy and supportive patrons, including Hancock (who was called Adams's unfailing "milch cow" in the *Chronicle*). The old friends came through, gathering a total contribution exceeding £1,000. Within a few years, the whole issue was put to rest.

In any case, there would be no stopping Adams's drive to broaden the base of the political process. Toward that end, and functioning in his key capacity as clerk of the House, he succeeded in having a roomy balcony built along the back wall of the Assembly Hall, where the House of Representatives met. Crowding onto the balcony at his invitation came neglected members of the Boston community; never before had they presumed to enter the halls of government, even to dream of doing it. Their swelling presence, Adams trusted, would help make his point to the gentlemen in their appointed chairs down below that these newly admitted people were the ones who held the true power. In fact, these tradesmen and carpenters and men of Boston's middling classes, most of whom held bits of property, were among the free white males (about a quarter of the town's total fifteen thousand population) already allowed to vote in the Town Meeting.* Yet they had always been made to feel too lowly to take any vocal part in the actions of the august House of Representatives.

As opposed to the characters who made up the no-longer-popular, once-violent waterfront mobs, these were the loyal citizens on whom Adams now counted to help reform the town and to

---

*Historian Dirk Hoerder made the point in his 1976 essay "Boston Leaders and British Crowds" that of the town's free white males, only about half (1,500) were actually enfranchised.

reconstruct the commonwealth with his complex policy of non-importation. While Hutchinson complained about the numbers of lower-class people who were coming into the House to intimidate the legislators, and while the governor wrote alarmed letters home, Samuel Adams attempted by politics, rather than by mob action, to reform the way government and citizens worked in Massachusetts.

Having succeeded in urging the Town Meeting to pass the Non-Importation Resolves at the end of 1767 and to renew and strengthen them early in the next year, Adams watched with approval the work of a new leader who strove to make sure that the populace conformed. This was the somewhat mysterious William Molineux, previously encountered in chapter 4 as one of Boston's most successful smugglers and most vigorous Whigs. Although Molineux did not share Adams's vision of the pure and gleaming Puritan commonwealth that would one day be restored, he did have a dynamic view of a province that would no longer be subject to Great Britain's restrictive maritime laws. Having helped to establish the Boston Society for Encouraging Trade and Commerce, he became the dynamic leader both of those unemployed townspeople who would accept jobs provided by the largesse of the elite and of those firebrands who wanted to march forth again against the authorities who were closing down the port.

Hot of temper and impatient with those of other opinions, Molineux turned all his considerable talents toward making Boston into a self-reliant society. Success in that effort would liberate Boston from control by British merchants and officials and would, of course, allow him to resume his freebooting ways. In pushing for that, he won the patriots' favorite nickname, "Paoli," after the Corsican freedom fighter, Pasquale Paoli (for whom, it will be remembered, Mackintosh had named his son). Molineux also won the special loyalty of the "mechanics" who were engaged in making the materials that were no longer allowed to be imported from England. Abigail Adams, for her part, approved of this fostering of Massachusetts's mechanics and coastwise shippers, believing that such strengthening would help break the domination of the province's old-line merchants.

Curiously, William "Paoli" Molineux was almost everything a revolutionary New Englander should not be. Unlike most of

Boston's other Whigs, he was not native-born but an immigrant from England; furthermore, he was not a Congregationalist or a deist but a notable Anglican, worshipping at Trinity Church. He had come to Boston in the 1740s and had begun his climb to moderate wealth as a hardware merchant. The interests of that trade led him increasingly to deal (illegally) with Dutch suppliers. Having entered the circle of the town's gentleman smugglers through that route, he became the operations agent for Charles Ward Apthorp in the 1760s. Apthorp, eldest son of one of Boston's richest merchants (who happened to be the partner of Hancock's wealthy uncle), eventually moved to New York, allowing the business and much of his property to be managed by Molineux. From this base, and after recovering from the grim depression of 1760 (for which he forever blamed the British), Molineux expanded his interests and his political connections.

At first, the cause of non-importation had been managed by one of the most powerful members of Boston's established merchant elite, the conservative John Rowe. He had emigrated to Boston from England in 1736, bringing with him an inheritance large enough for him to become quickly established as a merchant of consequence. Like Hancock, he had been alerted to the threats to Boston's maritime commerce by the Sugar Act of 1747 and had then presided over the drafting of a protest to the Crown from the newly formed Society for the Encouraging of Trade and Commerce. During the Stamp Act crisis, he had deigned to work with Samuel Adams and other radicals to keep the province's courts open despite the lack of stamps required for the legalizing of documents.

Called forth again to protest the Townshend Acts, Rowe became chairman of the committee that drafted Boston's Non-Importation Resolves and remained true to the concept of enforcing them by whatever means necessary. His reputation as a militant leader of Boston's non-importation crusade grew to such an extent that other conservatives began to whisper. One afternoon in October 1768, upon entering the British Coffee House, he heard himself accused of being a "Damn Incendiary," deserving nothing less than being "hanged in his shoes." Thereupon he commenced his gradual withdrawal from the cause, disassociating himself entirely from non-importation by the middle of 1770.

By 1768, Molineux had taken over as chief of the movement. He had indeed begun to focus less on the encouragement of various cottage industries, particularly women's home-spinning, and to concentrate more on initiating raids against people who failed to conform—particularly against import merchants like Hutchinson's two sons who continued to sell English tea. Unleashing street brigands and bands of reckless children, Molineux harassed the nonconformers in what would eventually be called a "Reign of Terror." By so doing, he raised new fears in the breasts of both conservative merchants and moderate Whigs about disruptions to regular business.

In fact, despite the best intentions of Molineux and others, nonimportation never could become a popular cause, for it kept even small traders from sending their ships to sea to bring back profit-making goods from the Indies. And thus it failed to help both the unemployed seamen and the impoverished veterans who wanted to find shipyard work. Nevertheless, Massachusetts led the other colonies in this homegrown American cause—with Harvard College demonstrating its concern for American rights by seeing to it that all academic theses were printed on paper inscribed "Made in New England." The more radical of Boston's merchants (some of whom cared little for the welfare of seamen and dockworkers) kept on pressing for that presumably patriotic effort.

Even the conservative merchant John Rowe believed that the vigorous campaign for non-importation was vital and should be seen as an effort to preserve for New Englanders the "Inestimable Blessings and advantages of the British Constitution." He was less concerned than Molineux, however, with the British Navy's stepping up its seizures of suspect ships in keeping with the spirit of the Townshend Acts. Indeed, Rowe, the stand-patter, reported with horror the scene made by Molineux, the unrepentant smuggler, among British officials when word came in mid-February 1767 that yet another ship had been seized on the waterfront. Rowe wrote in his diary that Molineux "used the Surveyor General Mr. Temple most Cruelly and Barbarously; he abused the Character of said Gentleman most shamefully."

Simultaneously, Molineux's brigades continued their "tumults" against nonconformers. Yet those were relatively mild actions compared with the violence that would be lavished upon the British customs inspectors after they arrived from England and settled into their duties. These were the officials charged with carrying out the dictates of the Townshend Acts to the letter and with setting up the American Board of Customs Commissioners. Their arrival would have raised hackles under the best of circumstances, but landing as they did on Pope's Day, whether by incredibly bad luck or dreadfully bad judgment, they ensured that they would become a primary focus for that season's mobs.

## "Liberty, Property, and No Commissioners!"

With the enforcement of the Townshend Acts formally beginning on November 20, 1767, and the Board of Commissioners commencing its labors, Boston suffered a sudden crackdown on petty smuggling and an aggressive tightening of customs regulations. Reactions, as forecast, were severe. Stories filled the town's newspapers of such unconscionable intrusions on normal affairs as customs officers knocking on the door of the respectable Captain Daniel Malcom. In quest of untaxed goods, the officers demanded that Captain Malcom open the room of one of his tenants (a certain William Mackay). But Malcom, honored in the North End as one of the Sons of Liberty (as was Mackay), aroused his neighbors in sufficient numbers to defend his home and beat back the invaders. Defensive and aggressive attacks on other customs officers became so numerous—most of them accompanied by shouts of "Liberty, Property, and No Commissioners!"—that Governor Bernard was tempted to take the dread step of calling in the British Navy. He was right to suspect that bloodier attacks would follow.

On the political front, James Otis and Samuel Adams struggled to bring the Assembly to the point of dispatching a strongly worded protest to London about the unfairness of the Townshend Acts. That failing, they drafted a so-called Circular Letter to the other colonies, urging that they join in informing the king of their collective hostility to the new duties. By clever maneuvering—that is, by pressing for a vote after conservative representatives had left for home on their winter recess in 1768–they managed to win enough votes to send off this provocative letter. It immediately brought down on their heads, and on the heads of other colonial leaders who had accepted its spirit, the ire of the king's haughty new Secretary of State for the Colonies, Lord Hillsborough. Demonstrating a lack of sympathy for both colonial history and the new American self-awareness, he demanded that all provincial legislatures deny the Circular Letter and ignore its call for unity. If they did not, they would be prorogued.

After the Massachusetts's House of Representatives declined to follow his orders, Lord Hillsborough ordered Governor Bernard to dissolve the province's General Court until it could bring together a new and more obedient House. Viewing this shutdown as an insult to the people and as precisely the kind of battle that independent thinkers in the Bay Colony had always enjoyed taking up, Adams was able to persuade ninety-two representatives, a majority of the newly convened Assembly, to vote against Hillsborough's orders. They became known throughout the colonies as the "Glorious 92," that number being used as a catchphrase for patriots everywhere. Fifteen members of the Assembly, all of them Sons of Liberty (Captain Malcom and Mackay among them), commissioned Paul Revere to design and create a silver bowl to commemorate the vote and its heroes; it may be seen today in Boston's Museum of Fine Arts.

Yet many of the Sons of Liberty, reverting to their roles as anxious members of the merchant elite, did what they could to keep affairs within bounds. They urged the captains of ships in port to calm down their seamen. Even Samuel Adams used softened words in his *Gazette* columns, once again urging, "No Mobbs [sic] . . . No Confusions . . . No Tumults." Ebenezer Mackintosh was snubbed and was allowed to disappear back into the anonymous poverty from which he had come. It was during this calming time in 1766 that Mackintosh married a respectable young woman named Elizabeth Maverick in the new North Church; with her, he had two children in the next two years. Perhaps the raising of that family is another explanation for Ebenezer's nonparticipation in actions after the Stamp Act riots. Nonetheless, events would not leave the young family alone: Elizabeth Mackintosh's half-brother Samuel Maverick would be one of the excited crowd at the Boston Massacre—indeed, one of its victims.

Communal celebrations of the Stamp Act's repeal tended to exclude the Mackintoshes and the Mavericks, involving only the "better sort" of gentlemen, they being the owners of the town's net worth. On one such occasion, 139 carriages were needed to transport the Sons of Liberty and other celebrants out to a fete in the shady suburb of Dorchester. Later, when the first anniversary of the repeal rolled around on March 18, 1767, the Loyal Nine appointed a man named Will Moore, who had been one of those jailed and released at the time of the Stamp Act riots, rather than Mackintosh, to be the master of ceremonies. Moore and his men hurried to take down the effigies of the commissioners that lower-class pranksters had strung up on the Liberty Tree.

The most prominent and troublesome effigy depicted Charles Paxton, a Boston native who had been run out of town the year before when he was functioning as Boston's surveyor of customs. Now, having returned and having sparked new hostility, he found that protesters of the new duties were stronger than ever; they followed him to his house and surrounded it, as a huge, ominously silent presence. For two nights thereafter, less-controlled rascals harassed him and his family with catcalls and yells. Records do not reveal whether Mackintosh, who at one point would have relished such a demonstration, was glimpsed among the participants.

Paxton had taken his first ribbing on that memorable day of the commissioners' arrival when he faced the Pope's Day celebrants. Those revelers, most of them school-age boys, had been cautioned like everybody else against violence and urged in the direction of "good Order and peaceable Behavior." One rather charming episode told about that day of cooled-down emotions concerned a lad who had come in from the country to help celebrate the anniversary. He was the son of the previously named Laommi Baldwin, and, having decorated the town pumps with flags in anticipation of a great event, he found himself face-to-face with gentlemen demanding that he take them down. This he swiftly did, saying by way of excuse that he "was just in from Woburn" and thus should not be held accountable.

But other lads were not to be intimidated; they could not pass up this opportunity to mock the Paxton fellow, who seemed such an ideal target. They refused either to hush their oft-repeated chant "Liberty, Property, and No Commissioners!" or to call off their traditional Pope's Day wagons. As ascertained by scholar John L. Bell, Paxton became the special butt of the wagon decorated by boys from the South End. Above their cart, the lads strung up a figure of a dandified man labeled with the words (taken from a recent issue of the *Boston Gazette*) "Everybody's Humble Servant & Nobody's Friend." Not to be outdone by the boys, the *Gazette* increased its mockery of Paxton, making a special point of his lack of manliness.

Another official who received frightening public harassment was Commissioner William Burch. The *Gazette* reported an incident that took place soon after his arrival, telling how "A large Number of Men with Clubs assembled before his Door." Frightened both for himself and for his family, Burch managed to slip out the back door with his wife and children. Seeing that such threats were growing stronger rather than weaker as the winter months of 1767–1768 went by (with the local merchants, even the Sons of Liberty, less and less able to keep the crowds under control), Paxton, Burch, and the other commissioners determined to write on their own to London and Halifax, asking for military support. Though Governor Bernard hesitated to call in the British Navy,* the commissioners did not hold back.

These actions of the Boston crowds, banging on doors and yelling epithets, hardly showed how deep lay the underlying hatred of British authority at the beginning of 1768 and how determined the waterfront populace was to take an active part in that authority's disruption. Men and women of the dockside populace reserved a special scorn for British agents called "tidesmen," minor customs officials who constantly pried beneath the tarpaulins and peeked under the hatches of newly arrived vessels. Patriots believed that there was only one category of vermin lower than they, and these

---

*A few months later, on September 9, 1768, John Rowe noted in his confidential diary that "The Governor told mee in Conversation Yesterday morning that he had Stav'd off the Introducing Troops as long as he could but could do it no longer."

were the tipsters, local seamen who for various reasons (usually money) informed on their smuggling skippers. In a key incident, two tidesmen had the effrontery to go below on John Hancock's successful packet *Lydia*. Speedy enough to reach London from Boston in a month's sailing, with a return trip of two, she was notoriously hard to catch. The inspectors emerged from *Lydia*'s hold with the unsurprising verdict that she carried goods on which no duties had been paid.

It was no accident, to be sure, that the officials had their eyes on Hancock's vessels. For all his desire to bring about a conservative consensus, he still seemed, in British eyes, to represent the most successful and outspoken of Boston's illicit traders. Indeed, he had been so bold as to state in public that he would "suffer" no officers "to go even on board any of my London ships." Yet he appeared to be playing all sorts of games. At one and the same time, he expressed admiration for the goals of the Non-Importation Association (perhaps because he wished to squelch those lesser merchants who could no longer trade) *and* he kept a number of his ships sailing back and forth to England. Also, he kept hiring laborers from the waterfront for "make work," while providing handouts to widows and orphans, *and* he associated with councilors and legislators at the highest level, dressing as opulently as they did and appearing to be the very image of fashion. A Boston wit concluded that Hancock was both courtier and demagogue, "the very Idol of the Mob."

The decision had apparently been made at the highest level to go after Hancock both on the waterfront and in the halls of government. Yet the seizure of the *Lydia* went poorly. A crowd gathered that seemed determined to defend her. Then Hancock himself came forth and, assisted by ten of his strongest employees, bodily removed the officers from the hold and the deck. Hancock's friend, the colony's attorney general, obligingly decreed that the search had been unauthorized: no request for special Writs of Assistance had been filed. Pushed aside, the customs officers vowed to be more careful in their next assault.

At the governmental level, things went no better. When the governor brusquely turned down Hancock's election to the council, Hancock made capital of the matter, claiming that he was "honored" by the rejection. Having been "martyred" and attacked, Hancock reinforced his hold on the public mind.

Before the next test of his stamina and his popularity occurred, Boston suffered what today might be called a "wake-up call." Into the harbor sailed one of Great Britain's mightiest warships, the fifty-five-gun HMS *Romney*, accompanied by two armed sloops. On board were sufficient marines and men-at-arms to convince the people of Boston both that obedience was expected—all ships that sailed in past the moored warship had to dip their colors by way of salute—and that more troops would follow. The commissioners' pleas for assistance had been answered; the king would use all necessary means to support his representatives and maintain his authority.

As if deliberately designed to remind the populace of bad days gone by, days when the mobs had had to rise against the Royal

*Accompanying Paul Revere's engraving of the landing of British forces on Long Wharf in 1768 is an indignantly voiced caption describing the troops as marching "with insolent Parade up King Street." Before the British had determined that a major military force was the only way to "awe the town," HMS Romney (anchored at right) arrived to support harassed customs officers.*

The Boston Athenaeum

Navy, the first move of the *Romney*'s commander was to send out impressment crews. They succeeded in halting a coaster that had sailed innocently into the harbor. From her, they removed a hapless seaman, one Michael Corbett, who, it was reported, fought fiercely "with several of his fellow tars against being forced on the man of war." The impressment crew succeeded, thereby, in arousing "a considerable crowd of young fellows and Negroes"—words heard often before in this town of supposed propriety. These townsmen, young and old, soon swelled in numbers, becoming a major uprising and a mass meeting under the Liberty Tree.

From there, the crowd's leaders decided that they should proceed to Faneuil Hall to make an official protest, but, on approaching the hall, it became clear that the crowd was so large that the people would have to move on to Old South Church. There, leaders calmed the people's fury by electing a committee charged with riding out to Bernard's residence and officially presenting him with their protest. Given this and the fact that the Assembly seemed poised to demand his recall, the governor declared that an "insurrection was at hand."

Having heard much about the political stresses and divisions within Boston society, General Thomas Gage, chief of British military operations in America, was interested in the precise size and makeup of the mob. He concluded, "This insurrection [was] composed of numbers of sailors headed by captains of privateers, as well as many people from the surrounding area, the whole amounting to some thousands." It was becoming clear to him that in Boston, the moderates' attempts to change the minds of those in Parliament by petitions or to form a conservative consensus were now viewed as failures. Apparently, "the captains" had concluded that the time had arrived to effect greater changes by renewed working-class riots. Or perhaps that was what the people themselves had decided.

## Liberty and "Further Mischiefs"

Knowing that they had at their backs the men and the guns of the *Romney*, the directors of the Board of Customs Commissioners believed that they need let no more time go by before taking another crack at John Hancock and his slippery shipping business. Hancock, for his part, believed that the commissioners were now out to ruin him but that, given the people on the waterfront who regarded him as their patron, he could manage to hold his own. The contest of strength was on.

Under the orders of Commissioner Benjamin Hallowell (the official whose house had been attacked before Hutchinson's), customs agents decided to make their move against another of Hancock's ships, this one the fast-sailing sloop *Liberty*. She had been named in honor of Isaac Barré, the British politician who seemed the very inventor of the liberty ideal, and with whom Hancock had struck up a mutually congratulatory correspondence. A month earlier, when a customs official had boarded the *Liberty* in search of reported cases of illegal Madeira wine, he had been rudely locked in a compartment, which permitted the crew to unload the cargo. After several hours, he was released with stern warnings that his actions were illegal and that he had better not report the incident.

When he finally summoned sufficient courage to make his report, it produced an expectable result. But this new move against Hancock was carefully planned. Thus, on the morning of June 10, Hallowell's men stormed on board the *Liberty*; they bore the right kind of papers to mark their seizure as legal. Their scheme this time was to coordinate the boarding and the seizing with the simultaneous landing of a boatload of Royal Marines; the military muscle would then tow the sloop from the wharf out within the protecting cover of the *Romney*. But before the *Liberty* could reach the open water of the harbor, a crowd of maritime roustabouts gathered, just the sort of men who, liable for impressment, were maddened by this display of naval confiscation. As reported in the press, these "vagrants" and "sturdy boys and Negroes" pelted the marines with stones and bricks.

When the *Liberty* was at last pulled out of range, the crowd turned their wrath on two customs officers who had remained behind, bringing down on their heads a steady rain of dirt and stones. That night, hundreds more people having joined the crowd, rioters charged through the streets wielding torches and clubs, focusing their attacks on the homes of the customs officers. Finally, they commandeered a handsome launch, a "pleasure boat" belonging to Commissioner Richard Harrison, and dragged it to within sight of Hancock's Beacon Hill mansion. There they triumphantly set it afire at the foot of the Liberty Tree and continued their carousing through the night.

Samuel Adams saw this action as his chance ultimately to gather all parties to the cause of resistance. But before that, as a master of well-timed politics, he persuaded Hancock not to press for the return of his ship—though British officials, appalled at the intensity of the riot they had caused, were willing to negotiate her return. Instead, the *Liberty* remained in the harbor, chained to the *Romney*, a reminder that Great Britain's military presence was now far more than a threat. At last, an arrangement was made whereby the *Liberty* was sold to one of the commissioners, who used her as an antismuggling cutter along the New England coast. But when the patriots of Newport, Rhode Island, had had their fill of her torment, they attacked and burned her to the waterline.

Back in Boston, Hancock, accused of smuggling, found protection and clever legal defense in the person of the fast-rising legal genius John Adams. All charges against the *Liberty*'s former owner were dropped without further review. As for the customs commissioners of Boston, they considered the harassments against them "sufficient notice" that they were now undoubtedly under a well-programmed attack by the dockside populace; this riot seemed to them but an overture to "further mischiefs." They dared not risk the lives of their families anymore in the face of the aroused "rabble" and transported themselves out to the *Romney*. From there, they withdrew to the safety of Castle William, renewing their pleas for stronger military support.

Governor Bernard, having survived four years of constant challenge, was now named in a petition from the General Court (written by Samuel Adams) as a factor hostile to the liberties of loyal subjects. Adams declared that Bernard's governorship was intolerable to the people. The Crown, to the surprise of many, listened: the governor was removed from his seat in Massachusetts. John Rowe portrayed the results of the riot and the departure of Bernard

(August 1, 1769) as joyful for seamen and townspeople alike: "The Flag hoisted on the Liberty Tree . . . the Bells Ringing . . . Great Joy to the People. A Great Bonfire in King Street & on Fort Hill."

The commissioners' fearful surmise that the *Liberty* riot would be the first of several mounting rebellions seemed happily true to Samuel Adams. Having concluded that the gradual policy of non-importation was getting nowhere, he hailed the new spirit of rebellion, referring to the latest uprising as "the spark that lit the fires of liberty." He glimpsed an opportunity to harness crowd action to political progress on wider fronts. Accordingly, he used the connections established by the Sons of Liberty across the province to bring together a convocation of Massachusetts towns at Faneuil Hall on September 22, 1768. Some sixty-seven communities sent representatives, in open defiance of the governor's refusal to authorize a new Assembly. But to Adams's disappointment, these representatives from the countryside, even while protesting the commissioners' actions and sympathizing with Boston's plight, declined to take up arms in support of the capital and its beleaguered merchants, smugglers, and seamen. Instead, they dutifully pledged obedience to the king and advised other colonists "to prevent . . . all tumults and disorders."

Yet the small and very intentional victory scored by the *Liberty* rioters led to a feeling that the imperial regulators could be successfully attacked; it was as if blood had been spread in the watery depths, causing a rush of voracious bluefish. The commissioners and other British officials were increasingly regarded as ready targets for men and women who saw themselves as defenders of their native land and property. Vengeful and rights-conscious seamen, as well as certain masters of ships and waterfront leaders, mindful of the success of vigilante actions in the past, concocted new means of intimidating authorities. Little more than a year after the *Liberty* incident, in October 1769, a tipster for the British named George Gailer, perhaps one of Hancock's crew who had informed the British of his smuggling activities, received a brutal tarring and feathering.

Historian Ben Irvin, the outstanding scholar of this fearful type of crowd action, reports that the event was witnessed by a Boston merchant named Elizabeth Cuming. She wrote that the attack on

Gailer had been carried out by "a large crowd of those who call themselves gentlemen." The victim later tried to get back at his assailants by filing suit, naming as his oppressors two merchants and five seamen and artisans. His suit was denied; the punishment had been sanctioned by the public.

Tarring and feathering, as can be seen from the employments of the men who made Gailer pay for his perceived sins, was clearly a maritime activity. Those seamen and laborers had the tar, they had the brushes, and they had the deep reservoirs of anger and resentment. It was a ghastly process, accompanied by the screaming of the tortured and the curses of those applying it. It was furthermore, as Professor Irvin points out, a folk ritual that, despite roots traceable to England, became a peculiarly American form of communal punishment, reaching a peak of intensity and popularity between 1768 and 1770. To put a "Yankee Jacket" on a perceived enemy was a cruel and inhumane practice, but it served its terroristic purposes.

Irvin describes how it worked:

> Having captured an official or informant, the crowd would first apply the tar. Pine tar was a familiar commodity in colonial America; it was used to waterproof ships, sails, and rigging. A thick, acrid dark brown or black liquid, tar was obtained by roasting mature pine trees over an open-pit fire and distilling the bituminous substance that boiled out. Some victims were fortunate enough to be tarred over their clothes or protected by a frock or sheet. Others were stripped, and the tar was brushed, poured, or "bedawbed" over their bare skin. When heated, tar would blister the skin. . . . In one instance, the crowd simply "knocked the top out of a tar barrel, and plunged" the offender in headfirst. Removing the tar, however, could be even more uncomfortable than having it poured over one's body. Once dry, tar clung tenaciously to the skin and could be removed only with a tremendous amount of scrubbing, possibly with the aid of turpentine or other chemical solvents that would further irritate the skin. After the tar came the feathers, also a familiar commodity in British North America.

Then came the traditional, deeply humiliating process (as one contemporary account described it) of hoisting the victim up on a "one-horse cart" and parading him through the "principal streets of the town," while a "great concourse of people" cheered, sang, and made rough music with pots and pans. This is the ghastly scene, staged at night with sputtering torches, that Hawthorne described so vividly in his short story.

More hideous in reality than in fiction, tarring and feathering caught on as a way for the maritime populace in Boston and other towns to torment and to wreak political retribution on their perceived enemies. Even while Samuel Adams tried and did not quite succeed in formulating a successful, quasi-legislative response to British repression, the people of the waterfront, by these "nocturnal paintings" and by increasing riots, were pushing affairs ever closer to open rebellion. Fearful of these terrorists in their neighborhoods, a number of anxious townspeople thought it wise to put exculpating advertisements in local newspapers, denying rumors that they had passed information about certain local skippers on to the authorities.

In the same month as Gailer's misery, another similar group of activists tried to punish a Scottish journalist in Boston named John Mein. As editor of the *Boston Chronicle*, he was a most outspoken opponent of the non-importation policy and the greatest defender of those who chose to break with it. He should have seen the inadvisability of such an attitude when one of his immediate neighbors and fellow resisters of non-importation, John McMasters, was carted through Boston to a gallows where he was threatened with hanging and instructed to leave town. Instead, Mein published even more stories (most of them accurate) about hypocritical citizens who, while pretending to go along with non-importation, were actually getting rich by violating the bans. He even went so far as to name John Hancock as the most successful of the violators.

For all their meanness and vindictiveness, Mein's articles had considerable success in weakening the supposedly united spirit behind non-importation. Reasonable people in Boston and abroad paid attention to his protests against both mob action and the resulting dictatorship by the unelected. For that outspokenness, as well as for his attacks on patriot leaders, Mein had to be "catechized." And so it was that attackers sought him out one autumn night in 1769 on his way to his lodgings. Drawing the weapon that he, like many other threatened citizens, now carried, he struggled to fight back against the sticks and the clubs of his assailants. In the process, his gun went off, unfortunately wounding a nearby trooper. The incident became a scandal; Mein had no alternative but to flee. Disguised as a soldier, he found refuge on a ship docked at the waterfront that was preparing to sail home to Great Britain.

Ironically, William Molineux, the chief proponent of the Non-Importation Association that Mein had fought so hard and effectively to refute, nearly met his end by the very torture that his crusade had fostered. Traveling to Salem early in 1770, he was assaulted by seamen working for a group of merchants who had tired of the strains of non-importation. They wanted it and its pressures and its advocates to back down. Fortunately, Molineux managed to break away from the intended tarring and feathering, escaping to take an active part in the rebellion that was soon to burst forth.

Before Molineux's misadventure, in the autumn of 1768, the British military establishment answered in full the requests for assistance that had been coming so constantly from Castle William. It sent forth a mighty task force of fighting ships and seasoned brigades whose purpose was to "Awe the Town." When he heard of its approach, Lieutenant Governor Hutchinson was so sure that the overreaction from all sections of Boston would be violent that he tried to hush the news, leaking it out in small, and what he hoped would be palatable, portions. Hutchinson's fears were totally accurate. This massive display of imperial power would, in ways unintended, shape the course of events toward revolution quite as effectively as would the actions of Bostonians themselves.

# 7

# A Dockside Riot and
# the Massacre

When the British armada anchored in Boston on September 30, 1768, crowding the capacious harbor with men-of-war, armed schooners, and transports, the cannons on all fighting ships were loaded, the sailors poised to fire broadsides at the town. For in the opinion of the royal government, the port of Boston was the seat of an active rebellion that must be quelled and not allowed to spread to the interior. This was, it will be remembered, shortly before the departure of Governor Bernard, at the time when the *Liberty* riots and actions against the customs officers had humbled authorities so thoroughly that radicals ruled the town; indeed, the Town Meeting, in which they dominated, had virtually taken over as the controlling body within the province. Just as the extraordinary waterfront mobs had helped shatter what used to be the regular forms of government, now the extraordinary application of military might seemed the only possible corrective response. Under the guns of the armada, American citizens within Boston and elsewhere were forced to consider the nature of colonial rule, as well as their proper place thereunder.

Benjamin Franklin, who had served as an upholder of America's cause in George III's court during the Stamp Act crisis and who remained in England during these years as agent for several of the American colonies, made a typically shrewd remark about the landing of the British troops. Discounting rumors of mob rule in his hometown, he said that the troops would not find a rebellion there, but "they may indeed make one."

Others who watched the coming ashore of some seven hundred soldiers and officers from the British army's 14th and 29th Regiments, accompanied by artillery and ancillary forces, must also have considered that they were looking into the kind of oppression that cannot be borne by freedom-loving people. The landing took place shortly before noon on Long Wharf; from there, accompanied by the beating of drums and shrilling of fifes, the soldiers in their bright red coats marched directly up King Street to the Common. Fully charged like the ship's cannons behind them, the soldiers' muskets were rigged with fixed bayonets. These prime foot soldiers, part of an eventual combined military force of nearly four thousand in a town of less than sixteen thousand people, had clearly come as backbreaking occupiers, not as peacemakers sent by a gracious king.

While Samuel Adams considered how to treat this disruptive enemy and as James Otis pondered how to spread the "Cause of American Freedom" ( John Dickinson's words), others decided that this was an expedient time to lower the rhetoric and toe the line. Even when the armada's arrival had been nothing but rumors in the wind, the representatives who had come in from outlying towns for a convocation about non-importation (as mentioned in the preceding chapter) had been disposed to turn their backs on Samuel Adams's proposals. With the fleet anchored so overwhelmingly in the harbor, Loyalist merchants believed that their safety and their status in town had now been secured and redeemed. They gathered around Governor Bernard to reinvigorate his rule. Their newspapers happily reported the fading away of the Popular Party. Bernard, though he was scheduled to depart, hastened to befriend Lieutenant Colonel William Dalrymple, the temporary British commander, and to promise suitable accommodations for him and his troops within the town in accordance with Parliament's Quartering Act.

But the governor's councilors, some of them still allied with Otis and Adams and all of them apprehensive, made bold to object, stating that it would be far better if the troops were quartered out of town, at Castle William. The selectmen of the town, though somewhat intimidated, interrupted Dalrymple when he pressed the accommodation problem upon them. They went so far as to claim that housing soldiers was no "cognisance" of theirs. Not until General Gage arrived from New York later in the month did the councilors grudgingly grant British troops the use of the colony-owned Manufactory House—the occupation of which had originally been denied Dalrymple by tenants who had barred the doors and the windows.

By that time, the colonel had begun to take the measure of the town's courteous reluctance; he commanded that some of the troops pitch tents on the Common and made arrangements to put up others in rental units and in certain available public spaces. William Molineux more or less cooperated, offering one or two of his empty storehouses at exorbitant rates. In return, Dalrymple attempted to keep his men in order, meting out brutal punishment, including execution, to captured deserters.

Yet the town was too small and too tense for military-civilian incidents to be avoided. Samuel Adams gave vivid interpretations of these offenses against the people of Boston. Using this opportunity to apply pressure both on the cooperating authorities and on the merchants unwilling to keep up the non-import effort, his outspoken letters under the names *Vindex* and *Candidus* went beyond Boston to appear in more distant journals. In the widely circulated *Journal of the Times*, he set forth a lengthy list of the troops' drunkenness, thievery, and "beastly" proposals to the town's women. Another account described how a uniformed "wretch" had assaulted an "aged," Bible-toting woman of renowned "piety."

The town's Whig magistrates were appalled, dutifully following Adams's lead and meting out harsh punishments to the erring troops. Dalrymple complained but only gently. He grumbled,

I don't suppose my men are without fault, but twenty of them have been knocked down in the streets and got up and

scratched their heads and run to their Barracks and no more
has been heard of it. Whereas if one of the Inhabitants meets
with no more than just a Kick for an Insult to a Soldier, the
Town is immediately in an Alarm and not one word the Soldier says in his justification can gain any credence.

Working with Molineux—who was in charge of carrying out
harassments on the noncooperating importers and on the rich by
means of his corps of pesky boys—Adams kept up a barrage of vitu-
peration against neutral and Tory New England merchants. He
was genuinely pleased to learn during the summer that in March
1770, Parliament had repealed the Townshend duties on all goods
except tea. Yet after praising the hard and occasionally painful work
of the colonists for this victory, Adams asked the people of Boston
to recommit themselves to the principle of non-importation. He
could not tolerate the idea of relapsing into dependency on Great
Britain.

Tensions on the waterfront heightened, with the practice of tarring and feathering informants becoming more frequent and with
inspectors spreading out from Boston and Salem to other maritime
communities. The tarring and feathering of George Gailer had
made an unforgettable impression on the region. Boston, despite, or
perhaps because of, the presence of the British regiments, seemed to
be the center of these brutal attacks, carried out by maritime mobs.
Anxious to find out what targets they would strike next, customs
officials considered kidnapping Ebenezer Mackintosh and taking
him for safekeeping to London, where he might reveal the Whigs'
secrets. The much-anticipated departure of Governor Bernard did
nothing to relieve stresses between the town's various factions. "I
live in hourly dread of disturbance," General Gage wrote to Dalrymple as summer ended.

Gage and Hutchinson continued to believe that the mobs carried out their strikes on the orders of certain irreconcilable Whigs.
James Otis, in particular, was identified by the Customs Board as
the chief instigator of the town's lawless behavior. In September,
Otis took an unfortunate step that seemed to confirm rumors of his
increasing irrationality and dangerous drunkenness. He strode into

the British Coffee House, where the customs commissioners were wont to assemble, and challenged Commissioner John Robinson to a duel. The scuffle that commenced as a fistfight degenerated into a general brawl, with other officers joining in. Otis ultimately emerged from the coffee house bleeding profusely from a blow to the head, probably as a result of a smack from Robinson's cane. The hard blow probably contributed to his rapid descent thereafter, from brilliance to insanity. It also contributed, as blood so often does, to the murderous mood of the town at the end of 1769.

## Boston's First Martyr

In the nonbloody sport of pestering importers, school-age boys played a conspicuous part. Acting both at the direction of Molineux and apparently on their own, they not only jeered and pelted with dirt the merchants who were marked as importers but also plastered their houses with mud and broke their windows. Historian Hiller B. Zobel, who has written the most complete book on the Boston Massacre, discovered in Loyalist Peter Oliver's writings the report of an old-fashioned but radical clergyman who spotted some boys smashing an importer's windows. Oliver quoted him as exclaiming, "See how those boys fight for us!"

At its best, this pestering might be seen as simply the kind of mischief to be expected in rude neighborhoods in rough times. At its worst, the harassment of importers became blatantly terroristic, as when their houses were coated in tar—that substance being, as already noted, the prime ingredient in New England's harshest form of social correction. Occasionally, the implication of a tarring and feathering soon to come was heightened by putting up a blackened sign in the form of a hand, a hand pointing to the house of the man to be punished.

One winter's day toward the end of February 1770, a black hand of this nature was erected in the gutter outside the North End shop of Theophilus Lillie, a storekeeper who had refused to sign the nonimportation agreement. What made his offense worse, Lillie had written in the *Boston News-Letter* a quite witty riposte to those who called themselves lovers of liberty, yet chose to "deprive others of *their* natural liberty." In that letter, he also framed the famous Tory line that if given the choice, he would rather be "a slave under one master" whom he knew (presumably the king) "than a slave to a hundred or more" (presumably the mob) whom he did not know.

It was indeed a mobbish crowd that gathered around his shop, a crowd of market-going adults, Sons of Liberty agitators, and restless boys whose intention that morning was to hang Lillie in effigy. At about ten o'clock, they saw a man approaching who seemed to be an ideal, additional target for the "frolics" (as they were called) of the day. This was Lillie's customer and neighbor Ebenezer Richardson, a notorious customs informer. An unflagging opponent of the radicals and of their non-importation policies, he had recently been heard to say of those self-nominated patriots, "Let 'em come on me. I'm ready, for I've guns loaded." In that same mood of impetuous hostility, he tried, upon seeing the hand outside Lillie's shop, to get control of one of the shoppers' wagons and use it to knock over the sign.

Prevented from doing so by a barrage of sticks and stones, Richardson was forced back to his own house. As he went, he shouted insults at all who were opposing him, telling them that it would be "too hot" for them before nightfall. He also berated the boys, who continued to pelt him with everything at hand, yelling at them to "Go off!" and get out of the road. Yet they stood their ground, just as free as he, they said, to stand in the king's highway. They surrounded the house and intensified their barrage, adding eggs to their variety of missiles. With all windows of the house broken, Richardson's alarmed family of his wife and two daughters came under attack. Just as his wife was struck by a rock, Richardson, who had been shaking a stick at the crowd, caught sight of an unemployed sailor named George Wilmot. Commanding him to come in the house and help, Richardson went in search of weapons.

The sight of the two armed men standing at the ready in the shattered upstairs windows did nothing to intimidate the crowd. Indeed, the sight seemed to double their fury; they charged the house and broke down the door. It was probably at this point that

Richardson decided to arm his weapon, loading it with so-called swan shot (pea-size pellets). Picking up the musket again and aiming it at the swirling mass of boys and adults below, he pulled the trigger, spraying the crowd with shot. One of the attackers was nicked, another slightly wounded, and yet another mortally wounded with the blast of eleven pellets. The last was an eleven-year-old lad named Christopher Seider.

With a surge, the crowd burst into the house, now determined to hang Richardson. Though he at first tried to defend himself with a cutlass, fighting off those who tried to seize him, he finally was overwhelmed and hauled out into the street. There the crowd had multiplied from hundreds to thousands, the tolling of the bell in a nearby church bringing in even more alarmed citizens. It was only the intervention of the authoritative William Molineux and other Whig leaders that saved Richardson from the rope. They conducted their captive to Faneuil Hall, where justices committed both Richardson and the sailor Wilmot to prison to await final judgment in a few weeks.

Speculation still goes on, particularly among conservative historians, as to why the Whig leadership took this moderating step at a time when they had a chance to seize wider and firmer control. But when viewed in the context of the many crises and crowd actions that preceded it in Boston's history, crowd actions that were almost always followed by attempts of the leaders to tone down the insurrection, Molineux's move toward justice rather than revenge seems right in the Boston spirit. He was certainly regarded at this point as the man who was controlling the opinions of the masses in town. After Lieutenant Governor Hutchinson subsequently agreed to calm the populace by removing two of the occupying British brigades (reducing the occupation force to six hundred men), it was Molineux, and Molineux alone, mounted on a horse and riding through the throngs of jeering citizens, who conducted the troops out of Boston, on their way to Halifax. For the moment, he ruled—and moderated—the town.

As for young Seider, he lay dying in a house near the site of the shooting. Among the doctors who rushed to treat him was a certain

Thomas Young, a recently arrived native of the Hudson River Valley, a deist and an iconoclast who, despite his lack of Boston connections, was beginning to play an increasingly important part in organizing the town's anti-British elements. He and the well-known Dr. Joseph Warren labored until evening to save the boy's life, but in vain; he died soon after 9:00 P.M. Dr. Warren performed an autopsy and removed the pellets, allowing the jury later on to conclude without a doubt how and by whose weapon he had died.

The word circulated that Christopher Seider had been "gratuitously" shot. And, in the sense that Richardson might have been aiming generally at the attacking boys, the comment may be correct. But it is equally true that the boy had thrown his lot in with others to strike back at the rich merchants and snobby shopkeepers who were blamed for keeping bread from his table. They were the ones who, by cooperating with the British occupiers, were preventing his German immigrant father from getting work on the waterfront. To Seider, it would surely have seemed as simple as that; such awareness and consciousness of apparent cause and effect should not be denied him. To call him a "martyr of freedom," as was soon essayed, would be to stretch the truth. But to withhold from him and other boys their open-eyed, deliberate part in the historic struggle then shaping up would be even more erroneous.

Martyr that he was perceived to be, Christopher Seider received a glorious funeral. Although heaps of sludge clogged the roads and pathways in the wake of a massive snowstorm, Samuel Adams and the Sons of Liberty succeeded in staging the funeral with full pomp. It began at the Liberty Tree; from there, accompanied by a cortege of more than thirty horse-drawn carriages, a procession of five hundred boys marching two by two preceded the casket on its way to the cemetery. As thousands of others watched and participated in the ceremonies, it became clear that by the Seider tragedy, Molineux and Adams (who was seen at the funeral in company with some of his roughneck "Mohawks") had won a major victory. Even Thomas Hutchinson agreed, concurring that it was "the largest [funeral] perhaps ever known in America." Thanks to the communication network established by the Sons of Liberty, the whole event received widespread notice throughout the colonies.

Newspapers in New York and Philadelphia reported the details of the lad's shooting in particularly gruesome detail, also pointing out the malfeasance of the customs officials and the effect of the incident on the rebellious mood of the oppressed town. Just five weeks before Seider's death, blood had been shed in New York. Violence had erupted when British soldiers hacked down the city's liberty pole, prompting a mob to set upon a band of soldiers with clubs and cutlasses. Soon more soldiers joined the fray, charging the crowd with fixed bayonets across a hill and up a slope, in a struggle that earned the name Battle of Golden Hill (January 19, 1770). Although the wounds were many and the injuries severe, no deaths resulted. Nonetheless, New York had seen the first bloodshed in a battle for liberty just as Boston had nominated its first martyr. The *Boston Gazette* concluded that "like the blood of the righteous Abel," these sanguinary affairs cried out for "Vengeance."

## Ropewalk Workers, Importunate Lads, and Former Slaves

Boys of about Seider's age also played a central part in the deadly episode that revealed the inflammatory condition of occupied Boston to the entire world—the so-called Boston Massacre. In addition to the fractiousness of the boys, there were a number of other irritations in the town's social makeup that contributed to the explosive evening of March 5, 1770. Outstanding among these were labor conditions. Accordingly, modern research indicates that the true point of origin of the Massacre was a certain sweaty ropewalk, Gray's ropewalk, in Boston's South End.

It might be helpful, first, to clarify more exactly what an eighteenth-century ropewalk was. One should picture a shed about a quarter-mile in length, within which a band of a dozen men, called "spinners," was employed to weave yarns of hemp together into heavy ropes under extremely stressful circumstances. The nature of the men's work has been studied most intensely by Louis Hutchins, a historian at the Boston National Historic Park. He describes how the chief spinner wrapped the cleaned strike of hemp around his waist, with the ends tucked into his belt behind his back. Then he would take a few fiber ends, depending on the desired thickness of the yarn, attach them to the "whirl" or hook on the spinning wheel, and, when another rope maker turned the wheel to set the spinning hooks in motion, he began walking backward down the full length of the ropewalk letting out the fibers and spinning as he went. The great difficulty in spinning lay not in merely twisting the fibers together but doing it in such a way to maintain a perfectly even thickness and twist. Paying out the fibers over the entire length of the walk required remarkable tenacity.

Like other laborers on the Boston waterfront, these men and the boys who assisted them worked between twelve and fourteen hours a day, six days a week. If they were fortunate enough to work year-round (most unlikely at this time of occupation, when the declining shipping business forced ropewalk shutdowns), spinners might make £40 a year. This was slightly more than what a seaman made and about half of what a craftsman like Revere earned. From their wages, they had to pay rent—often cruelly high—and other living expenses. Because of the stringent demands of the work and the need for tight coordination among the spinners, ropewalk workers developed their own kind of close-knit brotherhood, as close as the crew of a ship. Even when they were not performing their rigorous "rope walkers' dance," they tended to band together, often carrying with them the "willow wands" (more properly called wooldering, or wouldering, sticks) by means of which they straightened the ropes' threads. These sticks made handy weapons if the time came for a waterfront brawl.

And such times came often in the neighborhood of Gray's ropewalk. Named for its owner, John Gray, this shed earned a reputation for the rowdiness of its workers and the touchiness of their mood, particularly in the era of British occupation. To be sure, the reputation for violent behavior belonged not to the spinners of Gray's ropewalk alone; it applied to the entire industry—an industry founded on American shores in Boston in 1641. Ever since then, as the industry flourished as an essential part of all working harbors up and down the New England coast, ropewalk workers had felt the scorn of the straitlaced merchant society that they served. A parson in Salem remarked, typically, that ropewalks were congenitally evil. The sheds were "inhabited by the most lawless men, and on Sundays it is not unusual [for them] to crawl into such places and spend the day away in concealment."*

Added to the disorderly reputation of Gray's ropewalk was the renown of its owner, a man reportedly of "hardened" anti-British sentiments. Rumored to be one of the "Mohawks" who carried out the rough work of Samuel Adams and William Molineux, he shared with his men a hatred for the soldiers and the sailors from the occupying fleet who came around looking for extra work. Indeed, it was at his ropewalk's door that the fight flared up on March 3, the fight that began when one such "garrison rat" applied for work, the fight that kicked off the Boston Massacre.

It had gone something like this. When asked why he was hanging around, the soldier replied, "Yes, faith, I would like some work." The spinner who had asked the question then suggested, "Well then, go clean my shit house." "Empty it yourself!" the soldier snarled—and a melee broke out. Drubbed, knocked on his heels, and disarmed, the soldier soon fled. Almost immediately, he was back, supported by eight or nine of his cronies. Swinging into the fight, the soldiers at first carried all before them. But soon the men in the ropewalk, calling for additional help, outnumbered them and beat them back with their wouldering sticks. Eventually, magistrates separated the men and ordered both sides to return to their proper places. This they sullenly did, but all too soon they were ready to fight again.

---

*Given that reputation, it seems fitting that this proud counterstatement was discovered by Louis Hutchins, in his study of the ropewalk workers of Massachusetts: "I am a rope-maker, and I thank God for it!" boasted a Plymouth spinner in 1800. He went on, "It was the Rope-makers of Massachusetts who whipped the British soldiers in the streets of Boston with their willow-wands, which precipitated the so-called Boston Massacre, which was one of the leading incidents that brought about the Revolution and the freedom of this great country of ours."

They would not have long to wait. As that day of March 5 drew to a close, the indignant cries of a lad–a typically obstreperous Boston lad–could be heard as he ran toward King Street. This one was a wig maker's apprentice named Edward Garrick, and he was running to catch up with an officer of the 14th Regiment who, the boy loudly protested, had not paid his master for "dressing his hair." The argument soon caught the attention of other boys, girls, and adults, turning it into a major confrontation.

The fracas took place directly in front of an insecure sentry guarding the customs house on King Street, a certain Private White. Indeed, the position of the sentry, up the street from the head of Long Wharf and right in front of the hated customs house– headquarters of the system against which Bostonians had struggled so fiercely, with both their non-importation associations and their crowd actions–gives another key to understanding the sentiments behind the Massacre.

The nervous Private White immediately sided with the accosted officer, saying that as the officer was a gentleman, he must have paid his bill, so the lad should cease his lying wail. That was precisely the kind of insulting, offensive language that Boston's youngsters had come to expect, and to loathe, from British lobster backs. To drive home that point and to get the payment that he justly demanded, Garrick spat back some salty language of his own. Challenged, the private came out of his sentry box to take the lad on. He swung his musket at Garrick, striking him on the side of the head, producing more youthful caterwauling and outraged cries. The boisterous crowd of fifty or more that had gathered took up the cry, yelling at the "Lobster son of a bitch!" and moving between the buildings to surround his sentry post.

From the Town House at the head of King Street, a warning bell began to ring; cries of "Fire!" could be heard, as well as the ancient ancestral cry of "Town born, turn out!" Another Boston riot was evidently a-building. But it was scarcely a spontaneous event. Other well-rehearsed cries could soon be heard: "To the Main Guard! That's next!" For the details of that riot and the subsequent events, we are grateful again to the author Hiller Zobel. His coordination of the several eyewitness accounts of what happened on March 5 helps make the evening come alive.

Variously motivated, many citizens had chosen to go abroad that night of March 5, some armed with cudgels, cutlasses, or willow wands. Some from the waterfront community evidently expected a renewal of the ropewalk fight; other angry mariners came forth in response to a bleeding oysterman's report of how he had been beaten up by British troopers. There were also bands of soldiers, many of whom appeared to be in foul moods, jostling or even slashing members of the crowds they encountered on the snowy streets. Some of them still burned with rage for the ropewalk episode; they would get revenge. Yet they may have wondered whether this disturbance was leading to a battle with massed civilians, like New York's Battle of Golden Hill.

As the cool evening turned into a cold, clear night, a number of scuffles and snowball fights broke out. Above the ominous tolling of an alarm bell could be heard frightened shouts of "Fire!" Yet none of the uproar was accidental. The Reverend Andrew Eliot had been told that certain townspeople were pledged to fight the soldiers that night and that bells would be rung "to assemble the inhabitants together." Records show that a great number of sailors had been given leave from their ships and that they streamed ashore, ready to join in the confrontation. For their part, soldiers from the 14th and 29th Regiments had posted a public notice, saying that they were prepared to defend themselves—language of the day for "looking for a fight." The people responded as if released from football huddles, rushing at one another through the town's narrow passageways with whatever kind of weapon came to hand.

One who joined them was a seventeen-year-old lad named Samuel Maverick, the half-brother of Ebenezer Mackintosh's wife. An apprentice to an ivory turner, Maverick had worked until 8:30 that evening and then had gone to eat supper at the house of a keg maker. When he heard the bells, he told his host that he could eat but a few more mouthfuls, then must go to the "fire."

Another worker who was then eating supper was an extraordinary-looking forty-seven-year-old seaman named Michael Johnson.

He appeared distinctive, both in his massiveness—standing six feet two inches in height and with enormous strength—and in the personal history etched in his face. His racial lineage was, from the beginning, put to question. The Harvard librarian Justin Winslow, in his 1883 history of Boston, reported that Michael Johnson was "usually called a mulatto, sometimes a slave"; in the *American Historical Record* for December 1872, he is held to have been a "half-breed Indian." Not even his name was recorded with certainty. It was, in fact, Crispus Attucks; however, as he'd had to flee from slavery at a young age and had been constantly afraid of recapture and impressment, "Michael Johnson" was an identity that suited Crispus Attucks for the time being.

The history of the Attucks family, though difficult to trace (as confessed in the 1995 biography by James Neyland), is loaded with the kind of injustices that laboring-class and ethnically diverse people in and around Boston experienced and felt deeply about; they demanded violent counterstrikes. Again and again, the family (whose name is thought to mean "small deer") was cheated of what should have remained theirs. Crispus, most probably born in 1723, grew up in the supposedly secure Native American community of Natick, Massachusetts, founded by the missionary John Eliot in the mid-1600s (and described fully in the author's 2002 book *Gods of War, Gods of Peace*). But whereas this town of "praying Indians" had been guaranteed continuity even after the crushing inhumanities of King Philip's War, neighboring farmers had little by little dispossessed the inhabitants of their land and inheritance. Many of them were commandeered as slaves, including Crispus, though he had been born free.

Given his size, even as a youth, he must have seemed a great prize to potential owners. His tall and powerful father, whose name is given as Prince Attucks (presumably in memory of his Fulani or Tuareg ancestors), had come to America in chains. Sold to a farmer in Natick's neighboring town of Framingham, he had apparently married Crispus's mother, Nancy, soon after arrival. Their son Crispus had been enrolled in the Natick school before he was enslaved at the age of eleven. By the time he reached twenty-seven, he had been sold to different masters four more times, learning not peacefulness but an angry intractability that became his face to the world.

After his escape from slavery in 1750, his onetime owner William Brown placed an advertisement for Crispus's return, with a carefully drawn physical description to assist his recapture. But by then Attucks was safely off at sea, under the new name of Michael Johnson—the historical conjecture being that Brown's neighbors, the Johnsons, had helped him, hence his choice of that name. He had also been helped by Quakers in the whaling town of New Bedford. In that thriving port, few questions were asked of those applying for berths aboard ship, even of possibly escaped slaves. Indeed, some Quakers were even then in the forefront of pressing for abolition; they carried on that moral struggle with little help from the Puritans. In the decade preceding the Stamp Act (1755–1765), some 23,743 slaves were sold through the entrepot of Boston; the slave population of the province of Massachusetts itself at that time numbered between 5,000 and 6,000, about the same size as the capital's early population. Even a modest family like the Franklins had a slave; the institution was an accepted part of life, except for those who lived it.

Gradually, as the spirit of enlightenment spread into certain quarters, some educated Bostonians (including John Adams's wife, Abigail) came to see slavery for the horrible business that it was and joined the Quakers in opposing it. Under the influence of Samuel Adams, the Town Meeting voted in May 1766 for the "total abolishment of slavery from among us." But Governor Bernard and his council, then in control, turned their backs on the resolution, ensuring its nullification. In Massachusetts, on the waterfront and elsewhere, people who were slaves would remain caught within that accepted institution, unless their chains were removed by conscience-stricken masters or shattered by violence and escape. And to the Royal Navy, "Negroes" would always be the most likely target of impressment teams.

Attucks endured the stench and the hard life aboard the whaler, advancing to the rank of boatswain. He may also have played a seaman's part in the engagements of the French and Indian War. Sometime after 1760, he seems to have found a new home in the free-black community of Providence in the Bahamas, but then the sea (or poverty) called him forth again. In the months after the arrival of the *Romney* and the British armada, he is known to have sailed in and out of Boston several times, always fearful of impressment or apprehension, always aware of the British occupiers as the reason for the hard times. In the bitter cold winter of 1769–1770, he is thought to have been unemployed, waiting like others for a ship that never materialized or sailed, taking part-time work at Gray's ropewalk whenever he could get it. He certainly knew of the fight that had broken out there with British soldiers on March 3; he was certainly ready to take part in whatever might follow next.

## At the Sound of the Bells

Armed with a cordwood stick reported to be about the thickness of a man's wrist, Crispus Attucks went out that night to join his ropewalk colleagues and anyone else who might be engaged in further action against the British. He was joined by Samuel Maverick and many others, all rushing through the dark streets and alleys toward King Street and the customs house to see whether this truly was a fire, an armed fight, or another crowd action. Some of the people out that night, it was learned later, had been addressed by a tall man in a red cloak who had harangued all within earshot, passionately urging them, dispatching them to go "do for the soldiers." Guesses abound as to who this may have been, but since the presence of both Samuel Adams and William Molineux is quite well accounted for, and the role does not fit the intellectual Dr. Young, it may just have been one of Boston's many excited citizens.

Soldiers who had joined in the rush were described in a contemporary account as "quarrelling and fighting with the people whom they saw there." The question seemed not to be whether there might be a major fight but where the main action would take place. When the several groups of people arrived at the customs house, they could see that this was probably that anticipated place, here the crisis was at its most intense. Yet this was no regular, two-sided battle. Private White, having escaped from his penned-in sentry box, was standing on the customs house steps, attacked by boys throwing snow and ice balls and pressed by the weight of the throng. A solitary and scared figure, he turned away from the assault, yelling for help and banging on the door behind him to be let in. But the door remained locked; indeed, many of the people within had fled out the back way, wanting no part of the contest.

From a few blocks away at the main guardhouse, Captain Thomas Preston, the officer of the day, could hear the scuffle, as well as Private White's cries for help. He paced up and down, observers recalled, apparently trying to decide what course of action to take. Finally, putting himself in charge of a detachment of one corporal and six grenadiers (particularly tall enlisted men), he marched with them to the customs house. On his way, the captain was stopped by a young bookseller named Henry Knox (later to be George Washington's chief of artillery). "For God's sake," Knox pleaded of Preston, "take care of your men. If they fire, you die." Preston replied that he was well aware of the danger.

Apparently, the captain's first thought had been to rescue White and march him under the squad's protection back to the guardhouse. But when the press of people proved too great for that, Preston told White to "fall in," and he lined the eight men up in semicircular formation right where they were. Standing in front of them, Preston hollered at the crowd, commanding it to disperse. The people returned his yells with insults, followed by taunts daring the soldiers to shoot. The men leveled their bayonets, some thrusting at jostlers who came too close. They had a reputation, these soldiers from the 29th Regiment, for quick tempers. Zobel quotes Lieutenant Governor Hutchinson as having said of them, "They are in general such bad fellows in that regiment, that it seems impossible for restraining them from firing upon an insult or provocation given them."

The standoff continued for some ten or fifteen taut and frightening minutes as more and more excited people arrived on the scene, including Crispus Attucks and Samuel Maverick. As the level of the taunts increased, the redcoats, poised at attention, set themselves to raise their muskets. "Damn you, you sons of bitches, fire!" shouted someone, perhaps a drunk, adding, "You can't kill us all!" Then a push and a shove, a club and a counterthrust, and a grenadier slipped on the ice and fell on his back, his musket slipping free and clattering across the street's surface. Picking it up in fury, the soldier fired what turned out to be a harmless shot. It maddened the crowd. But Preston yelled, "Recover!" seeking to tighten the formation and prevent further shooting.

It was too late. Soldiers had begun firing at will, presumably aiming at those who threatened them most immediately. That was too much for many of those brave (or desperate) men to resist; Crispus Attucks, among others, reacted by deciding not to flee but to charge ahead. Apparently caught right at the moment of hurling his heavy stick at the hated redcoats, he was hit by two balls in mid-chest. More muskets were fired. Maverick, hearing the blast and seeing blood flow, tried to run from the scene. But as he raced toward Town House, he was hit by a ricocheting bullet and fell, dying a day later.

The first to fall seems to have been Samuel Gray, one of the regular workers at John Gray's ropewalk (maybe a relative). Perhaps he had rushed to the site in company with Attucks; certainly, according to reports, he had been in the vanguard of those who taunted and physically challenged the soldiers. Another who fell was the young sailor James Caldwell, who, in somewhat the same manner as Maverick, had been turning away from the gunfire when hit. Two balls struck him in the back, one in the body, one in the shoulder. He died on the spot.

The fifth to die from the redcoats' fire was an interesting young Irish immigrant named Patrick Carr. He had had his fill of British oppression when participating in crowd action in the Old Country and, on this evening, had rushed to the fray with weapon in hand. Though persuaded by a neighbor to leave his sword at home, he was still eager to have a crack at the soldiers by means of whatever else might come to hand. Hit by bullets in the hip and the backbone, he suffered several days of agony before dying on March 14. A merchant standing in his doorway and watching the terrible sight of the chargers, and the firing and the dying, was struck in the right arm, a nonfatal wound. Six others also felt the sting of bullets that night but lived to tell the tale. All this happened in just a few minutes, after which the soldiers reloaded and cocked their pieces to fire again.

But Captain Preston, appalled at what had happened, commanded them to cease firing and lower their guns. As soon as he could reestablish order, he marched the squad back to the guardhouse. There he had to face Lieutenant Governor Hutchinson, who, hearing of the fray, had hurried from his home in the North End to the center through the enraged populace—an act of considerable personal courage. Emergency action was called for, however great the danger to himself. Through Hutchinson's many contacts, he may well have known that a tar barrel had been prepared that evening on the crest of Signal Hill; by igniting it and raising it to the top of a pole, signalers planned to bring in additional thousands of people from the countryside. When Hutchinson reached the guardhouse and demanded of Preston what had gone on, a hot exchange of defensive answers ensued.

Gathering what facts he could and pressed on all sides by the angry crowd, Hutchinson decided that he must try to keep the riot from becoming a mass rebellion by returning to Town House and reasserting authority. William Molineux was waiting for him there, demanding the immediate and official withdrawal of all British troops. But Hutchinson, caught in an uncomfortable position between the army and the citizens, sidestepped that issue, wanting to show favor to neither side. He went out on the balcony to address the immense, roaring crowd below. "The law will have its course!" he called. "I will live and die by the law." And he urged all to return to their homes. Cooler heads prevailing, the tar barrel on the hill was never raised.

Yet the night's events did not end until, arrest warrants having been issued for Captain Preston and his second in command, those two men were found and brought into the Town House chamber by the ever-faithful Sheriff Greenleaf. In a brief hearing involving the statements of a few witnesses, the justices determined that Preston might well be guilty of having ordered the troops to fire and should therefore be tried. Attempts thereby would be made to let justice bring peace to a town on the brink of rebellion, if not self-destruction.

# "A Rabble of Saucy Boys, Negroes and Mulattoes, Irish Teagues, and Outlandish Jack Tars"

Almost immediately, the bloody affair of March 5 was given its everlasting, exaggerated title, the "Boston Massacre."* Though the event itself had sprung so obviously from that one peculiarly impacted town, these words were shocking enough to help swing the minds of Americans up and down the Atlantic coast toward armed resistance. If the British soldiers were going to invade this continent and massacre its people, to fight back seemed the only noble—or even reasonable—response. Yet curiously, as the adept pen of Samuel Adams and the vivid artwork of Paul Revere strove to advertise the horrors of the Massacre, nothing much was said about who had actually been massacred.

The fact that the five victims were typical men and boys of the waterfront—a sailor, a ropewalk worker, an unemployed Native American/African American escaped slave, an Irish immigrant, and a youthful apprentice (in fact, Ebenezer Mackintosh's brother-in-law)—received absolutely no attention from the forces that were making the Massacre a cause for American liberty. Nor was it considered that they were more than victims, that at least some of them had known what they were doing. It was only much later, in the nineteenth century, that the historian John Fisk could perceive that the deaths of these men and boys, where they had not been accidental and collateral, had been combative and purposeful. They had, Fisk wrote, "effected in a moment what seventeen months of petitions had failed to accomplish"—namely, the repeal of most of the Townshend Acts and the withdrawal of the British military from Boston.

Not concerned with the volitional aspect of the Massacre, the contemporary Bostonian Paul Revere, when he chose to rush into print a copy of Henry Pelham's picture of the event, made sure that those who fell looked like victimized first-class citizens. Not a sailor,

---

*Historians today tend to refer to it as the "King Street Riot."

*A masterpiece of Whig propaganda, Paul Revere's engraving of Henry Pelham's*
Boston Massacre *painting bristles with exaggerations: over the customs house's
door are the words "Butcher's Hall"; from an upstairs window, someone (a Tory?)
fires an extra shot. Those who were killed are shown not as a number of onrushing
waterfront laborers but as proper gentlemen.*
The Boston Athenaeum

not a spinner, not a youth, and certainly not a Negro is to be seen
falling to the bloodstained ground in front of the customs house;
instead, periwigged gentlemen take the blast, fall into one another's
arms, and register looks of Bostonian indignation. The print,
accompanied by screaming headlines and vivid text (including emotional verse), soon appeared on broadsides around the town and in

newspapers throughout the colonies. Revere and Samuel Adams tried to stretch the facts somewhat and link the town's noncooperating merchants to the shooting by the redcoats. Had not certain well-known figures been seen firing from upper-story windows along with them? Was this not a Tory plot? Though that effort failed to win many adherents, Hutchinson and other conservatives realized that they must try both to present the affair rationally and to bring matters under the control of law.

Hutchinson, who would not be named governor of the province for yet another year, deliberately procrastinated in setting up the trial of Captain Preston and his eight soldiers. On the other side, not wanting passions to be allowed to cool, Samuel Adams, at the head of a group of Whigs, indignantly marched into court to demand more haste. Yet the Massachusetts Superior Court seemed unable to complete arrangements for the trial until October 24. It determined that the order of judicial affairs should be that Captain Preston would be tried first, followed by the rest of his men. The attorney to lead the defense would be none other than John Adams, deemed Boston's most outstanding trial lawyer, seconded by the "sprightly genius" Josiah Quincy Jr.

Hearing of his son's decision to take on that unpopular—indeed, dangerous—role, Josiah Quincy Sr. exclaimed, "Good God! Is it possible? I will not believe it." To this, the young man replied that the soldiers were "not yet legally proved guilty" and therefore were entitled, "by the laws of God and man, to all legal counsel and aid." Patriots were also surprised at John Adams's acceptance of a defense attorney's role (though, tellingly, his cousin Samuel found no fault with this move). To objections, John made the high-minded retort that "Council ought to be the very last thing that an accused Person should want in a free country."

It seems clear both that the pleas for assistance from John Adams's merchant clients had influenced his decision to aid the defense and that his willingness to help calm matters down was in the tradition of Boston's conservative reaction to all major disturbances. Scholars also agree, however, that Adams, this very judicial man, even while taking a different path from his radical cousin, had at this point reached the conclusion that Great Britain had demonstrated its "determination . . . to subjugate Us." Henceforth, he could be counted on the side of the patriots.

Hutchinson's slow-down tactic worked fairly effectively. Preston's trial dragged on until the end of October, when he was declared innocent; only two of the soldiers were found guilty, not of murder but of manslaughter. Even these escaped with but a token punishment, John Adams having pleaded "benefit of clergy" on their behalf. This meant that they would receive nothing more than a brand on the thumb. It can also be said that Adams's professional services on behalf of the defense had been as effective as Hutchinson's delays. He took the slant not only that the soldiers had been provoked into firing (confirmed by many who testified) but also that the provocateurs who were slain came only from the lowest levels of society.

Adams referred to them as this "motley rabble of saucy boys, Negroes and Mulattoes, Irish Teagues, and outlandish Jack Tars." However regrettable their deaths might be, such types should certainly not be allowed to influence justice or the course of governmental affairs. Behind this appallingly haughty attitude, scholars have found that Adams had at least done his research and was struck by the maritime character of those slain. Historian Alfred Young, in combing through Adams's notes for the trial, spotted constant seafaring references such as "appear to be sailors" and "sailors on vessel aware of plan" and "Attucks dressed sailor-like" and "entire crews from vessels, from taverns (around 190)." Adams manipulated those facts so as to convince the jury of non-Bostonians [!] that the deaths of mere sailors, brought on by their own misbehavior and that of other drunken waterfront characters, should not be considered as a serious deviation on the part of the king's grenadiers.*

The people of Boston, for their part, were more willing to accept Samuel Adams's version of the Massacre story, which was that the

---

*Though John Adams seems to have had little regard for Attucks as a sentient human being, going so far as to call his appearance "terrifying," he felt free to use Attucks's name as a pseudonym and as a symbol when writing about liberty to Lieutenant Governor Hutchinson.

murdered men should be seen as sacrificial reminders of British oppression. Leaving aside what these men's real purposes in life may have been, he painted them in death as valiant martyrs for liberty. Because the Irishman Patrick Carr had not yet succumbed to his ultimately mortal wounds, the funeral that Adams arranged for the afternoon of March 8 featured only four black-painted coffins. Carried on the shoulders of mourners and accompanied by unbelievable numbers (ten to twelve thousand people), the coffins processed through the streets of the town, around the Liberty Tree, and finally to the burial ground at the Granary. Carr's body would join them at that revered burial site on March 17—a site still marked today by a simple, eroding stone.

Because of Samuel Adams's hyperbolic magnification of the Massacre and because of John Adams's derogation of those massacred, the real-life importance of the wronged Crispus Attucks and his fallen comrades was allowed to fade away. No longer workmen and apprentices to be considered in their own worlds, they became patriotic abstractions. Whenever liberal civic leaders suggested erecting a memorial to these men and boys that would contain their real names and occupations, loud cries of opposition were heard (even from the Massachusetts Historical Society). The danger was that if those "heroes" were considered for what they were, they might be recognized as "ruffians" and provokers of violence. Indeed, no monument was built and dedicated until 1888, when abolition and the Civil War had done their parts, and African American leaders could overcome continuing objections and construct a fitting monument on Boston Common.

Samuel Adams's intention had been to use the glorified Massacre as a powerful springboard from which to launch further Whig-conceived actions for liberty and against the strangling strategies of the British. In that spirit, he succeeded in expanding the membership of Boston's Town Meeting to include most of "the body of the people." Ironically, with the cancelation of almost all the Townshend Acts and the withdrawal of most British troops from Boston, the port began to function smoothly again (though the customs officers remained in place). What it was that Attucks,

Maverick, Gray, Caldwell, and Carr must have wanted most of all for themselves and for others—namely, the reopening of the shipyards, new business in the ropewalks, and the sailing forth of ships—did indeed begin to happen. This was the kind of liberty they had cared about.

# 8

# The Maritime Workers' Tea Party

When news of the repeal of most of the Townshend Acts' provisions sailed into Boston Harbor in the early summer of 1770, the town's tensions relaxed. Samuel Adams and William Molineux tried to keep public attention focused on the remaining tea duty—which constituted, Adams cried unceasingly, taxation without representation—and on maintaining the spirit (if not the precise letter) of non-importation. To him, British tea became the very symbol of non-importation; by eternally forsaking it, patriots might "save this country from Ruin and Slavery." But, as mentioned in the preceding chapter, Molineux nearly received a coat of tar and feathers when he, often a bully, pushed his cause too hard in Marblehead. And Adams, now fifty years old and less vigorous than in earlier years of combat, was referred to as one of those "gloomy mortals" whose warnings of British "tyranny!" rang somewhat hollow.

To be sure, ardor for resistance still warmed the hearts of many Bostonians. Their favorite piece for tavern singing was the "Liberty Song," an American version of the British sailors' favorite melody, "Heart of Oak." The new words, which commemorated the *Liberty* riot of a few years back and which pushed the claim of taxation without representation, had been written by the best-selling author of the day, the pretend "Pennsylvania Farmer," John Dickinson. His words lurched along somewhat awkwardly but with a point:

> In Freedom we're born, and in Freedom we'll live.
> Our purses are ready,
> Steady, friends, steady,
> Not as slaves but as Freemen our Money we'll give.

Also recalled in verse and prose was Boston's subsequent riot, the near-rebellion of seamen and others that had broken out on the night of the Massacre. Indeed, March 5 became recognized as the prime holiday of the year for all patriots who loved liberty; this tradition endured in the town until July 4 took its place a decade later. In that spirit, Samuel Adams blasted away in the columns of the *Boston Gazette* at jury and judges for their leniency toward the British soldiers in the Boston Massacre trial. To Adams's disgust, many fellow Bostonians reacted much as they had after other waterfront disturbances: a hush was allowed to fall over both the legal proceedings and the deaths of the five shabby unfortunates; the town reassumed its posture of social propriety.

Whereas Governor Hutchinson had had the sagacity (and the gall) to move the General Court across the Charles River to Cambridge as a safety measure, he now brought it back to its proper location, threats of mob action against it having died down. John Rowe, the wealthy merchant who had once chaired the committee for the boycott of English goods, announced that there was no further need for such actions; to continue them would be "prejudicial to the Merchants & Trade of the Town of Boston." Even the hated Board of Customs Commissioners, whose members had wisely exiled themselves to Castle William when the bloody battle commenced, were now invited to return. To their pleasure, they received neither the "Insults" nor the "Molestation" (meaning, presumably, the tarring and feathering) that had plagued them earlier in the year. Samuel Adams's "coalition of thugs and lawyers" seemed to have lost its dominance.

Throughout the American colonies, it was as if some great storm had battered coastal cities and then blown out to sea, leaving in its wake a fading memory of bloodshed and rebellion. In New York, where the Liberty Boys had been bold enough to defend their liberty pole by waterfront rioting and by the Battle of Golden Hill, and where the non-importation agreement had been so tightly maintained that grass was seen to grow in unfrequented streets along the harbor, "political lethargy" became the recognized mood of 1771. In Philadelphia, as radicals and mob leaders quieted, Dickinson and other moderate lovers of liberty resumed control. One of them wrote that "Everything is as we would wish, and nothing but some unhappy misunderstanding with the Mother Country can hurt us." It was beyond anyone's imagining that 342 chests of tea would upset that dear relationship.

## Tying the Rebellious Ports Together

Prosperity returned to Boston. Merchants rerigged their ships and sent them forth to Europe and the West Indies, instructing captains to bring home cargoes legal and otherwise. British manufacturers, happy to recommence trade with their New England cousins, supplied them once again with the rich textiles and the elegant coaches that the upper class had learned to enjoy before the boycott. Samuel Adams blamed his crisis-time collaborators, the merchants, for this surrender of non-importation principles (a surrender in which they were preceded by their New York colleagues) and this lapse in Puritan restraint. He watched with disgust as John Hancock once again became a close associate of the governor, even to the extent of accepting Hutchinson's invitation to become the colonel of his fancily rigged-out cadet corps.

That seductive British coziness was indeed a threat to the patriot cause. Through the tough times of the 1760s, John Hancock had seemed to be the eternal champion of the poor, driving his carriage into poor streets where politicians had never before been seen, dispensing his largesse wherever he heard tales of destitution and unemployment, and contending face-to-face with British officials when they increased shipboard inspections. He had so vehemently backed the cause of non-importation that as late as 1770, he stocked his swift brig *Lydia* with a variety of disallowed English imports—the total cargo valued at more than £15,000—and shipped them back to London. He had also donated a fire engine to the people of Boston. Now, a peace of some sort having been achieved with the imperial authorities, and he having accomplished his objective of taking power back from the radical Whigs, he set off on a summer's cruise along the coast of Maine, the privileged executive on vacation and in denial.

For there was no doubt about the splits within the society of this new Boston. The rich and competitive merchants, always numbering more than the town's economy could easily justify, were once again striving to become even richer; the poor of the waterfront, whose ownership share of the wealth of the town was approaching zero, faced intensifying privation and starvation. Though the town's slaves, some eight hundred in number, managed to have a petition for their freedom submitted to the Assembly, it—and they—were as usual ignored. This was also the time when Ebenezer Mackintosh and George Robert Twelves Hewes found themselves sharing the same debtors' prison. None of the other merchants and high-and-mighties who had been so willing earlier to give them a drink or march with them came forth with assistance. Mackintosh, overwhelmed by the death of his wife, seems to have lost himself in drink. Hewes, once he managed to regain a measure of freedom, apparently went off fishing on the Banks, unable to earn a living at shoemaking. So desperate were the unemployed that some merchants feared a waterfront uprising, one that might resemble the slave breakouts simultaneously dreaded by their southern colleagues.

Samuel Adams must have recognized with some bitterness that there never had been much cohesion between even the most liberal of the Whig merchants and the men like himself who wanted a return to the social principles of a people's commonwealth and the casting-out of British affectations and imperial regulations. Bleakly, he identified his personal cause as "the fiction of a political enthusiast." Neither in his hometown nor in his province at large did the concept of freedom seem to have sufficient dynamism for success. The two men on whom he could still count were definitely not from traditional Boston families. There was the strong-armed William Molineux, the English-born smuggler who was surely running his own illegal games with the Dutch even as he sought, with apparent sincerity, to find weaving jobs for the poor. And there was Dr. Thomas Young, the impetuous and outspoken freethinker from Albany who wanted to break the back of British authority. By preaching that message, he had gained the disdain of the more sedate Whigs, along with enormous credibility among the long-shoremen and the craftsmen.

When Dr. Young, one of the founders of the North End Caucus, was asked to give the oration in honor of the first anniversary of the Boston Massacre, he went so far as to select as his theme the occasional advisability of treason. For this, he was roundly condemned. A member of the Roxbury Town Meeting declared that Dr. Young was a known deist and thus, as a godless and profane man, should not be listened to. Samuel Adams attempted to defend his colleague, pointing out that as a man of "political integrity," Young had been "an unwearied assertor of the rights of his countrymen." In that time of reinstated calm and reinforced authority, such men could feel the ebbing of their political strength.

Yet ironically, the bloodred seeds of rebellion that Boston patriots—patriots either by conscience or by their desperate circumstances—had planted in the decade from 1760 to 1770 had begun to germinate and sprout in other localities, near and far. The same maritime factors that had stimulated thoughts of independence and rebellion in Boston could be discerned acting on people of other ports in an obviously correlated and synchronous way. In the fishing community of Essex, which lay eastward up the coast from Boston, adjacent to the towns where the Reverend John Wise had stirred up his rebellion against Governor Edmund Andros, the local newspaper came out for the formation of a new, republican government—a "commonweal" such as the one the Dutch had recently formed in the Republic of the Netherlands.

Down the Delaware River from Philadelphia, when a boat containing tea on which no duty had been paid was seized by customs officers, waterfront freebooters went on the attack. Casting the boat adrift, they abandoned her on a mud bank. More alarmingly, the law-abiding people of that community declined to chase after the "ruffians" who had been involved in the incident; not even the appointed authorities of the province seemed much interested in pursuing the matter, even though the attackers had made off with the smuggled cargo. Similar breakdowns of royal regulations were occurring up and down the coast. By writing about and tying together those events, Samuel Adams, frustrated by the back-pedaling in Boston, tried to make of what had been local disturbances an intercolonial campaign of resistance to British oppression.

Specifically, it was through his invention of the "Boston Committee of Correspondence" that Adams was able to further his plan of creating a functioning, united body of resistance. In 1764, even before the Stamp Act crisis, he had actually set up a prototype of the committee when he was carrying on his father's campaign against the Currency Act. But that early version enjoyed the short life of many other ad hoc patriotic groups in Massachusetts and elsewhere. Now, with thoughts and actions fermenting throughout the colonies, Adams sought to establish a more permanent bond between them all, with riders committed to dash across appointed distances whenever information or alarms needed to be spread abroad.

The first such alarm occurred in September 1772 when Governor Hutchinson committed the gross tactical error of deciding that the salaries of both himself and the province's judges should be paid not by the legislature but by the Crown. This move was instantly seen as an effort to deprive the people of their power of the purse over local officials. Adams believed it to be the kind of usurpation of authority that would outrage citizens far beyond the capital port of Boston. That was when he persuaded the Sons of Liberty to create the town's more permanent Committee of Correspondence. The response to messages carried by that committee's riders across the province was so intense that within the next three months, more than eighty other committees had been established throughout Massachusetts.

An explosive piece of intelligence then fell into Samuel Adams's hands. This was, in brief, that Governor Hutchinson—whom Adams had always held responsible for the Boston Massacre and other threats to the citizens' lives and fortunes—had warned the king's ministers that "there *must* be an abridgment of what are called English liberties" in Massachusetts. He had also written that the Crown's functionaries should be "in some measure independent of the people" and that a British military presence in Boston was probably an advisable thing. These tremendously unpopular sentiments, which seemed to Adams definite proof of Hutchinson's criminal attitude toward the people and their government, were contained in a series of letters that had been obtained by Benjamin Franklin under confidential and slightly mysterious circumstances.

Franklin, still in London as an agent of the Massachusetts legislature, sent the sizzling packet of letters on to Thomas Cushing, Speaker of the House, with instructions that the contents should be shown only to a few; the letters should definitely not be published. But it seems unlikely that he could have believed that they would have stayed out of the public eye (and the press) for long. Almost immediately, they were shown by Cushing to Samuel Adams and others; Adams began a campaign of subtly referring to the letters, a campaign that ultimately revealed them all. They proved ruinous to Hutchinson. Such a cry was raised for his removal by the Massachusetts General Court that not even George III could resist the appeal.

It was an out-and-out triumph for Adams, though the end of Franklin at the royal court. The Boston Committee of Correspondence, given such marvelous fuel, succeeded in setting afire committees elsewhere. The Hutchinson-Oliver letters, as they were called, created a sensation wherever they were published. They not only revitalized the somnolent Sons of Liberty in ports and towns up and down the coast but also gave new power and more votes to radical politicians. Once again, the patriots' faction seized control of the Massachusetts legislature. They were prepared to defend the people's rights (including the rights of those who held slaves and exploited seamen) whenever Great Britain might oblige by supplying a new challenge.

# New England Seamen's First Attack
## on the Royal Navy

In retrospect, Samuel Adams wrote that his Boston Committee of Correspondence "gave visible shape to the American Revolution, and endowed it with life and strength." As if to echo that point, Virginia's House of Burgesses set up a "standing committee" in March 1773 that had the effect of granting life, strength, and even legislative sanction to that province's previously independent and illegal Committee of Correspondence. The legislatures of many colonies soon followed suit, choosing to establish a system that would endorse and facilitate communication on matters of mutual interest concerning relations with Great Britain. That step-by-step process would lead in due course to the First Continental Congress of 1774.

While the echoing action of the House of Burgesses probably did not result from sympathy on the Virginians' part for British-harassed ship captains in Massachusetts Bay, an incident in Rhode Island's Narragansett Bay did serve to highlight maritime outrages and to boost the intercolonial cause. As in Massachusetts, the ruling elite of Rhode Island treasured certain precepts of autonomy, as spelled out in the ancient charter that Roger Williams had kept out of Governor Andros's grasp. Nicholas Brown stood at the head of that elite, running a well-established mercantile business that conducted lucrative and only occasionally illegal trade with the West Indies (including slave trading). His brother John Brown (1736–1803) had left the family firm to set up his own considerably more adventurous enterprise. He had, in addition, become a political activist in the 1760s, raising a notable protest against the Sugar and the Stamp Acts and leading the pro non-importation forces in the Rhode Island Assembly. In that capacity, he not only won influential friends throughout New England but also made contacts with the maritime subculture that would serve him well in the years to come.

John Brown, in his personality and operations, resembled many of the new elite in the American colonies—gentlemen who were equally determined to fight against the restraints of the British and to utilize the restless energies of the mixed hoi polloi on their port's waterfront. In Bostonian terms, he might be described as a combination of William Molineux and John Hancock. Like Molineux, John Brown was a chief of smugglers, a brigand who had won the loyalty of his skippers and their families. But because he was an integral part of the old-line gentry of his province, he commanded far more authority than Molineux did in the upper reaches of society. More like Hancock, he made his personal cause, meaning the making and the retaining of his wealth, seem to be the cause of his constituency. And to some extent, despite John Brown's slave-trading elitism, he *was* their best hope for leading the drive for liberty at this time in their history.

He demonstrated that leadership in the famous HMS *Gaspée* incident. This armed schooner had been a blight in Narragansett Bay ever since she arrived there in March 1772. The official assignment of her captain, Lieutenant William Dudingston, was to seize any ship trying to enter a Rhode Island port while carrying contraband cargo. Providence stood out as the busiest and most suspect of those ports, but Newport and Warwick were also known for harboring fleets of smugglers. In the eyes of the province's population whose living came from the sea, Lieutenant Dudingston seemed more of a pirate than a respectable naval officer. In the words of a local commentator: Dudingston "personally ill treat[ed] every Master and Merchant of the Vessels he boarded, stealing Sheep, Hogs, Poultry, &c. From the Farmers around the Bay, and cutting down their Fruit and other Trees for Fire Wood."

It seemed that no respectable Rhode Island shoreman—indeed, no rightful Englishman—should "patiently bear" such arrogant behavior. Also fresh in local minds was the successful burning of Hancock's captured *Liberty* in 1769. A groundswell of public sentiment arose to take action against the *Gaspée* and her captain whenever the winds allowed. Then, as afternoon turned to evening on June 9, the *Gaspée* ran hard aground off Warwick's Namquit Point. Given the timing of the tide's rise and fall, she would probably be unable to get free until after midnight; word of this fortuitous misfortune quickly spread to Providence and throughout Rhode Island's maritime communities.

John Brown sprang into immediate action, ordering eight long-boats to be brought into Fenner's Wharf. A drummer was dispatched to parade along Providence's Main Street, beating out a rhythm and inviting all those to come along "who felt a disposition to go and destroy the troublesome vessel." They were to assemble that evening at the public house across from Fenner's. In the well-established pattern of seamen responding to their officers' orders, many heeded the call as darkness fell. Among them were Rhode Island's most capable skippers, Abraham Whipple and John B. Hopkins. Guided by their orders, an assemblage of some fifty volunteers rowed the gathered longboats out to the *Gaspée*, gliding through the water so silently that the ship's lookout was not aware of them until they were a mere sixty yards distant. When Whipple hailed them and Lieutenant Dudingston came over to the starboard side to investigate, Whipple is said to have replied, "I am the sheriff of the county of Kent, God damn you!" He went on, "I have got a warrant to apprehend you, God damn you; so surrender, God damn you!"

At the same time, one of his crewmen raised his gun and took a shot at the hated lieutenant. Dudingston fell back wounded, unable to marshal resistance to boarders. Those who swarmed up over the *Gaspée*'s rail saw to the dressing of Dudingston's wound and swept on below to search his cabin for possibly incriminating papers. Rounding up the British crew, they sent them ashore in their ship's small boats. They then set fire to the *Gaspée* and, as they rowed home, had the satisfaction of watching her burn to the waterline.

As soon as he heard of the blow struck by Rhode Island patriots, Massachusetts's Governor Hutchinson understood that this was of the same stripe as the assaults that royal officers had endured in his province. Had it not been carried out in Boston by captains and their everlastingly obedient sailors? He believed that this latest spectacular act of rebellion had to be met directly if Great Britain were to retain any degree of respect in New England. As he fumed, torch-bearing demonstrators in Boston and other coastal towns paraded through nighttime streets in support of the Rhode Island activists. Hutchinson wrote to London that "If the *Gaspée* rioters are not punished, the Friends to Government will despond and give up all hopes of being able to withstand the Faction."

But demands to turn the suspected perpetrators of the *Gaspée* attack over for Admiralty trial in London were met with such shouts of unified horror from the American colonies that the royally appointed commission agreed to conduct its investigations and hearings on the spot, in Rhode Island. One of the most incriminating factors that the prosecution advanced was the testimony of a black indentured servant: he claimed to have direct personal knowledge that John Brown had been among the chief leaders of the affair. To counter that, the defense soon produced four discrediting affidavits that indicated that the servant had never been present at the scene. Other obstructions from all sides impeded the work of the commissioners. Frustrated and intimidated, the judges adjourned with the conclusion that not enough evidence was in hand to arrest anyone.

Admiral William Montagu, who commanded the British fleet off Boston, also took the measure of the *Gaspée* affair as news spread to the newly tense Massachusetts capital. He concluded that the people of that town, excited by that report even beyond the passions raised by the Boston Massacre, were now "almost ripe for independence."

## "With Our Lives and Fortunes"

To the men, gentlemen and otherwise, who met regularly at the Green Dragon Tavern in Boston's North End in the summer and the fall of 1773, rebellion and revolution were undertakings rarely discussed in public but on occasion considered in private. Beneath a still-surviving sketch of the tavern, the artist, a certain John Johnson, carefully wrote these revealing words: "Where we Met to Plan the Consignment of [a] few Shiploads of Tea Dec 16 1773." As Johnson well remembered, it was this unloading of tea that, more than any other action, incited the British to take the retributive action against the port of Boston that brought on the Revolution.

Significantly, Johnson's sketch is also marked by a Mason's emblem in the upper left-hand corner, for there was something of an overlap between the meetings of the notoriously radical North End Caucus and the sessions of St. Andrew's Lodge; the lodge members certainly knew that the Green Dragon Tavern was often used as the patriots' covert place of assemblage. Many of the Masons were deeply involved in the port's patriotic activities but had no desire to let their participation be known. The leaders of the North End Caucus, organized by Dr. Thomas Young and his colleague Dr. Joseph Warren, had to operate with both caution and force. An important power shift was about to take place in Boston, and these two men were at the heart of it. Once, long ago, all power had been in the hands of the merchant scions of the "Codfish Aristocracy"; then, briefly, there had been the rule of the crowd ("Ochlocracy," Governor Bernard had called it); now other players were coming to the fore.

But one might ask: what really happened to the once-mighty Ebenezer Mackintosh and Captain Henry Swift? Apparently, those lower-class leaders of rebellion had served useful purposes only during certain crises, after which they were regarded by higher-ranking Bostonians as untrustworthy blabbermouths, incapable of keeping to themselves the names of gentleman-patriots. By contrast, the new breed of middle-class Bostonians who were joining the anti-British cause in ever greater numbers, including ambitious artisans such as Paul Revere and printers and distillers such as Benjamin Edes and John Avery, seemed more reliable in the eyes of the elite Whigs. Though not truly gentlemen (as witnessed by their lack of wigs and their workingmen's clothes), they seemed sufficiently dependable for admission to clandestine political discussions. Furthermore, they maintained strong family and social connections with the people of the waterfront; they could serve to bind the patriot factions together.

To those secretive men, wont to meet at the Green Dragon, it became clear as autumn advanced that the issue of what to do about certain ships carrying tea to Boston from England had reached a point beyond mere discussion. Those trouble-freighted ships would be arriving in a few weeks. On October 23, caucus members attending a key meeting at the tavern agreed that opposition must take a definite, physical form—that great numbers of people, including the violent maritime labor force, must be rallied. The caucus voted to "oppose the vending of any tea, sent by the East India Company to any part of our Continent, *with our lives and fortunes*" (author's italics).

The act of Parliament that sent those tea ships on their way, the Tea Act of May 10, 1773, had been crafted with exquisite care. Lord North had designed it to appeal to all Americans. Because the tea would be virtually duty-free, the bill would seem fair and nonintrusive even to those sensitive to taxation without representation. And, in fact, the price of tea sold to American colonists would be further lowered by the innovative provision that the East India Company would ship its casks directly to the warehouses of certain consignees—a scheme that would effect considerable savings. Those fortunate consignees (two of whom happened to be the sons of Governor Hutchinson) would receive a 6 percent profit on their sold merchandise. It seemed a good deal for all. The king still viewed the leveling of taxes as an essential part of his rights over the colonies. Yet he and North trusted that the Townshend Acts' tea duty would be ignored in general jubilation at the lowered retail price. They were wrong. In Boston, where no duty or tax ever went undisputed, the argument was not persuasive.

Samuel Adams, backed by the radical caucus, led the opposing faction. In speeches and articles, he accused the king's ministers of trying to bribe colonists with cheap tea so they would forget about the tax that subverted their liberties. He and other opponents made much of the fact that Lord North, in his efforts to aid the financially imperiled East India Company—which was the second-largest financial institution in Great Britain after the Bank of England—sought to establish a virtual monopoly. And that would set a dangerous precedent for all future commercial relations between the mother country and the colonies. For in the wake of that monopoly, what essential industry might next come under the total control of the Crown?

That bell-ringing theme, heard up and down the land, had some effect in rousing American resistance—more evident in Philadelphia and New York, in fact, than in Boston. In all three towns—but not in Charleston, South Carolina, which was the fourth port named as a recipient of the East India Company's shipped tea casks—the loudest opposition came from the smuggling fraternity. What angered those mariners about Lord North's Tea Act was, first, that it allowed the consignees (the fortunate merchants who had been selected to receive the tea) to make a handsome profit and, second, that those privileged merchants could purvey tea to customers at a price about equal to what the smugglers themselves charged for their Dutch-derived product.

The smugglers had been dealing, for the most part, in tea shipped from China (specifically, Canton) to Batavia in the East Indies and from there to St. Eustatius in the Dutch West Indies. Lawless merchants such as William Molineux and Meletia Bourne would regularly send their skippers down to that foreign, thus forbidden, island to pick up chests of the Bohea tea that Bostonians had come to love. Even John Hancock's respectable Uncle Thomas, in his day, had been known to have dispatched his swift ship *Lydia* to "Statia," assuming that no one would point a moralistic finger at him.

By the 1770s, American colonists were consuming about 1.2 million pounds of tea a year, with bootleggers supplying nearly three-quarters of that total. It was a very profitable business, and the smugglers, even those like Molineux who detested the British and their supposed command of the sea, did not join those who protested against the imperial tax of threepence on each pound of legal British tea. Yet they joined in heartily with the chorus of cheers that was raised when Parliament revoked most of the Townshend Acts.

Some patriots, particularly in Boston, believed that it had been thanks to their merchants' protests over reduced business and to their town's severe ban on buying or drinking tea—still regarded by old-line Puritans as a British affectation—that Parliament was then forced to back down. But Lord North's mollifying Tea Act (also called the Regulating Act) actually resulted from quite a different cause—namely, the alarming financial situation in Great Britain. The misguided managers of the British East India Company, whose prime business was the tea trade, had attempted to make affairs look better than they were in the eyes of stockholders by issuing liberal dividends at the end of 1771 and the beginning of 1772. They had succeeded thereby in plunging the company into a condition of deep indebtedness. Disaster loomed even more imminently when the government declined to renew a life-saving loan to the company of £1.3 million. The king told his First Lord of the Treasury, Lord

North (who rarely deviated from the king's will and, oddly, looked very much like him), that something must be done to salvage the East India Company and the Empire along with it. Might the solution to the crisis lie in the 17 million pounds of tea that were awaiting sale in London warehouses? Possibly. Hence, Lord North's seemingly generous Tea Act.

So it happened that those troublesome vessels packed with some two thousand chests containing nearly six hundred thousand pounds of tea cast off from their London docks very soon after the passage of the Act. They rode the tide downriver to the mouth of the Thames and raised their sails to the generally contrary Atlantic winds. Headed for Boston were the ships *Eleanor* and *Dartmouth* (the latter owned by a Quaker merchant from Nantucket named Francis Rotch) and the brigs *Beaver* and *William*. Others turned their bows toward New York, Philadelphia, and Charleston. Heavily laden and sailing against the prevailing westerlies, the vessels were not expected to arrive in America before autumn.* By then, news of their approach would have spread across the colonies, provoking a variety of reactions.

From Philadelphia and New York came blusterings of outrage at the Tea Act, a storm of patriotic verbiage in which smugglers' shouts against the "unjust monopoly" could be heard prominently. At the fore of the New York demonstrations were the vibrant waterfront patriots John Lamb and Isaac Sears, undiminished in popular eyes since their leadership in the Stamp Act crisis. They were joined by a vociferous retired seaman named Alexander McDougall. Together, the three called for a mass meeting of citizens in October 1773, during which the tea consignees in New York were denounced as trying to get away with "public robbery," words sufficiently terrifying to force those gentlemen to resign their commissions. In mid-December, at about the time of the conclusive Green Dragon Tavern meeting in Boston, they demanded of the governor, William

---

*The news of the ships' departure from London actually reached Boston by the end of August. But only three vessels made it to that destination: the *William* never arrived. She was wrecked off Cape Cod and deemed a total loss.

Tryon, that he send back New York's tea ships untouched. Fearing mob violence, the governor did nothing, hoping the problem would be taken out of his hands.

The Philadelphia consignees also came under considerable pressure from the city's radical leadership to resign. They dodged this way and that, stating that having not yet received their commissions, they could not truly know what they were appointed to do and therefore could not decide one way or the other. Ultimately, however, when pilots in the Delaware River were strenuously warned against admitting the tea ships, with threats of tarring and feathering accompanying the warnings, the consignees agreed to abdicate. Thus, when the tea ship *Polly* finally appeared below Philadelphia, she was sent home on the governor's orders, no tea having been allowed to be unloaded.

In Boston, during the months before the three surviving tea ships sailed separately into the harbor, it appeared that there would also be nothing but endless debates between conservative merchants and roused patriots. The recent years of prosperity had done much to strengthen the conservatives' hand; flocking around Governor Hutchinson, these cautious merchants had successfully advocated a measured reaction to the Tea Act. The governor himself, newly emboldened against the threat of mob violence by the ships of war in the harbor and by the officers and men in the fortresses, believed that he was equipped to ride out this storm. He even took the rash step of dismissing the ambivalent John Hancock from his council, replacing him with the seemingly impeccable Dr. Joseph Warren (who was, Hutchinson had yet to learn, even more deeply committed to Samuel Adams than was Hancock). The town's minority of radicals, moderately encouraged by reports from Philadelphia and New York, could do little more than attempt to stir up anger at the Tea Act and to intimidate the consignees.

## Summoned to the Liberty Tree

A little more than a week after the patriots pledged their lives and fortunes to the anti-tea cause and six weeks before the decisive

December meeting at the Green Dragon Tavern, on November 2, a delegation of townsmen went on the attack. Knocking violently on the front door of the home of the most powerful consignee, Richard Clark, they awoke his family from their sleep. They demanded that Clark come downstairs to receive a message: he and the other tea agents (including the two widely detested sons of Governor Hutchinson) were "expected to appear" at the town's Liberty Tree at noon on November 3 in order "to make a public resignation" of their consignee commissions. Notices would be posted all over town indicating that the gentlemen would not only resign but would "swear" to return the tea to England whenever it arrived. Though thoroughly frightened, Richard Clark and the Hutchinson brothers declined to accept the invitation.

On Wednesday, November 3, the town's bells having summoned citizens by the hundreds and thousands to the Liberty Tree, the radical leadership put before them the scandalous fact that the consignees were deliberately refusing to come to this public place and to honor the people's will. Nominated to head a new committee to pay a visit to Clark, William Molineux led the selected committee, followed by a roaring crowd, to that storekeeper's shop at the foot of King Street, where they noisily demanded compliance. When their requests were rebuffed by the consignees as the rantings of an illegal mob, the crowd ripped the shop's door off its hinges and rushed inside, the occupants fleeing to the second floor. From there, Clark stood firm against the crowd's howled demands, telling Molineux directly that "I shall have nothing to do with you."

His adamant stance at length cooled the ardor of the mob, which gradually dispersed. But Loyalists were generally terrified, seeing the episode as an indication that the Boston underworld was again on the point of rebellion—particularly with the approach of Pope's Day. Hearing of this new confrontation in King Street, the Hutchinson brothers, who were generally called the "two children," fled Boston for their country home in nearby Milton.

With increasing expectation of new crowd action, Boston's leading Whigs watched the furor mount. It now seemed possible that whether as a result of Samuel Adams's and the radicals' patient maneuvers or because of the explosiveness of the people, the balance was again shifting away from moderation. John Hancock, recognizing that shift, agreed to head a committee to deal with the consignees appointed by a massive meeting of the people in Faneuil Hall on November 5. The committee was prepared to receive, in a more formal and less threatening way than before, the resignations of the tea agents. Sheriff Greenleaf was brushed aside when he strode in with word from the governor that the committee was illegal. Yet legal or otherwise, the committee failed in its purpose—the consignees would not budge. Indeed, all such temperate steps seemed to be in vain; even another attack on Clark's house on November 17, after definite news of the tea ships' approach had been received, failed to move them toward resignation. Something more must be done.

The governor ordered Hancock, his recently appointed colonel of the cadet corps, to ready the corps for any possible action, but Hancock declined to do so—a telling response from someone who usually knew which way the wind was blowing. The town's radical leader had apparently let it be known in the right circles that in keeping with their vow made on October 23 to prevent the landing of the tea, some action beyond wordy resolutions and personal attacks would be taken. Boston would once again resort to violent measures, carried out by those who were used to obeying orders, the seamen of the waterfront.

Early rumors of the tea ships' arrival proved accurate. The *Dartmouth*, carrying 114 chests of tea, anchored in Boston's outer harbor on Saturday, November 28; the *Beaver* and the *Eleanor* were not far behind. The activists who counseled mass action knew that from that November date, they had only a certain number of days in which to make their move, because pertaining laws stipulated that every ship entering the port had to be registered and pay charges within twenty days of arrival or have its cargo seized and sold. Therefore, within less than three weeks the fate of the tea must be determined—the cargo must be officially recorded as having been landed—and thus salable—or the ship would have to take it back to London. Although the town meeting met twice on that Sunday (an emergency measure that must have made old Puritan bones rattle in their graves), its flustered merchant members could not agree on the landing of the tea. The ever-vigilant Committee of Correspondence, which had been in close touch with other towns in the region, as well as with the cities to the south, appointed itself to take charge of Boston and its destiny.

Calling a mass meeting in Faneuil Hall on Monday, November 30, and summoning people there with the ringing of church bells, Samuel Adams proposed that the British tea be forcibly returned to whence it had come. With a roar, the people approved. Swelling to a total of five thousand, they then moved on to Old South Meeting House. There the representative of the *Dartmouth*'s owner, Francis Rotch, was informed by Adams and William Molineux that the people "had now the Power in their Hands"; Rotch must bend to their will. He was also instructed that his ship must be moved to a wharf in the center of town, Griffin's Wharf, and that in that secure position she would be boarded and watched over night and day by appointed patriots. Soon the other two tea ships that had succeeded in crossing the Atlantic joined her there, all under tight guard. The people had no intention of allowing the tea to be removed from their holds by the governor's agents.

Francis Rotch, the twenty-three-year-old son of the wealthy whale-oil merchant Joseph Rotch, had been raised by his family's Quaker precepts to be peaceable and to avoid political dustups of this nature. Francis's branch of the family, though they had made their fortune by monopolizing the whaling fishery off Nantucket, had recently (1765) moved from that sequestered island to the mainland, joining an industrial community within the Massachusetts town of Dartmouth and setting up a spermaceti (whale oil) factory. That community, founded by a Quaker named Joseph Russell and named New Bedford, represented one of the few booming capital centers of New England. It was not interested in altering the economic status quo. In keeping with that stance, Nantucket and New Bedford had shown little interest in the new philosophy of patriotism that was sweeping the province; indeed, Nantucket stayed neutral during the entire Revolution, adhering both to Quaker principles and to sensible business practices. Young Francis Rotch, despite his salty origins, was therefore viewed as an outsider in

Boston and had, himself, no concern for the politics of the day. His main interest was to unload his cargo, see to the proper payments, and preserve his father's ship.

When the patriot leadership, backed by large crowds, demanded of Rotch that he and the ships' captains return all three cargoes to England, he protested vehemently, perhaps hoping that the large neutral portion of the town's citizenry would respect his stance. And when the patriots' tough-minded spokesman William Molineux made it clear to young Rotch that the unloading of the tea would not be tolerated, he appealed to the Governor's Council for clarification. Because the appointed consignees had fled from the mob to the safety of Castle William, Rotch had to deal with a series of official committees, all of which agreed that in the name of the king, the tea must be registered, unloaded, and sold. Otherwise, he would not be permitted to leave the port.

Caught between those unyielding authorities, Rotch continued to hope that some kind of compromise could be worked out, advanced by sensible and neutral merchants in opposition to those who were then controlling the waterfront and, in effect, running the town. But John Hancock and the majority of merchants understood perfectly that a climax involving the people was now at hand. One by one, they came out more and more openly to oppose the king's will. With customary grandiosity, Hancock proclaimed, "My fellow Countrymen, we have put our Hands to the Plough and Wo Be to him that shrinks or looks back."

In other ports, resisters to the Tea Act watched and waited to see what would happen in Boston, the American colonies' center of radicalism. Would the town's patriots fail the cause? On December 13, a letter from Philadelphia expressing impatience appeared in the *Boston Gazette*. "All that we fear," wrote the Pennsylvania patriots, "is that you will shrink at Boston. May God give you virtue enough to save the liberties of your country!" One can imagine the reaction by Adams and Molineux to this challenge.

On the next day, they formed a committee to march Francis Rotch to the customs house for his ship's clearance papers. They wanted him and the *Dartmouth* to sail away. The same action had to be repeated the next day, December 15, because the customs officers stalled, saying they had no orders. Therefore, on December 16, the last day before the tea had to be landed, when it was apparent that Rotch would obtain no such pass, he was told by the committee to ride out to Governor Hutchinson's residence in Milton to obtain official permission for his ship to leave port. It was an utterly miserable day, cold and rainy, yet the young skipper complied.

When he returned, wet and bedraggled, it was with word of Hutchinson's refusal—an act of stubborn defiance on the governor's part that many see not as the first shot of the Revolution but as the last chance to prevent it. Hutchinson thought that he was on firm ground—that there were still sufficient property-owning men of sense who, combined with the king's officers, could and would prevent any destruction of officially sanctioned goods. But he could not have been more incorrect. His refusal to let the *Dartmouth* leave port before unloading made the ruling powers of New York and Philadelphia seem extraordinarily wise in their final decisions to send the tea vessels back home. Hutchinson's proud unwillingness to lend his endorsement to the mob leaders' defiance of the Tea Act was precisely the kind of royal arrogance that had always caused explosions in Boston.

While Rotch was riding to and back from Milton, the radical leadership had called for and obtained a vote from "the body of the people" that the tea must not be landed. A kind of signal seemed to have been given. A witness reported that he heard "an hideous Yelling in the Street as of an Hundred People, some imitating the Powaws of Indians and others the Whistle of Boatswain." Samuel Adams released the crowd on its errand with the charged words "This meeting can do nothing more to save the country." Obviously, he intended that some form of planned action must then go into effect. The crowd responded, shouting out their new rallying cries: "Boston Harbor—a tea-pot tonight!" And "Hurrah for Griffin's Wharf!"

It was on that night, the night of December 16, that the ultimate meeting was held at the Green Dragon Tavern. The word was passed down the line. A large number of "nobodies," including tradesmen, apprentices, and seamen, plus a few gentlemen, responded, donning their disguises and going to their assigned locations. Patriots would indeed risk their lives and fortunes to reject the imperial rule of Great Britain.

## Mackintosh: "It Was My Chickens That Did the Job"

The story of Boston's Tea Party has been told often and well: how that great variety of men, totaling perhaps two hundred, many with blackened faces or done up as "Mohawks" in paint and blankets, took guard positions or swarmed over the *Dartmouth* and, having obtained the keys from her intimidated captain, unloaded the cargo of tea; how on that black and rainy night, so many torches lit the scene that it was easy for the watching crowd to see the uplifting of the chests from the three vessels, the cracking open of many of them, and the dumping of all 342 of them over the side into Boston Harbor; and how, after three hours of that heavy labor, the moon came out to reveal the wondrous sight of tea chests drifting out to sea. There is also the story of the two politically incorrect participants who attempted to grab some of the tea for themselves: the first had his boat capsized by other members of the workforce and had to swim for it; the other, who had tried to pack away some in his pocket, was stripped naked and given "a coat of mud, with a severe bruising in the bargain."

It was all carried out with remarkable precision. The decision reached at the Green Dragon had been followed up by the most exact kind of operations planning, recruitment of volunteers, and systematic execution. This mode of operation—the levelheaded orderliness and the lack of destructive violence—was emphasized by Boston's new elite from the very beginning of the telling of the Tea Party's story as it evolved from fact to history to myth. John Adams referred to the "sublimity" of the event, as if it had been managed by angels. When Paul Revere rode to Philadelphia on December 17 with the "Glorious Intelligence" of what had happened in Boston Harbor, the letter in his saddlebags spoke of those who had dumped the tea in most respectful terms: "Their conduct last night surprised the admiral [Montagu] and English gentlemen, who observed that these were not a mob of disorderly rabble, (as they have been reported) but men of sense, coolness, and intrepidity."

But this stressing of the solid bourgeois character of those involved in the Tea Party gave the story of that action a certain tilt. As with the first histories of the Boston Massacre of 1770, it appeared that the people involved in the dockside action of December 16, 1773, were all of the most upright kind, guided by a superb kind of patriotism. Just as the true character of the five young and old, black and white, home-born and foreign-born maritime characters killed in front of the customs house was downplayed by contemporary and later narrators, so the lofty rank and the political intrepidity of the Tea Party perpetrators were exaggerated by those who chose to write about it. As the most recent chronicler of this event, Alfred Young, discovered and disclosed in his 1999 book *The Shoemaker and the Tea Party*, this great expression of across-the-board communal accord (which is what the event really was, even though planned by certain leaders) had been muffled in Boston for more than a half-century. When coined in 1834, the unfortunately memorable name "Tea Party" (connoting an action by the elite alone) helped to disguise who had been involved.

To demonstrate who had really done what, Professor Young brought to the fore one of the actual participants in the event: the very short, very strangely named George Robert Twelves Hewes, (mentioned previously as having been cast into debtors' prison with Ebenezer Mackintosh in 1770). Because Hewes had first been honored and interviewed as something of a celebrity in the 1830s, Professor Young was able to delve into published recollections of the Tea Party from that time. Hewes recounted how he had dressed as an Indian on that cold, damp night and covered his face and hands with coal dust. He went on,

> I fell in with many who were dressed, equipped, and painted as I was. . . . When we arrived at the wharf, there were three of our number who assumed authority to direct our operations,

to which we readily submitted. They divided us into three parties, for the purpose of boarding the three ships which contained tea at the same time. . . .

The commander of the division to which I belonged, as soon as we were on board the ship, appointed me boatswain, and ordered me to go to the captain and demand of him the keys to the hatches and a dozen candles. I made the demand accordingly, and the captain promptly replied, and delivered the articles; but requested me at the same time to do no damage to the ship or rigging. We then were ordered by our commander to open the hatches, and take out all the chests of tea and throw them overboard, and we immediately proceeded to execute his orders; first cutting and splitting the chests with our tomahawks, so as thoroughly to expose them to the effects of the water. In about three hours from the time we went on board, we had thus broken and thrown overboard every tea chest to be found in the ship, while those in the other ships were disposing of the tea in the same way, at the same time. We were surrounded by British armed ships, but no attempt was made to resist us. We then quietly retired to our several places of residence, without having any conversation with each other, or taking any measures to discover who were our associates.

Hewes asked himself (or his editor did) why he, as a lowly shoemaker, had been selected to be one of the leaders. And he seemed satisfied with the easy answer that he was known on the Boston waterfront for having a talent to whistle—a talent that might prove useful in such a clandestine operation. But another, more significant answer may be that he, having sailed and fished along with many of the others, had the seaman's understanding that a skipper's command is to be obeyed immediately. He knew how to carry out the boatswain's function of receiving an order and swiftly getting the appointed men to do the job right.

As Hewes pointed out, the participating men from the North and the South Ends were divided into three groups, each with a commander and a boatswain. Of the perhaps 200 who boarded the ships or simply served as guards, the scholar Dirk Hoerder has identified some 123 men from available lists. Interestingly, a sizable fraction of these (a third or more) were very small property holders and another third possessed no property at all. That is why it seems totally justified that Ebenezer Mackintosh referred to the men who actually did the work of heaving the tea chests overboard as "my Chickens." He did not mean that he himself was involved as a commander (for no record of his presence exists) but that the waterfront characters he had been working with for nearly a decade were the ones who deserved the credit for this operation. They were the ones who had at various times been impressed, gypped, and pushed aside by British soldiers (as Hewes had been) and treated little better than slaves. They were the ones who saw in this one spectacular maritime action a chance for themselves to be part of the process of change, along with the rest of the right-thinking community.

Another participant who has been identified by historians is the seaman John May, whose family proudly preserved in the following words their memory of John's adventure that night:

> On the afternoon of December 16, 1773, he went in haste to his home on North Square, and said to his young wife, "Nabby, let me have a beef steak as quickly as possible." While he was eating it, a rap was heard on the window, and he rose at once from the unfinished meal and departed. He returned late, tired and uncommunicative. In the morning there was found in his shoes, and scattered upon the floor, a quantity of tea.

Given such revealing pictures of who was involved and how if not why, it hardly seems proper that the Boston Tea Party is so often presented as having been planned and carried out by "gentlemen in disguise." Yet neither does all praise or blame for the event belong exclusively to that so-called elusive social group, the seamen who have played such a large part in this book. The hot-and-cold, on-and-off-again Whigs and the ambitious artisans who teamed with them, all of whom passed the daring resolution at the Green

Dragon Tavern, also deserve credit. Indeed, the Tea Party is best understood as one of Boston's many historic social actions, with seamen and other citizens of all levels of society and property ownership (or lack of it) uniting in a seaport exercise.

Professor Young also finds great significance in the fact that three weeks after the Tea Party, George Robert Twelves Hewes took it upon himself to upbraid a gentleman who was beating a small child with a stick for some act of "impertinence." When the gentleman, a notorious customs informer and Loyalist named John Malcolm, snarled at Hewes that the beating was none of his affair and that Hewes himself was merely a "vagabond" with no right to address him, Hewes presumed to argue back that although a poor man, he was in "good credit in the town." For this, Hewes received a nasty slash on the head from Malcolm's cane. By that time, a large crowd had gathered, several of whom came to the little man's aid, carrying him off to Dr. Joseph Warren's office for treatment.*

The rest of the crowd pursued Malcolm to his home, from which refuge he answered their taunts with angry threats. Finally dispersing, the people vowed to carry the matter to its end later in the day. In the meantime, Hewes, his wound patched, obtained a warrant for Malcolm's arrest. But the crowd had in mind a treatment more severe than could be obtained by legal action: they rousted Malcolm forth from his home and dragged him on a sled into King Street "amid the huzzahs of thousands." A group of gentlemen tried to break up the affair, exercising their authority in a commanding way that had always worked in days gone by. But not now. The crowd would not be put off: they stripped Malcolm to the buff, tarred and feathered him, and, threatening to hang him, rigged a rope around a tree limb. Only then did they leave him alone. To George Robert Twelves Hewes, this might have seemed wonderful vindication. As pointed out by Professor Young, Hewes's newly

---

*This was a function on behalf of stricken crowd members often performed by the sympathetic Dr. Warren. He had also been called upon to assist the dying Christopher Seider and to examine the corpse of Crispus Attucks. He carried out the latter mission in company with the ambivalent Whig Dr. Benjamin Church (see chapter 9).

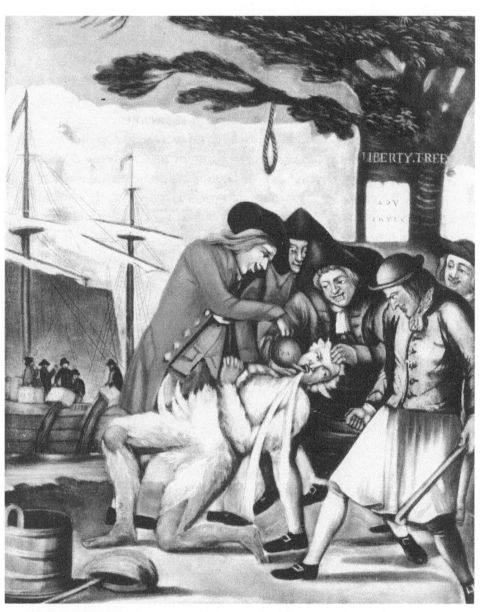

*After the Boston mobs and the Whig leadership had turned the Stamp Act upside down, as shown in this 1774 British cartoon, their next organized strike was against the British East India Tea Company, an action visible in the background. Less-organized mob actions, such as the treatment given to John Malcolm (center), were regarded by Whigs as dangerous to "the cause of Freedom."*

Courtesy of the John Carter Brown Library at Brown University found place in society, his right to confront any other citizen on equal terms, had been supported. That, even more than the looming punishment of the port of Boston by British officials incensed at the loss of eighteen thousand pounds' worth of royally sanctioned tea, was the profound effect of the Tea Party and of the Revolution that would soon follow. Even though men and women of the waterfront and the town would have to keep on struggling and dying for their civil rights, deference to someone of the presumed upper class would no longer be expected in Boston or, eventually, anywhere else in America. Yet, ironically, Hewes was aghast at the violent treatment given to Malcolm, having put all his courage and hope into the power of the arrest warrant.

# 9

# The Fighting Spirit of a Besieged Boston

Ebenezer Mackintosh crossed the Neck and left Boston behind him in the summer of 1774, a widower trudging inland with his two very young children. As they walked northwestward to New Hampshire, they marched in company with many other emigrés, for Boston, by now a garrison town, was no longer a healthy place for poor, unemployed families—particularly when the father was a known rioter and may have had a price on his head.

General Thomas Gage, who had been cordially received on his arrival in Boston in May 1774 by Loyalists and many of the well-to-do, swiftly carried out his orders to replace Thomas Hutchinson as governor. It was believed that his orders also instructed him to apprehend "several Persons, who had been declared by His Majesty's Law Servants to have been guilty of High Treason." A patriot newspaper circulated warnings that Gage therefore intended to pick up and take away for trial in Great Britain four notorious patriots—Samuel Adams, John Hancock, John Rowe, and Ebenezer Mackintosh. The British believed that "the latter has been very active among the lower order of people, and the other [three] among the higher." It was definitely time for Mackintosh to head for the hills.

Besides the fear of apprehension, there was a total disruption of the waterfront, where all shops on Long Wharf were closed and charities had set themselves up to pass out food to starving families. Not a ship moved in the harbor; not even the ferry was allowed to cross over from Charlestown. The desperate conditions in Boston resulted directly, as Americans understood, from four special acts passed by Parliament in May and June. Crafted by the government of Lord North with the specific encouragement of King George, these vengeful acts were designed to punish Boston for "baptizing" the East India Company's tea chests. Coming one after another in rapid succession, they were named, respectively, the Boston Port Act, the Quartering Act, the Administration of Justice Act, and the Massachusetts Government Act, but they were known collectively, far and wide, as the Coercive Acts. Samuel Adams went further, referring to this collection of laws that destroyed the shipping business of the port of Boston and exposed the province's population to the brutalities of a military occupation as the "Murderers' Act."

Since the only business that had ever mattered in Boston was the commerce generated by shipping, including shipbuilding and the importing of molasses for distilling rum, the population of the town was forced to depend on already wealthy merchants for a penny here, an odd job there. Although the local craftsmen had begun to be a force in the town's affairs, they, no less than the ship-yard workers and the seamen, could survive only as secondary beneficiaries of the merchants' wealth. Deep resentment continued to churn in the breasts of craftsmen and mariners toward the wealthy few, who, by selling hoarded English goods or by accepting royal appointments, lived in a luxurious world quite removed from those being punished.

For the estimated three thousand men out of work (from a total population of about fifteen thousand) and for all others, there was the additional punishment of being deprived of their own government. The Coercive Acts did away with Massachusetts's political touchstone, its "ancient charter," canceling that document's semiautonomous provisions even more thoroughly than what had been attempted by Governor Andros. By the new laws, Governor Gage was granted unprecedented mastery over all of Massachusetts, including authority to dismiss the legislature and any town meeting. Although patriots had succeeded in impeaching and removing the chief justice from office before Gage's arrival, their maneuverings were soon smothered by Gage's omnipotence across the province. When some of the towns sought to run their affairs by patriot-controlled meetings and extra-legal forums, he moved without hesitation to prohibit all such sessions. In Boston, he severely restricted the town meeting's agenda, permitting only one session a year. Civic trials were no longer to be conducted by judges responsible to the people but by special mandamus councilors appointed by the governor.

To back up his extraordinary jurisdiction over the province, Gage requested additional troops beyond the four regiments originally assigned. In response to that call, an eventual total of eleven of the Empire's finest regiments came into the punished province, not only from England but also from other American colonies and from Halifax and Quebec. To quarter them before barracks could be built, Gage now had the power to bypass the town's selectmen in order to demand of Boston's residents that the troops be garrisoned in private homes.

Although the general-turned-governor had served long in America, being the dauntless officer who had carried the wounded Braddock from the battlefield in the French and Indian War, and although he had an American-born wife, Gage had a narrow and lordly view of colonials. He was determined to make the Bostonians pay for their crime. He and Lord North's government were of the informed opinion that the Tea Party had not just been the work of the common mob (which he called a "despicable rabble") but that it had been carried out on the orders of certain known leaders. As ordered, he intended to bring to heel these radical Whigs, whom he labeled "the Faction," by whatever method seemed most effective.

Gage could not see or appreciate the delicate connection between those leaders and the poor, that hungry and now idle populace on whose shoulders the military government's restrictions fell most heavily. As food became scarcer, prices rose; both men and women (there still being seven hundred more women than men in Boston) became beggars. As the scholar Dirk Hoerder has pointed out, daily life in Boston at this time suffered a moral breakdown. Robberies and assaults increased; the localized gangs turned away from political demonstrations to desperate attempts to get whatever they could by any means. Brothels and liquor shops multiplied. The middle and the lower classes, enduring outbreaks of smallpox and assaults by roaming jack-booted troops, regarded the sympathetic attitudes of the upper-class Whigs as generally worthless.

The Sons of Liberty formed and promoted a Solemn League and Covenant that was designed to bind all citizens, high and low, to the principles of non-importation and noncooperation with the British occupiers. To the unemployed, this appeared to be little more than patriotic posturing. By setting up a Committee of Ways and Means, Samuel Adams and William Molineux sought to make jobs for their constituents. The committee's work-fare program was supposed to give out food to all who cooperated. That worked with some men and women; others preferred not to accept such partisan charity, viewing with well-justified suspicion any moves by the wealthy to manipulate or obligate them by means of handouts.

Donations began to arrive from outlying towns and more distant points in New England: a pig from Wrentham, Massachusetts; a sheep from Windham, Connecticut. Boston's Committee of Correspondence thought it wise to set up a Committee of Donations in order to organize food distribution. Though appreciated, this, too, was viewed in the ranks of the indigent and by the gangs in the town's diseased, crowded districts as attempts to chain their loyalty to the patriots' cause. After all, a sane man might think, why not get the rich to repay the money lost by the East India Company in the dumping of the tea and open the port for the benefit of all?

Indeed, such farsighted American patriots as Benjamin Franklin (still in England) and John Dickinson from Philadelphia urged that Bostonians swallow their pride and come up with the funds to pay for the damages. They felt that although active resistance to the worst sort of imperial impositions was necessary, the people's liberty could best be preserved by some sort of reconciliation with the Crown—a gesture, a petition of apology, a payment. Gage, too, maintained the hope that sensible, conservative merchants of the town still had enough power in the community to arrange for a conciliatory payback of the tea's cost. At first, most of the merchants were inclined to agree, but as reports of the successive Coercive Acts came in and as their consequences were understood, many merchants swung in the direction of Hancock.

General Gage saw any residual hopes for cooperation dashed at a June town meeting when, as he wrote, "A number of the better sort of people" tried to bring forth a motion for the payment but were "outvoted by a great number of the lower class." In fact, the merchants had regrouped in a position of considerable strength and had gone to that meeting with high hopes of defeating the Sons of Liberty, figuring out some sort of moderate policy, and bringing the fractious town back under their control. But they had underestimated the effectiveness of Molineux's and Adams's operations, and by that miscalculation they had lost a crucial battle. Their loss of similar battles for control in towns across the province, particularly in Concord, which became the coalescing point of patriot activity outside of Boston, would result in the need for General Gage to send battalions marching northwestward toward that destination on a warm and memorable day in April of the following year.

## Massachusetts in Resolutions and in Arms

Craftsmen, mechanics, and skilled laborers of the town, seeing the jack-booted regime as nothing more than a foreign fist in the face, decided on a type of action far more direct than Whiggish committees and Puritanical covenants. They joined local militia units and became increasingly outspoken about their unwillingness to work for the British. Boston dockworkers, known for their obduracy, refused to unload the navy ships. Carpenters declined to construct new barracks for the redcoats, making it necessary for General Gage to send to New York for workmen. Paul Revere, who had many talents but was not much of a petition writer or political orator, dedicated himself to freeing the town from the unfairly privileged and the British military. He appeared ready to ride anywhere any time and began taking a more strenuous part in the illegal caucus meetings within his part of town.

As a North Ender, Revere had invaluable contacts both with waterfront characters who were suffering such unremitting hardships and with liberal Whigs who were seeking to find a way around the imposed government. As a Mason, Revere was encouraged by social higher-ups to speak out in operational planning sessions; he was also trusted to execute those plans swiftly and discreetly. In his later writings, he recalled that "In the fall of '74 and the winter of '75, I was one of upwards of thirty, chiefly mechanics, who formed ourselves into a committee for the purpose of watching movements of the British soldiers, and gaining every intelligence of the movements of the Tories." Their twin objectives were to see which of the local citizens were continuing to profit from the sale of stored British goods and to get an idea of troop movements and armament placements. They would spread word of those deployments to the communities that might be threatened.

The outlying communities of Massachusetts, patriotically aroused–meaning that they began to fear what restrictions the British might be planning for the interior of the province–sent delegates into the capital for a massive meeting in August 1774. This altogether illegal convention was in part a province-wide demonstration on behalf of the starving and beleaguered people of Boston, a salute to them for what they had done and were enduring. But its central purpose was to select representatives for the forthcoming Continental Congress to be held in Philadelphia in September. Despite some countermoves and objections by conservatives, the majority of the seventeen elected representatives were known radical leaders, including Hancock himself and Thomas Cushing, plus John and Samuel Adams and the latter's friends Elbridge Gerry and Robert Treat Paine. Because this was Samuel Adams's first opportunity to stand forth personally in the company of patriots from other colonies (indeed, his first trip out of greater Boston), his colleagues pitched in to outfit him in a proper suit.

John Hancock decided not to join the delegation to Philadelphia, choosing instead to stay behind for the time being and do whatever he could to keep in touch with the North and the South Enders and to aid the poor. Another Bostonian deeply involved in these political decisions was the eminent physician Dr. Joseph Warren, a warmhearted politician with excellent contacts in both the polished and the rude sectors of Boston society. In an attempt to diminish him, a Tory pamphleteer had described him not as one of the most handsome men in America (which he was, by all reports), but as this "crazy doctor," as well as, "One of our most bawling demagogues and voluminous writers." He was called by Lord Rawdon, who would be one of the British combatants at Bunker Hill, "the greatest incendiary in all America." Not quite true. Both of those characterizations failed to get the point of the man: a graduate of Harvard and a notable intellectual, he had long ago committed himself to service among the oppressed and stricken citizens of the port, a commitment for which he would ultimately pay with his life. His years of medical service among people of the waterfront, even more than his strong and staunch friendship with Samuel Adams, made him the credible and noncompromising leader that he was.

Immediately after graduation from medical school in 1763, he faced the challenge of a smallpox outbreak. Though hundreds of his class fled from Boston, he stayed behind to fight the epidemic with the controversial weapon of inoculation. Contending against the protests of many in authority, he finally received permission to open clinics, one on the Mystic River waterfront in Chelsea and the other at Castle William in the harbor. There, he and his volunteer colleagues treated more than a thousand patients from all walks of life. As reported by historian Louis Birnbaum, Warren's clinics inoculated 4,977 people, with only 46 contracting the disease and dying. By contrast, of the 699 persons who had contracted the disease naturally, 124 had died. By mid-August 1764, not a person in Boston had smallpox; the town honored him.

Long a protester against the impressment of seamen, Warren came to the fore as an activist and a trenchant penman during the Stamp Act crisis when his articles, under the name of A True Patriot, raised the hackles of the irascible Governor Bernard. Not bothered by the governor's charge that he was involved in "seditious libels," Warren went on to take a leading part in the *Liberty* riots of 1768 and in trying to save the life of poor Christopher Seider. After the Boston Massacre, he became one of the most popular members of the Special Committee of Safety, charged with the assignment of keeping rebellious Boston united. Now, with impressment by British naval officers threatening once more and smallpox endangering the populace (having probably been spread by the British troops, careless as they were about general hygiene), he once again urged patriots to work together against the occupying forces.

The kinds of action that patriots had in mind against their entrenched enemy during 1774 varied from armed resistance to conscious revolution. John Hancock said that, for him, his delivery of a speech on the fourth anniversary of the Massacre was "the most important" day of his life. In the course of writing that address, he apparently made up his mind that resistance had to be of the most militant kind; he called on patriots across the province to arm themselves and to form militia units. He also went so far as to speak of "a general union among us and our sister colonies." Samuel Adams went even further, stating later that at this time, he saw "the entire separation and independence of the colonies." Yet, ironically, he understood that there would be wide support for that move only if the British attempted further destruction of American liberties.

The Whig leadership also viewed that summer of 1774 as a period of tremendous risk, when the dangers to their own lives, as warned in the venomous Tory press, were extreme. Dr. Thomas Young, having been assaulted by British army officers, thought it best to remove himself to Rhode Island. Dr. Benjamin Church, despite his early espousal of the Whig cause and his grandiloquent speeches and artful essays in favor of the patriots, seems to have chosen this difficult time to start delivering intelligence to his friend General Gage.* Dr. Joseph Warren, on the other hand, chose to stay in Boston, believing this to be the galvanizing moment when all

---

*Paul Revere kept his keen eyes on the two-faced Dr. Church before and during this period, writing that "I was a constant and critical observer of him, and I must say, that I never thought him a man of Principle; and I doubted much in my own mind, wether [sic] He was a real Whig." In November 1775, some of Church's letters, in cipher, were intercepted. Tried and found guilty after what was generally conceded to have been a brilliant defense, he was sentenced to life imprisonment. Subsequently, he was allowed to leave the country in exile because of illness contracted in prison. The ship on which he embarked for the West Indies was lost at sea.

Americans might be led to believe in the wickedness of the oppressor. "I can assure you," he wrote to Adams, "that I never saw a more glorious prospect than the present."

Although blessed with charm and looks, Warren was a large and somewhat awkward man, lacking the polish of the gentlemen who moved in Boston's British-influenced upper class. Yet because of his popularity and grand speaking voice, he was invited to give the formal oration on the Boston Massacre's fifth anniversary in 1775—an invitation that involved considerable peril at that time of British occupation. The grand public event was staged at Boston's capacious Old South Church. As the tale is told, Warren was obliged to clamber in through the small windows at the rear of the building, because British officers blocked the church's front doors. When he ascended to the pulpit to address the crowded congregation of fellow townsmen, he saw another group of officers seated in the back pews, prepared to heckle him. In order to keep the peace, he modified his peroration slightly. And when he noticed that one officer, moving to sit on the pulpit stairs, had taken several pistol bullets from his pocket and was holding them in his open hand, Warren simply leaned over the side of the pulpit and dropped a white handkerchief upon the threatening hand.

Despite such politesse, his opinions on the subject of government tended to be radical and outspoken. In an earlier speech, he had put forth a revolutionary vision of the function of an ideal regime, saying that it "must contribute to the good of the whole."* Small wonder that the people, even before his subsequent heroic death, loved him for his mettle.

Warren's oratory became even more rash during the Suffolk County Convention held in Milton. Though it seems curious that this unauthorized meeting of September 9 could be held at all, it was apparently not banned by the military regime because the

---

*This quotation, one of many indications that the patriots at this time were considering what manner of government might be imagined beyond that of the all-too-well-known British monarchy, sounds notably different from to a statement by the radical Dr. Thomas Young, that it was "for the people to take the government into their own hands."

governor had never heard of such a thing as a county convention before. While acknowledging King George III as America's sovereign, Warren indicted Parliament's "unparalleled usurpation of unconstitutional power." He had brought to the convention a set of bold resolves, one of which demanded the resignation of Crown officers in Massachusetts, another of which denied all taxes to Gage's government. Most important, the resolves stressed the importance of establishing an armed militia in all communities. With the unanimous adoption of the so-called Suffolk Resolves by the convention, it was clear that this part of the province was in a state of defensive war. The accepted resolves were immediately put into Paul Revere's saddlebag, to be carried as swiftly as possible to the Continental Congress (the intercolonial body that would lead in 1776 to the first government of the United States)—where, to the surprise and dismay of many provinces' delegations, they were formally accepted.

It was indeed a time in which both patriots and Loyalists were looking to their governmental structures and to their weaponry. General Gage took the cautionary step of fortifying Boston's main gate with cannons. William Molineux, active as ever, made a daring attempt to seize eight or nine cannons and to transport them on a scow up the Charles River to a patriot strong point. This incident, discovered in the researchings of John Bell, unfortunately ended in failure, the scow running aground and the guns being recaptured by the British Navy. Bell also reports that on the other side of the political fence, a Loyalist merchant, having sold artillery supplies to the redcoats for £500, was threatened with hanging by a crowd of North End townspeople. Boston's authorities struggled to maintain the peace between the contending parties.

It was shortly after the attempted theft of the cannons, during the summer of 1774, that Molineux mysteriously expired, the victim either of British agents or of suicide prompted by his own financial overreaching. Chances are that if he did die as a result of foul play, he did not go gently. He and the waterfront characters who worked with him as reinforcers of non-importation were seen by the Loyalists as criminals determined to terrorize the town. Nonetheless, the not particularly sympathetic John Rowe recorded in his diary that at

Molineux's funeral, there was "A Great Concourse of People." In summing up the career of William Molineux—this inveterate smuggler, master of "dirty tricks" for the radicals, and sincere advocate of the maritime poor and disenfranchised—the nineteenth-century Boston historian Richard Frothingham laid the patriot to rest as if he had never been anything but a gentleman: "A distinguished merchant, an ardent friend to the country, whose labors proved too much for him."

With her usual acuity, Abigail Adams, observing from nearby Braintree the increasingly fraught scene, noted that Loyalists, seeking security, were streaming from the countryside into the heavily defended port. She now called the capital she had once admired so much "Boston Garrison." In her own town of Braintree, once quite removed from the fray, she also observed men carting away and sequestering the community's stored gunpowder ". . . because," she said, "we had so many Tories here they dare not trust us with it." Another fear, according to Abigail Adams (for whose letters to her husband, John, historians are eternally grateful), was what was stirring among the region's African American population; she wrote of a "conspiracy among the Negroes." There were rumors that should warfare break out, they would fight with the British, General Gage having promised them freedom for such service.

And so, in a rather strange dance, the two opposed factions hardened in their convictions—and changed places. More and more of the outvoted and harassed Loyalists left their no-longer-conservative towns for the safety of occupied Boston; behind them, they could see pillars of smoke as their houses were broken into and put to the torch. Simultaneously, more and more of the impoverished and rebellious townsmen and women left their hub of radicalism for the formerly conservative, now well-armed, countryside; behind them, they left the closed and profitless town, once the trading headquarters of the New World. Governor Gage let the Bostonians go, hundreds and hundreds of them, feeling that the town was well rid of such rabble.

As a result of this leakage, the town's civilian population was reduced from 15,000 to 6,753. By then, the British military establishment had reached a total of 13,600, counting attendant families, servants, and camp followers. Wherever troops encountered "saucy boys" and unemployed laborers, brawls intensified, despite Gage's historic order that street lamps be set up and turned on at dusk; he had hoped that their illumination would cut down on the nightly bloody incidents. He also forbade officers to wear their sidearms in the streets—an order that they regarded as humiliating and that they avoided whenever possible. Gage's failed idea of calming the capital by letting its most troublesome group depart became a failure twice over as those emigrés carried their radical message and their arms with them into the countryside. At the end of September, when Governor Gage saw what had happened, he wrote to Viscount Barrington in London that nearly all of Massachusetts was in a state of armed preparedness. Loyalist Henry Bromfield agreed, observing that to his consternation, "Our Country people spend half their time exercising and preparing for War."

## Mirroring the Boston Mobs in the Western Hills

The writings of a rural revolutionist from Billerica, Massachusetts, named William Manning (1747–1814) give a close-in view of how the radical spirit had spread from Boston to the countryside. As well as describing the process by which the political sentiments of his fellow townsmen changed during the middle of the eighteenth century, Manning's papers tell how the town of Billerica became less self-contained and more connected to seaport communities, particularly Boston. He also tells a poignant story of what happened to one of his neighbors, a luckless fellow named Thomas Ditson, who went into Boston at summer's end in 1774 to see if he could buy one of those excellent fifteen-pound Brown Bess muskets from a British soldier. Ditson took with him into town and across the Neck the not-small sum of four dollars, suspecting that his yearning for a really good musket might cost him dearly. Little did he know how much that would be.

At first, luck seemed to be on his side: in some tavern or other, he located a soldier willing to discuss the sale. But when Ditson came up with the precious dollars, the soldier took them and disappeared.

Fearing that he had been bilked, Ditson went outside to see what might be salvaged from the deal. Immediately, he was set upon by a number of the soldier's companions. Not content with roughing him up, the gang proceeded to tar and feather him, giving him what had come to be called a "Yankee Jacket." Then they paraded him through the neighborhood to the tune of "Yankee Doodle." Humiliated, scorched, and barely alive, Ditson returned home with a tale that left no doubt about who was then in charge of the streets of Boston.

As ever, the tough treatment handed out to local residents by in-charge British soldiers fell most heavily on the backs of the defenseless (and not necessarily politicized) waterfront laborers, be they deserter sailors, black slaves, or merely seamen trapped in that no-man's land of paralyzed marine activities. Historian Carl Bridenbaugh, in his seminal *Cities in Revolt*, wrote of an unfortunate black sailor who was set upon by a gang of British sailors. When Constable John Syms attempted to intervene, he was roughly pushed aside, and the fight went on to a bloody and lethal end. Although the selectmen managed to add new watchmen to the civilian force in an attempt to control waterfront disorders, the brutalities continued, with "lobster backs" the usual winners.

Less rough but more consequential than the British soldiers' drubbings of the down-and-outs in Boston were the patriots' actions in Massachusetts country towns. The towns, even farther beyond Boston than Billerica and Concord, have been described by historian Ray Raphael. In Great Barrington, located in the province's western hills, patriots boldly drove superimposed judges from their benches. Throughout Berkshire and other western counties, aristocratic Tory judges and officials came under attack, many resigning in the face of harassment by patriots. In the proud town of Hadley on the Connecticut River, patriots constructed a liberty pole some 130 feet high, rivaling even New York City's. Almost every town in western Massachusetts passed a resolution proclaiming its preparedness to resist "invasion." As conservatives cringed from these acts of perceived terrorism, the newly zealous patriots armed their militias and collected powder casks in apparent recognition of the fact that war was at hand.

The remarkable militant readiness on the westerners' part, involving small landowners and well-established gentry alike, was to a certain extent a reflection of the rebelliousness in Boston. But it arose mostly from the westerners' long-simmering conviction that they had been deliberately left out of the councils of the capital. In this conviction, they greatly resembled upcountry contingents in several other colonies, where antiauthoritarian actions had broken out that were quite different from the better-known struggles in coastal ports. Massachusetts's westerners, underrepresented, overtaxed, and expected to obey whatever the eastern merchants decreed, were impatient to claim a greater part of their own destiny. To strike against the royal government and its courts in their displeasure for taxes charged, mortgages foreclosed, and rights abrogated seemed a necessary and urgent step. But it was a step in what turned into a decades-long campaign, for that struggle against the eastern establishment would continue even after the Revolution.

More than seven months before Paul Revere's famous ride to Lexington, when word of British columns coming forth in search of hidden powder spread across the hills and the valleys, this western rebellion built to a kind of climax. An estimated ten thousand farmers responded to the alarm, taking muskets down from their hanging places and forming themselves into units for the expected battle. Although the alarm proved to be false and the men returned to their farms, the number of men who rallied on this occasion (called the "Powder Alarm" of October 1775) must have given General Gage something more to think about as he pondered his next move. In the same season, a crowd of five thousand men and women swarmed on Worcester to prevent that town's foreclosure-prone Court of Common Pleas from sitting. In that effort they succeeded, contributing further to Gage's conviction that with Boston under his control and that of his jack-booted troopers, the seat of the rebellion had shifted out of Boston into the interior—most obviously to Concord, where the illegal Provincial Congress had organized itself and begun to meet regularly.

It was along the coast, however, that the first actions occurred that involved heavy weapons of war and the possibility of heavy human losses. Just before the turning of the year into 1775, Paul Revere was sent riding hard over icy-muddy roads to Durham, New Hampshire, bearing reports of a move by General Gage to reinforce Fort William and Mary downriver from Durham at Portsmouth. There, at the mouth of the tidal and treacherous Piscataqua River, the fort held a strategic position. But more important to the patriots than the fort's location were its armaments and military stores. Since these were guarded by a squad of only five men, it seemed highly likely that they could be captured in one bold strike before the reinforcing task force arrived.

Revere delivered his message to militia captain John Sullivan, an Irish immigrant who had struggled, like Mackintosh, to find a place for himself in Yankee society. Though just as rough and ready as Mackintosh, he was far better educated. And having established himself as a battling lawyer in Durham, he had won enough cases and acquired enough landholdings to advance his status in the militia. Promoted through the officer ranks, he served in George Washington's forthcoming siege of Boston and went on from there to command forces in many of the Revolution's most effective, though high-loss, campaigns. What gave a special edge to his hatred of the British was Parliament's recently passed Quebec Act, which seemed to favor that province's Roman Catholic establishment—the denomination he had abandoned early on and mistrusted eternally. The Act also granted to Quebec much of the northwestern territory that New England frontiersmen considered rightly theirs. Sullivan was more than ready to rally his militiamen to pursue the course that Revere suggested.

Because the men he commanded were both seamen and farmers, many of them possessing what are now called saltwater farms, Sullivan had no doubt about their ability to guide their dorylike sailboats down the perilous Piscataqua River. Landing successfully at the island, they waded ashore and rushed the walls of the fort. Easily overcoming the commander and his men, they carried away 97 kegs of powder and 1,500 small arms, including more than 100 of the highly prized Brown Bess muskets. Sailing back upriver to

Durham, they hid their booty under the town's meeting house (it would be used later by New Hampshire soldiers at Bunker Hill). This was the first capture of royal property by American colonials. Although no shots were fired, it was a dramatic indication of what militia men and American seamen at arms could, with clever timing and a bit of luck, accomplish against the British.

Not many weeks later, on February 26, the British conducted an arms-collecting raid on the port of Salem that foreshadowed their April attack on Concord. Salem Loyalist spies had informed the British command in Boston that the militia company in their town possessed several brass cannons and gun carriages. Lieutenant Colonel Alexander Leslie took charge of the mission; his plan was to approach Salem from the north, by its Northfields Bridge. But when his force of regulars reached that lift bridge, they found it pulled up, and on the other side appeared a militia force prepared to prevent the British from lowering the bridge and crossing.

As more and more fishermen-turned-militiamen gathered on the town side and as the regulars prepared themselves to fire what might be the first shots heard in the Revolution, a respected parson named John Bernard (mentioned in chapter 3, with the Louisbourg campaign) stepped in to see what might be done. Knowing and trusting to the militiamen's salty humor, he proposed that the bridge be lowered, that the regulars be allowed to march over it, but that the British then turn around and head back to Boston. This ridiculous solution was accepted by all parties and dutifully acted out, and the episode lived on in local song and story.

But the British were far from amused at the prospect of more and more communities arming themselves, training their militias, and developing command structures. General Gage wrote to London that "Civil government is near its end. Furthermore, conciliation, moderation, reason is over; nothing can be done but by forcible means." At one point, in a mood of despair, he went so far as to suggest the repeal of the Coercive Acts—a suggestion that convinced Parliament he should probably be removed. Then he saw what he must do as his duty: the time for strenuous military action had come.

## Great Battles within Boston and Without

The two celebrated battles that started the American Revolution—Concord and Lexington in April 1775 and Bunker Hill in June of that year—have provided generations of historians with rich opportunities to reshuffle old facts and build new constructions. One strong theme that runs through most of their reconstructions is that General Gage's outstanding intelligence force allowed him to have a hawk's eye, cross-country view of the patriots' activities, but that it ultimately misled him by underestimating the farmers' readiness.

The converse of that is equally true: the patriots also had an extremely active intelligence force, but it was fashioned in a different manner. Rather than being sparked by inquiries from officers on high directed to sources in the field, it was energized by the sources themselves, whose information was screened by Joseph Warren and others. This gave them a locally detailed, scavenger's view, or what might be called a seagull's view, of the enemy—a capability quite in keeping with Boston's waterfront community. Indeed, it could also be said that both the origins and the outcomes of those great battles, so important to what would happen after 1775, were dramatic results of the unique history of Boston and its maritime character. Nor would Massachusetts's Governor Gage disagree. In reviewing the American Revolution, he wrote, "This province began it—I might say, this town. For here the arch-rebels formed their scheme long ago."

As the lives of constrained citizens within Boston grew more unbearable, with neither fresh food nor dependable firewood available (only salted-down fish and torn-apart houses), and as tensions tightened, the Provincial Congress, meeting in Concord, advised that all right-thinking citizens should leave the capital. If they were recognizable patriots and known troublemakers, they would have to disguise themselves. Yet some Bostonians, as records of the time point out, managed to remain determinedly neutral, resenting with equal fervor the bullying of the patriots and the overbearing attitudes of the Loyalists and the British. The courageous Dr. Joseph Warren remained in Boston, as did many other less eminent men and women of singular zeal, some of whom were pledged, like Revere, to keep sharp eyes on the British.

Having accepted responsibility for organizing and training patriots to observe and, where possible, to subvert the British forces, a Bostonian named Richard Devens set about recruiting a network of informants from his base across the river in Charlestown. That responsibility had been given to him by the powerful Special Committee of Safety, which was, in effect, the war department of the Provincial Congress. Some of Devens's men, mechanics and seamen among them, concentrated their activities on discouraging merchants and farmers from breaking the embargo on supplies for the occupiers and on encouraging desertion among British troops. The latter subversion met with much success. More than two hundred redcoats left the army in a ten-week period. Other spies and couriers were told to focus their attention particularly on the dispositions of the British warships. Regarding these as key to what might happen next, Devens reported those movements directly to Warren. The strange behavior of HMS *Somerset* on the morning of Saturday, April 15, caught the attention of one of his agents. Why had she been moved to a new mooring near the crossing lane of the Boston-Charleston ferry?

Curiosity about that unusual relocation deepened when it was reported that the ship's boats from a number of the troop transports had been collected under the sterns of several battleships. The word had been spread about that they were being brought in merely for painting and repair. But Dr. Warren and others saw a pattern forming. They put no stock in a suspicious-sounding report issued from British headquarters that grenadiers and light infantry squads had been given leave. Rather, suspecting that British troops were to be transported on a large-scaled invasion of the interior, the Special Committee of Safety ordered the number of observers—the trained seagulls, as it were—to be doubled.

From these observers, the committee learned that British headquarters had issued general orders stating that a Lieutenant Mackensie would be in charge of certain "new maneuvers" on the next day—which happened to be Easter Sunday. For Warren, this was a clear indication that a highly unusual exercise was being planned.

Because he and other patriot leaders had long suspected that the British intended to dispatch a major force out to Lexington (to which town John Hancock and Samuel Adams had escaped) and on to Concord (where the Provincial Congress was meeting), he concluded that this was the true purpose of the observed maneuvering. At once, he sent for Paul Revere, who, on the strength of his five successfully completed rides to Philadelphia and New York, was regarded as the patriots' boldest horseman. Warren instructed him to carry the news to Lexington as early as possible the next day.

Gage's hawklike spies, it was known, had carried out several scouting forays toward Concord. They had reported to Gage that there, in Concord, only twenty-two miles from Boston, the patriots had created one of the province's two major supply depots (the other was at Worcester, forty-seven miles away). The spies had also mapped the preferred marching routes to Concord, paying special attention to such military features as bridges and potential ambush sites. They brought back with them to British headquarters and safety the endangered Loyalist Daniel Bliss, who had, he believed, a good idea of where the patriots had stored their cannons and powder.

Gage's informants were less successful in portraying how Concord, like other towns in New England, was going through political and military metamorphoses in preparation for an attack. Once known for its desire to be left alone, left out of the antiauthoritarian tumults in Boston and the push for non-importation, Concord and its town meeting had gradually been taken over by radicals. They succeeded in passing a resolution praising Boston patriots for the "Preservation or Recovery of our Rights and Liberty." The town was swept by what the remaining Loyalists called the "contagious spirit of mobbing." People, they noted, were forgetting their proper places in society and were forming new allegiances.

At the direction of its Committee of Safety, Concord deemphasized the traditional militia units, in which officers had been democratically elected by their men, and in which strict command systems were therefore rarely achieved. Instead, it emphasized the new, elite Minute Man companies, in which the town's fittest men pledged to obey the commands of their appointed officers, and in which the soldiers were far better prepared than the militia to meet British regulars. The new command scheme also set up backup alarm squads, in which older men served on call as ancillary forces. Concord, as the hawks advised, was a ripe target, with its supply depot bulging with prohibited arms, but it was also a ready target, prepared for attack.

At Warren's command, Paul Revere made a preliminary trip to Concord on April 16 in order to warn the town of the suspected British move. A second purpose of that trip was to set up an alarm system to be triggered when the British actually marched forth from Boston. Revere and the intelligence expert Richard Devens agreed that the lofty belfry of the Old North Church (a few blocks away from Revere's house in the North End) should serve as the signal tower. As has been memorized by successive generations of American schoolchildren, one lantern up in the belfry would indicate that the enemy force was taking a southern route by land across the Neck, through Roxbury, and on to either Worcester or Concord. Two lanterns would indicate that the British brigades were proceeding at first across the Charles River (transported in those boats the seagulls had seen assembled astern the warships), then on land by a more northern route to Lexington and ultimately to Concord.

All this was a prelude to the famous Battle of Concord and Lexington, in which the British lost a horrendous 18 percent of the fifteen hundred troopers who had so boldly marched forth. That loss on April 19, 1775, signaled to all who would open their eyes not only that a war had begun between Great Britain and a certain part of the American colonies, but also that those in rebellion were well equipped and well organized to carry on that war. In the words of Lord Hugh Percy, "Whoever looks on [these rebels] as an irregular mob will be much mistaken. They have men amongst them who know very well what they are about."

Although Lord Percy was quite right that there were men who knew what they were about—Joseph Warren and Samuel and John Adams, to name three of them—he would have done well not to have dismissed those less informed but no less bold. These were the people of Boston who had always come forth previously in the town's history at a time of alarm; these were the seamen who knew about the tides and the movements of ships; these were the neighborhood men and women who knew very well what all the business in the Old North Church belfry was about. It is no wonder that the British, in a pointed act of cultural vandalism, destroyed the neighboring Old North Meeting House before abandoning the town in 1776.

In the days after Lexington and Concord, with fifes and drums picking up the beat of war on all sides, every man and woman was forced to choose on which side to fight. Under British military command, Boston closed its gates and doubled its guard force. Meanwhile, from towns around Boston and from distant parts of New England, armed and trained farmer patriots streamed in to surround and make it a citadel under siege. It now seemed impossible to escape. John Rowe, the cautious merchant, wrote in his diary on April 28 that "This day I apply'd to get a Pass to go out with my Effects but could not prevail." One who did succeed in escaping was the massive bookseller Henry Knox from the North End, who would soon serve as George Washington's artillery chief.

In the streets of the suffering town, hatred blossomed between resentful patriot captives and frightened Loyalists, no longer friendly neighbors. Violence would surely erupt. Paul Revere wrote to Samuel Adams that "something must be done to stop this growing evil or we shall eat one another." Carousing British soldiers and frequently inebriated officers made the streets increasingly perilous; in March, when celebrating St. Patrick's Day, they had attacked patriots' property, including the mansion of John Hancock. General Gage and the British command observed all this, concluding that they faced not only an army forming without the gates but also other battles within. Against the advice of many of his councilors, Gage decided that rather than intensify the struggle within the town, a wiser course was to let more of those constrained people depart.

Furthermore, Gage decided that he must make an arrangement whereby Loyalists from surrounding towns would be granted safe passage into Boston. The selectmen, having obtained the Special Committee of Safety's consent for this delicate matter, agreed with the switch. At the end of April, Governor Gage therefore proclaimed that if a citizen would ask permission and would surrender his weapons to the proper authorities, he and his family could leave. Some two thousand men and women applied and were released—leaving behind them only about a fifth of the town's population.

As the military contingents assembling around Boston swelled in size (to an eventual total of seventy-five hundred men), confusion grew correspondingly. Not until Congress's appointment of George Washington as commander in chief and his arrival in Cambridge at the end of June would the squabbling of provincial generals cease and the Grand Army become a reality. Massachusetts's cautious General Artemas Ward debated with Connecticut's impetuous General Israel Putnam what might be the most effective course of action. On their minds were the twin questions of how to prevent the British from striking out beyond their encircled position to the mainland and how to attack that formidably fortified position in a way that would be effective.

Richard Ketcham's book *Decisive Day* carefully sets forth those and other issues faced by the divided commanders before and during the Battle of Bunker Hill. With its all-encompassing scope, the book succeeds extraordinarily well. It does fail, however, to note adequately that the battle enjoyed a peculiarly local character. There were, to be sure, military components from the surrounding states that made vitally important contributions, but Bunker Hill was truly a greater-Boston affair, shaped for good and ill by the conditions of that landscape and that society.

After scouting out the hills above Charlestown early in May, intelligence chief Richard Devens had recommended that an American position be constructed on the highest point on that ridge—namely, Bunker Hill. Rumors and more solid reports had continued to come in to the Special Committee of Safety (chaired by Dr. Warren) that the British might indeed move north across the channel to seize Charlestown or possibly south by land to take Dorchester Heights. The erection of a redoubt on Bunker Hill, Devens assured the committee, would keep at least that peninsula free from enemy "sallies." The more distant Dorchester was a less urgent matter.

But it was not until Thursday, June 15, that the Special Committee of Safety, having received more definite news of the British intentions, made the historic decision to "post sufficient force" on Bunker

Hill to ensure "the Security of this Colony." Israel Putnam and Colonel William Prescott proposed immediate action, their theory being that the British might be tempted to come forth in a hasty, defensive effort without adequate preparation. Other patriot leaders, led by Artemas Ward and Dr. Warren, were concerned about the Americans' own preparedness. Finally and reluctantly, Ward was won over (though he would keep the major part of his force in Cambridge); on June 16, Ward issued orders for Colonel Prescott to proceed to Bunker Hill to erect a fort. After he assembled bits and pieces of three Massachusetts regiments by evening, the colonel started off toward Charlestown Neck at 6:00 P.M. With him marched a detachment that he must have considered perilously small—little more than eight hundred men.

The next important command decision made before the battle proved central to what happened on the slopes above Charlestown on that next, bloody day. Having crossed the Neck and reached the first rise of land, Colonel Prescott—who stood more than six feet tall and was the very model of a Massachusetts Minute Man, coming from the Boston suburb of Groton—met with two other officers in the darkness and debated where precisely to build their fort. Although the highest-ranking member of that meeting is not known to history, to Richard Ketcham it seems a good bet that General Putnam was there—he, along with Prescott and the sixty-five-year-old artillery colonel Richard Gridley. Whoever gave the individual command or however a consensus was reached, the decision was terribly wrong: they ordered their men to proceed with entrenching tools not to Bunker Hill, the highest point of land, but to Breed's Hill, slightly below it.

Indeed, Breed's Hill was and is only a slight hump in the ridge that runs down from Bunker Hill (altitude: 110 feet above sea level) to the peninsula's foot, half a mile across the harbor from Boston. From the British gun batteries at Copp's Hill on the Boston shore, it was thus an easy lob for a cannonball up and over the channel to Breed's Hill. It was an even easier shot for ships' cannons aboard the *Somerset* and other British warships moored in the harbor. General Putnam must have known that an emplacement so near to the British guns would be subjected to a most brutal pummeling, from

Copp's Hill, from the warships, and from the guns aboard barges that could easily be moved into place. But he, as had been evident in all the prior meetings of which records have been kept, was determined to bring the British out, to fight with them nose to nose, and to drive them off. So let us put the fort right in their faces, he may have thought.

How much this erroneous decision affected the fighting and the loss of life in the Battle of Breed's Hill is very well known. Perhaps if the general had come from Boston, he would have been more aware of the advantages of choosing the true summit. Perhaps then he would not have veered away from the Special Committee of Safety's order and would not have directed Prescott's men to defend the lower, more easily stormed site, just down from Bunker Hill.

Perhapses aside, "Bunker Hill" stands in history books as a notable American victory and proportionately the greatest loss ever sustained by the British in a single battle. Appalled at the 1,154 men killed or wounded and impressed by the Americans' firepower, General Gage stated, confidentially, that "the loss we have sustained here is greater than we can bear." Then, in anger, "I wish this Cursed place was burned!" Instead of burning Boston or making further forays, the weighty British forces stayed passively penned inside the exhausted, starving citadel. It was not until George Washington and Henry Knox leveled at them the cannons brought from Fort Ticonderoga (captured the next winter) that they would depart. Their sailing away is still celebrated in town on Evacuation Day, commemorating March 17, 1776. Before leaving, a British soldier made sure to chop down the infamous Liberty Tree, which had seen the birth of so many peculiarly Bostonian actions. As the tree fell, it killed the soldier, signaling, it seemed, that the genius loci, the rebellious spirit of the place, lived on.

The spirit of Bunker Hill, however, has suffered much buffeting as it has been reexamined down through the American centuries. John Trumbull's famous 1786 painting of the event, with flags massing, a noble hero dying gloriously while held in protective arms, and a Connecticut courtier aghast at the solemnity of it all, did much to prevent an understanding of what really happened. The true spirit of the battle is caught far more accurately in one phrase uttered by

Colonel Prescott as he and his men came under early fire from HMS *Lively*, whose lookouts had caught sight of the American entrenchments and started to lob shells at Breed's Hill even before dawn.

While some of his men stood stock still in terror at their lack of protection from the bombardment and others chose to run for cover, Prescott was told by his panicked officers that he must either send immediately for reinforcements or withdraw. They feared that the mission had gone terribly wrong, that daylight would reveal them as betrayed, caught by mistake in a deadly trap. But Prescott believed that no reinforcements could handle the situation better than those men from the Boston area who were with him at that moment. "The men who have raised these works," he replied, "are the best able to defend them."

*The Boston artist John Trumbull was an eyewitness of the Battle of Bunker Hill, actually Breed's Hill. His heroically styled painting correctly reports the death of General Warren (left) and the carrying-off of wounded Major Pitcairn (center). Yet with the exception of the black soldier Salem Prince (far right), it fails to show the racially and socially mixed character of the local fighters.*

Yale University Art Gallery, Trumbull Collection

The colonel was indeed a remarkable leader. Ketcham quotes a veteran of the battle as recalling, "I tell ye that if it had not been for Colonel Prescott, there would have been no fight." Another testimonial was bestowed on him at the time of the battle by his own Tory brother-in-law, Abijah Willard, who happened to be standing then at General Gage's side. Gage, looking through his telescope across the channel to the battlefield and seeing Prescott positioned atop the barricade, asked about him, "Will he fight?" To which Willard responded, "I cannot answer for his men, but Prescott will fight you to the gates of hell." The only thing inaccurate about the reply, as it turned out, was that both the colonel *and* his men fought like hell.

Although there were some driftings away from Prescott's regiment at Breed's Hill (some going up the slope to join others out of cannonball range on Bunker Hill) and some additions to Prescott's companies (most notably, General John Stark's regiment from New Hampshire), the corps of men who stood firing together against the three assaults by oncoming British grenadiers seems to have numbered about 1,500. Of these, 140 were killed, 271 were wounded, and 31 were captured. The British troops sent up the hill against them by General Howe totaled about 2,000. Of these, 226 were killed and 928 wounded—a grim casualty rate of 52 percent. When Howe's wounded and dying men were brought back on litters to Boston, observers noted that their blood literally ran in the streets.

The hometowns of those Americans who died in battle, as listed in memorial tablets in Charlestown, tell the story of how people from the Boston area cast localisms aside and responded to the crisis of their anguished capital. The fishing communities of Gloucester and Marblehead contributed six of the fallen; the small, close-knit town of Groton contributed nine. Men who had marched in with their companies from more distant hamlets also fell in great numbers: nine from Connecticut and six from Hollis, New Hampshire. These men had served in Dow's Company of Prescott's regiment. Indeed, the volunteers who came down from the New Hampshire hills in Stark's regiment served with special valor and sustained dreadful losses; thirteen of them would never return to their farms.

Because of Massachusetts's large African American population—5,249 in total, compared with the province's 343,845 whites—it is small wonder that there were so many blacks to be seen among those who fought passionately and lived or died at Breed's Hill. Some 103 of these African American soldiers have been counted, as revealed in a probing 2002 study of the subject by George Quintal. Of these, 3 were killed, 5 wounded, and 1 taken prisoner. Indeed, it is believed that the last man killed during the vicious hand-to-hand struggle that raged after the Americans' ammunition ran out was a black soldier. Quintal also makes the point that of those African Americans who survived the so-called Battle of Bunker Hill, many went on to fight heroically in other battles of the Revolution. A Boston-area infantryman named Jamaica James, for example, served well at Saratoga.[*]

Several reports survive of exemplary action by the blacks who fought on Breed's Hill. Quintal found this entry in the journal of a sixteen-year-old white participant named Aaron Smith:

> Just as I came near the place [of battle], a negro man, wounded in the back of his neck, passed me and, his collar being open and he not having anything on except his shirt and trousers, I saw the wound and the blood running down his back. I asked him if it hurt him much as he did not seem to mind it; he said no, that he was only going to get a plaster put on it, and meant to return. You cannot conceive what encouragement this immediately gave me; I began to feel brave and like a soldier from that moment, and fear never troubled me afterward during the whole war.

Richard Ketcham, in his vivid book, allows us to catch a glimpse of a black fighter named Coffee Whittemore whose hat was shot

---

[*]Because of the widely acknowledged bravery of African American fighters at Bunker Hill, attempts by such southern representatives in the Congress as Edward Rutledge to have blacks excluded from the Continental Army were consistently defeated. The American fighting force of 1775 was completely integrated.

through by a British musket ball. In the final moments of the battle, he seized a sword from a fallen British officer and carried it off in triumph. But, needing funds more than triumph, Whittemore sold the sword a few days later, to the disgust of his friends.

A black fighter with the resonant name of Salem Prince is said to have been the American who killed the British marine major John Pitcairn, a leader and a victim of the second attack up the slopes of Breed's Hill. Although Prince's name recalls that of Crispus Attucks's father, there was, in fact, no relationship. This Prince served as an assistant to an officer from Connecticut who had rushed into the fight, perhaps in company with General Putnam. In the celebrated Trumbull painting, Prince is depicted holding a musket, in step and mood with that natty officer.

At the center of the painting, Joseph Warren dies dramatically, the deserved focus of attention: his loss was surely the most grievous suffered at Bunker Hill. Warren had been roused from his sickbed by the ringing of the Cambridge alarm bell. Forgetting the attack of headache and exhaustion that had prevented him from chairing the most recent meeting of his Special Committee of Safety, he borrowed somebody's horse and galloped toward Charlestown. He arrived on the battlefield in midafternoon, at the time when the British, led into battle by Major General William Howe, had commenced their full-scale attacks. Taking up the musket of a wounded soldier, he rushed toward the redoubt that seemed to be the center of the action. Because he had recently been given the rank of major general, both General Putnam and Colonel Prescott assumed that Warren, when they saw him approaching, would take command. But after reporting that reinforcements were on the way, he stated, "I have no command here; I have not received my commission." Then, after a courteous word to the effect that it would be an honor to serve under Prescott, he took up his weapon and joined the fray.

Warren had come not to issue orders but to give encouragement and to fight. On the redoubt's fire step, shoulder to shoulder with those who sought to hold back the last of the British troops' three assaults, he blazed away until ammunition ran out. Then, called by name to join the retreat, he turned to reply, was struck in the head by a ball, and fell beneath the feet of oncoming grenadiers. In the aftermath of the battle, a British officer recalled that Warren had "died in his best cloaths; everyone remembers his fine silk-fringed waistcoat." But even with that and other clues, his body was not located and positively identified by grief-stricken Bostonians until several days later. It was necessary for Paul Revere to confirm, definitively, that a certain body was that of Dr. Joseph Warren; Revere had made and installed those wire-and-ivory teeth himself not long before the battle.

Immense as was the loss of Warren—since the departure of Samuel Adams from Boston, he had not only led the radical wing of the Whigs but had also, as head of the Special Committee of Safety, taken the lead in conducting the war—the significance of the battle was even larger. That significance lay in both the dead and the living, in the fishermen and the farmers, the African and the Native Americans, all of them having chosen to fight then and there for what they perceived as *their* land. Although the traumatized people of Boston and the withheld reserve squadrons of General Artemas Ward's Grand Army had watched in static horror as the battle right across the channel worked out its frenzy for two and a half bloody hours, enough Americans had rallied and fought at Breed's Hill to make an undeniable point. This province and its neighbors had pulled themselves together as an effective combat force. The point was not lost on the British.

After learning of the earlier battle, the action at Concord and Lexington, King George III had written to Lord North, "The die is now cast, the Colonies must either submit or triumph." By "Colonies," the king had surely meant each one of them, individually; the forthcoming war for a united independence for all of Great Britain's North American colonies was by no means manifested in the springtime of 1775, but a war of some kind was obviously on. A remark made by the French foreign minister Charles de Vergennes after the Battle of Bunker Hill was also prescient. "Two more such victories," he said, "and England will have no army left in America." He was quite right. Men from New England had demonstrated that certain Americans were going to fight against old England and for

Boston or for whichever their community might be. They were far more potent than "raw lads and old men," as one scoffing British officer had characterized them. No, sir, they were going to win.

## "The Liberties of the Country Are Safe"

The destruction and the carnage on the Charlestown peninsula were so stunning that another significant fact about the battle was difficult to notice: it was fought from within the town of Boston, as well as across the harbor. Battle losses among the patriots might have been much worse had it not been for certain tricks and treasonous acts carried out, on various local Boston fronts, that impeded the British forces. For example, in an early phase of the battle, General Howe's artillerymen striking against the Americans' right flank were chagrined to find that their cannonballs were the wrong size; at that critical time, their cannons could not do their damage. Later, after certain papers on the body of Dr. Joseph Warren were discovered by the British before his burial, a connection was traced between the clerk of the artillery stores, one Benjamin Lovell, and his brother James, a young master at the Boston Latin School. It explained the mystery of the wrong-size cannonballs.

For many months it had been known that James, a Whig who, over his father's objections, had delivered one of the orations in honor of the Massacre, was inclining more and more in favor of the rebels' cause. Fortunately, researcher John Bell has scrupulously examined the case of the Lovells and the Boston Latin School at this time of shifting loyalties. He makes the case that James's students, mere youngsters who had protested the British troops' blocking of their coasting course, through their youthful courage had helped to firm up their master's mind that he should go ahead and speak in praise of those patriots. Here, once again, it was the "saucy boys" of Boston who provided at a particular time a needed thrust for freedom.

But alas for James Lovell. He became an example of Boston's war at its harshest of times when General Gage had declared martial law and all townsmen were under suspicion. Certain papers captured on him showed that in addition to having switched the cannonballs, he had drafted reports describing the disposition of British troops. He was therefore imprisoned and shipped off to a British jail, not to be exchanged and brought back to his town until near the Revolution's end.

When George Washington was on his way to Boston to carry out his new assignment from Congress as commander in chief, word reached him of the battle at Breed's Hill. Although Congress had not yet then, in 1775, voted for war against Great Britain, the representatives agreed that Boston must be defended and that a chief was needed to pull the American armies of resistance together. Washington was assigned, it might be said, to turn what had been Boston's local war fueled by internal desperation into a war energized by anger and frustration throughout the colonies. According to Daniel Webster, when Washington heard of the recent battle, he asked with understandable urgency how American troops had done in their first fight against attacking British warriors. Learning that they had held their ground, and that they had fired with devastating effect against the charging redcoats until ammunition ran out, Washington softly made a profoundly grateful reply: "The liberties of the country are safe."

It was a typical reply for that classical gentleman (if those were, in fact, Washington's words and not Webster's). But what neither General Washington nor the myth-maker Webster could foresee was that the liberties of the country, once protected and advanced by the blood of seamen, mechanics, freed slaves, and other common people at Bunker Hill, can only be truly safe when the heirs of those and other Americans are willing to fight additional battles both bloody and bloodless and to achieve victories against newly emerged elites.

# Epilogue

# "Public Liberty": An Enduring Dream

In 1777, the year after the Declaration of Independence was signed, and when Ebenezer Mackintosh was forty years old, he enlisted as a private in the Army of the United States. Rumors were sweeping Vermont, where he then lived, that a massive British army headed by General Johnny Burgoyne was headed south to split apart the newly formed Republic. So Mackintosh, the veteran of other less-recognized battles (as we have noted), went back into uniform, taking a modest part in the regional contest that would terminate in the great American victory at Saratoga. Later in the war, he functioned as an army scout against a threatened assault from the west by the notorious Major Guy Carleton.

These facts about Mackintosh at midlife were discovered in the 1920s by his one and only biographer, George Anderson. They help us understand how Mackintosh, the sometime mob leader, carried on the fight against the British and how the rebellion that he had helped raise in Boston was a significant part, albeit a disconnected part, of the nationwide revolution. That War of American Independence, as it is formally called, would finally, in 1781, end in a kind of victory that he and his "chickens" had never anticipated or intended.

Anderson relates how Mackintosh, well after the war, when he was sixty-five, walked all the way to Ohio in order to visit his son Paschal Paoli and to leave another one of his later children there with Paschal. Returning to Vermont, he died in a poorhouse in 1816. Neighbors, having heard some of his tales and wishing to honor him in death as they had not in life, carved a tombstone, using the not-quite-right name Philip McIntosh. They wrote on it that he had been "A Leader of the Boston Tea Party, 1773," which is what he may have told them. Actually, of course, what he had led most successfully in Boston was not any one of the well-coordinated Tea Party teams but a formless group of angry and drunken mariners in the Stamp Act riots of 1765.

Yes, he had led a *mob*. But, as this book attempts to demonstrate, it should not be believed that the waterfront mobs of Boston in the pre-Revolutionary era were purely destructive and mindless. Nor were they always spontaneous and isolated demonstrations of social outrage. In the opinion of the contemporary observer Gouverneur Morris, such popular gatherings as were observed on the dockside streets and in the squares of Boston and New York *evolved*, becoming more definitely political after the events of 1765, 1770, and 1773. That is why it seems no stretch for the modern analysts of mob actions, analysts led by scholars mentioned in the preface, to conclude that the American Revolution had its genesis on the waterfront, in violent actions that were vitally important in pushing other patriots of other classes and places toward the future.

As one of those historians, Paul Gilje, wrote in *Liberty on the Waterfront*, "Maritime workers . . . helped propel the resistance movement toward greater social change and gave voice to a call for equality. As resistance moved toward revolution, and as mobs parading with effigies or tarring and feathering an opponent gave way to armed conflict, the American maritime worker continued to play an active part." Local gangs transformed themselves into militia units; townspeople who protested against specific regulations and commissioners enlisted as soldiers in a long and difficult war.

Yet along with that process of Boston's working people beginning a victorious war went a great contradiction: this war's winning and its ultimate victory would not belong to them. Historian Dirk

Hoerder paints a memorable scene of how Boston's Committee of Correspondence rounded up townsmen in the summer of 1776, ordering them to appear on the Common for a military draft: "Just as in 1765, when gentlemen-volunteers had guarded the property of the wealthy, a similar unit [consisting of the elite] now surrounded the draft-age population with lowered guns." The gentlemen had bought substitutes for themselves and now pushed them into the ranks, but the majority of people were forced to serve, like it or not. Hoerder goes on, "The people rioted against the gentlemen and the Whig committee, shouting 'Tyranny is Tyranny, let it come from whom it may!'"

Tough as it was to serve and tyrannical as the Revolutionary leadership may have been, Boston's mariners and other townspeople somehow had to fight a war for survival, a war against the

*Around the rim of this classically shaped silver bowl appear names of the patriots, many of them from the maritime community, who requested Paul Revere to create it. The bowl celebrates the action of ninety-two Massachusetts legislators who refused to rescind a Circular Letter summoning all colonies to resist the Townshend Acts. It also salutes the British politician John Wilkes, displaying symbols of the Magna Carta and the Bill of Rights.*
Photograph copyright 2005, Museum of Fine Arts, Boston

greatest empire in the world at that time. Then there was the free-
for-all struggle to find an improved life within post-Revolution
Massachusetts and ultimately within the emergent United States of
America. Unfortunately, old hierarchical ways would not give way
easily to more equal systems, either during the lifetimes of these
people or ever. In Boston, the new elite closed its ranks, determined
to hold power through the war and afterward. That system was,
one might say, a quite natural and expectable formation, clearly
preferable to the old aristocratic order—a small step into what was
called republicanism. Yet it left the workers trying to grasp the rules
of the new, quasi-democratic game while looking for new leaders.
Even the sagacious John Adams admitted that he "never understood what a republic was."

There were, fortunately, young and vital and liberal men in
Boston who had a pretty clear idea of how the Republic might work
and "what they were about" (to repeat the words General Percy had
used at Bunker Hill). One of those men was the energetic artisan
Paul Revere, a patriot with excellent contacts among both the
entrenched merchants and the waterfront rioters. He identified the
objective of the war with admirable clarity, saying that what he
desired most of all was "public liberty" for his fellow Bostonians.

This was clearly a definition of liberty rooted in the communal
and maritime traditions of the town. It bespoke not the liberty of
Dr. Thomas Young's antiauthoritarian individualism nor that of
Samuel Adams's Christian Sparta, but that of a mutually responsible citizenry. Like New England fishermen, each person would be
"on his own hook" but would answer to the captain for the security
of the ship. That might not have been precisely the governance
desired by Ebenezer Mackintosh and his fellow rioters—not sufficiently free or wide open. And it was clearly not the one advocated
by such Loyalists as Peter Oliver. Oliver viscerally detested any sort
of democracy, any pretense that the people could be constructively
involved in government. Indeed, he characterized Boston's townspeople not only as the "mobility" but also as "a winch wound by
any hand," for he saw Mackintosh and his ilk as inevitably the tools
of more powerful forces. But Revere, for his part, had far more

confidence in people of all sorts, particularly in those who lived in the port of Boston's closely packed neighborhoods. For them, the concept and the practice of "public liberty" had both an ancient heritage and a revolutionary reality.

A close look at Boston's North End after the British occupation had ended, as depicted in Carol Ely's 1983 study (see the acknowledgments), reveals that this location may well have been the model of liberty that Paul Revere had in mind. These North Enders, it will be recalled, were the highly stressed people who had supplied one of Boston's angriest and most effective mobs. Furthermore, as a consequence of the British aggressions that their own and others' actions had provoked, they had paid a heavy price in lives lost and property vandalized. After the evacuation of the port by royal forces, North End families returning home from outlying towns found "little more but a heap of ruins" left to greet them.

Yet Ely points out that even with the central church torn down and many houses destroyed for firewood, the homecomers were gratified to create a place for themselves once again in their old neighborhood. As the war went on unrelievedly elsewhere, and as strictly enforced rationing and runaway inflation made life difficult for them, they found ways to get along. And most happily, the returnees found a different spirit in their old Boston. The former political hostility had been blown away with the removal of the rich loyalists; even the raging gangs had dispersed, their anger abated— for the moment.

Gone, too, of course, but by no means forgotten, were the horrors that had been visited upon the two or three thousand people who had remained in town during the British wartime occupation. Ely tells of a sailor and a navigator named John Leach of the North End who, during that time, had been seized by an officer and a sheriff and dragged back to his house, where all of his possessions, particularly his notes, were subjected to the closest scrutiny. He recalled berating himself for not taking up a "hanger" (a seaman's short sword) and cutting his attackers down but then reflected that he "could not escape, as the whole Town was a prison." Convicted of being a spy, Leach was imprisoned for many months. On release, he had to live with his family on relief money supplied by charitable Quakers. He concluded his memoir with the warning to other Americans: "Put not your faith in Princes!"

And so the Revolution both removed the king, his princes, and his royal rule and it permitted another, more people-based regime to begin. Indeed, for those who came back to the post-Revolutionary North End, a condition of collective harmony and political consensus seemed to have been achieved. Factional and religious schisms had been healed, and responsive representatives were trusted to carry on the business of government.* Paul Revere's cousin, Nathaniel Hichborn, who appears on the tax rolls as a boatbuilder and who was blessed with eleven children to provide for, was asked to carry out certain official duties on the waterfront. He was also given the position of "scavenger," making him a town functionary at about the same level that Mackintosh had been when he served as sealer. Many other poor men, previously disregarded and in the shadows of society, now came forth into the light of public service. This greatly improved, more democratic situation appeared to be, in fact, a realization of Revere's "public liberty."

Yet it was a brief phenomenon. The new elite of merchants and magistrates that had begun to establish itself as the ruling power in Boston and throughout the new Commonwealth of Massachusetts during the Revolution extended its power within the federal government that was promulgated soon after 1781. These new rulers looked quite familiar. With names like Hancock and Adams and Rowe, they had never hesitated to assert their authority. As the smoke of battle blew away, they seized uncontested control once again.

Yet the people's dream of a harmonious social/political state, the state that was glimpsed *in parvo* and momentarily in the North End, endures both as a dream and as a demand. Toward that objective,

---

*From his recently established New Brick Church in the North End, Deacon Tudor wrote, "To me it was Agreeable to see former Bigatree so far gon and going off, and God grant that for Time to come boath Churchmen and Desenters may live in peace and Love."

successive generations of Americans have continued to strive, by other disconnected insurgencies and revolutions, by constitutional amendments, and by almost all other means imaginable except for sailors' tar and featherings. Once long ago, in an exceptional phase of violence and terror, a maritime and tradition-minded populace living at a time of social panic did what they could with the means available to them to assert themselves as self-respecting Americans. Their example must be understood.

# Acknowledgments, Sources, and Interpretations

Writing this book was a maritime adventure from start to finish, having to do with merchants and seamen operating out of the port of Boston before the Revolution. I therefore feel obliged to present this retrospective section in nautical terms. The individuals who counseled me and the institutions that assisted me served truly as pilots and beacons along the way; without them, the work would surely have foundered.

Chief pilot of them all was the generous and incisive Alfred F. Young, professor emeritus at Northern Illinois University and senior research fellow at the Newberry Library in Chicago. Author of the soon to be published *Ordinary People of the American Revolution*, Al is rightly considered the dean of all those who write early American history "from the bottom up" (see bibliography for all books mentioned here). Just as he guided me through the varying interpretations of who aroused, controlled, or countered the mobs of Boston, Pat Leehey, director of the Paul Revere House in North Boston, helped me navigate through the local dynamics of the town's dockside neighborhoods. It was in those neighborhoods that Boston waterfront politicians came up with what might be considered their greatest invention: the caucus. Pat was also kind enough to review much of my manuscript in an early stage. Yet neither he nor Al

Young should be tarred and feathered for any errors or misjudgments that occur in the book; my hand alone steered the narrative.

To William Fowler, director of the Massachusetts Historical Society, and to that institution's librarian, Peter Drummey, as well as to his assistant Kim Nusco, I am also deeply indebted for their encouragement and for their leads to pertinent sources within their own collections and elsewhere. Many other seasoned Bostonians also deserve my thanks for their helpfulness. Marty Blatt, director of the Boston National Historical Park, is positioned high on the list, for it was he who, at various sites on the seaport's working waterfront, helped give me the personal feeling that I stood exactly where the men and the women of Boston had labored under such duress and had vented their anger so significantly. Similarly, the exemplary young researcher of Boston's early history John E. Bell introduced me to another important but not often considered aspect of the town's society: its impetuous, impudent, incendiary children. Another prime source for interpretations of the social/political scene was historian Benjamin H. Irvin, formerly of Brandeis University and now at the University of Arizona, whose 2002 biography of Samuel Adams shone as a veritable North Star amid the whirling galaxies of opposed academic opinions.

At pain of repeating points made in the narrative, I would like to be more exact in acknowledging what sources proved most helpful in solving problems encountered as I charted my course through the respective chapters. For the purposes of the introduction and chapter 1, where I needed to catch on to the peculiar, inbred character of Boston society, I was grateful for Bernard Bailyn's 1974 biography of Massachusetts's pivotal colonial governor Thomas Hutchinson. Yet I found myself asking again and again, as Professor Bailyn portrayed the shifting political scene of the 1760s and 1770s, why he could not credit Hutchinson's harassers, the mobs, with possessing any positive intentions. Hutchinson did indeed, as Bailyn so accurately presents him, focus his narrow mind on the Whigs and the caucus clubs and the merchants who opposed importation from Great Britain—in sum, on all those tricky convolutions of Boston's emerging political consciousness. But given his special, aristocratic background, Hutchinson could not view the people themselves, as

THE Merchants and Traders in the Town of *Boſton* are deſired to meet at *Faneuil-Hall* To-Morrow, at Three o'Clock, P. M. when Matters of the utmoſt Importance will be laid before them for their Conſideration———It is earneſtly deſired there may be a general Attendance.

TUESDAY, *July* 25, 1769.

*Typical of announcements made when Samuel Adams was organizing the Sons of Liberty, this broadside of 1769 was written as an appeal to the leadership of Boston, its merchants, and its traders.*

Massachusetts Historical Society

they committed their sometimes organized and occasionally spontaneous deeds of violence, as anything but townsmen "verging on hysteria" or rabble-rousers contributing to "plebiscitarian tyranny." Thus Bailyn's generally sympathetic depiction of that aloof governor seemed to demand an answer to his caustic put-downs from what might be called the people's side.

It was then that I discovered Professor Al Young and his associated school of from-the-ground-up historians. Al encouraged me in the strongest terms to concentrate on the role of maritime workers during the historic developments preceding 1776. In beginning that work, I turned to his own wonderfully rich anthologies on the Revolution, the two volumes subtitled *Explorations in the History of American Radicalism,* and there I encountered scholars willing to answer my question about the people's intentions by analyzing their actual doings and by risking the Marxist word *class* when dealing with group reactions. Most helpful to me of these radical historians was Dirk Hoerder, whose subsequent book *Crowd Action in Revolutionary America* became an essential part of my research.

Three other founding members of this radical school, the seminal writer Pauline Maier (*From Resistance to Revolution* and *The Old Revolutionaries*), Gary B. Nash (*The Urban Crucible*), and Paul A. Gilje (*Rioting in America* and *Liberty on the Waterfront*), helped me see the vital role played in those dramatic times by working-class people for whom mob action was a mode of political expression. Two historians usually considered more classical than radical—Carl Bridenbaugh (*Cities in Revolt*) and Gordon S. Wood (*The Radicalism of the American Revolution* and *The Creation of the American Republic*), also helped me form what I hoped was a balanced view of pre-Revolutionary mob violence. That awareness took a more nautical turn when I encountered two particularly salty historians, Jesse Lemisch (*Jack Tarr vs. John Bull*) and Marcus Rediker (*Between the Devil and the Deep Blue Sea*). Through their lively writings, I learned, even while reading disquisitions on the intellectual aspects of the Puritans' independent thinking, that it was wise to keep an eye on how the fishermen were faring in competitions with the French Canadians on the Grand Banks and what the merchants were doing to build trade with the West Indies and other lands beyond the horizon.

I also had to accept the challenge of identifying and confirming Boston as the town where those fishermen and maritime workers made a special and causative impact on American history. Hearing of that task, my friend John Reps, professor emeritus of city and regional planning at Cornell University, arrived in my driveway with a whole backseat full of books that he lugged up the steps to my study. These included such works as Justin Winsor's three-volume *Memorial History of Boston* and the compendious *Mapping Boston*, edited by Alex Krieger and David Cobb.

They were a huge help. Yet I still had leagues to go before I could feel truly in company with those rebellious New England merchants and seamen. To approach them more closely involved my not only rereading Admiral Samuel Eliot Morison's *Maritime History of New England* and Benjamin Labaree's *New England and the*

*Sea* but also studying anew Perry Miller's *The New England Mind in the Seventeenth Century*. It also involved, fortunately, many discussions and e-mails with Professor Miller's student, my friend Cushing Strout, a professor of American studies and humane letters at Cornell, who also introduced me to that most haunted of New England observers, Nathaniel Hawthorne.

For the development of chapter 2, which involved examining the deterioration of Boston's traditional civility, Al Young suggested that I read William Pencak's *War, Politics, and Revolution in Provincial Massachusetts*. This brilliant, if now slightly outdated, work stresses the constant strains that were imposed on maritime workers and their families—on them far more than on other social groups within the region and in Boston far more than in other colonial ports. Pencak also focuses on the generally inept leadership of Massachusetts. Small wonder that the people of the province, after disposing of the lordly Governor-General Andros, commenced a history of throwing subsequent governors overboard. With my friend and Bay State kinsman John Kingsbury, professor emeritus of plant biology at Cornell, I enjoyed several conversations about high-level provincial peccadillos, including those of Governor Phips, most of whose heirs became Loyalists in Revolutionary times. One of Jack's papers on the subject is titled "Whatever Happened to the Phipps Family Fortune?"

It was also necessary to sail beyond local considerations and try to get a more comprehensive view; that is, to figure out the fraught relationship between war-exhausted seamen and expansive merchants in Massachusetts as part of the sweeping drama of British global imperialism. For in the mid-eighteenth century, that Empire's world-girdling mercantilism helped to create a storm on the Boston waterfront that resulted ultimately in blowing the Puritan ethos out and bringing the new rich in. Merchants were observed riding in ornate carriages from London; tea became the preferred beverage in polite society. Meanwhile, the poor, who had never before considered themselves as such, suffered starvation and penury. To be a seaman or to be a shipwright—once crucially necessary and well-respected callings—was no longer to be a significant part of society. I caught a glimpse of this stressful change in Mary Lou Lustig's biography of Governor-General Andros, *The Imperial Executive in America*. It was spelled out to me even more completely by yet another Cornell friend and professor, Michael Kammen, in his early work *Empire and Interest*.

But even after being introduced to this broader perspective, I still found the New England fisherman, for all the elusiveness of his character, central to and determinate in this story of the violence that led up to the American Revolution. That conclusion seemed historically validated when I read about John Wise (1652–1725), the pastor of fishermen in Ipswich. George Allen Cook's biography *John Wise, Early American Democrat* tells of how he stirred up the royal government with his arguments on behalf of his parishioners so memorably that his town (less than thirty miles from Boston) won the title "Birthplace of Independence."

In researching chapter 3, I wanted to find out more precisely how mob action, or reaction, became almost a way of life in early-eighteenth-century Boston. As described in a second book by William Pencak, *Riot and Revelry in Early America*, that tradition of crowd behavior had its earliest roots in medieval England but took on spectacularly new forms in America. And as further examined by Jack Tager in *Boston Riots*, this port—which had been a singularly placid, religiously constrained town for most of the sixteenth century—suddenly, after the 1693 ouster of Governor-General Andros, became not only a hotbed of "tumults" but also the headquarters of American protest against British "tyranny."

Simultaneously, it appeared that the town's staid "Codfish Aristocracy" had lost its position of control to certain daring entrepreneurs. These avid merchants and smugglers, of whom John Hancock's uncle Thomas was the epitome, had pioneered in the so-called Triangle Trade and had little patience with new regulations visited upon them by Great Britain's successive administrations. In the opening chapters of his immensely helpful book *Smugglers and Patriots*, the historian John W. Tyler demonstrates how this new group of risk-takers, linked in a variety of ways to the riot-ready underclass, began to dominate Boston's political structures.

In chapters 4 and 5, I therefore sought to focus on the major personalities who were primary factors in this drama of maritime politics. Harlow G. Unger's recent biography of John Hancock provided much-needed insight into the differing aspirations of Whigs and merchants. Many years ago, I had received an introduction to two of these major players: James Otis and Samuel Adams Jr. That introduction was provided by the historian Lillian Miller, with whom I produced a publication for the Smithsonian at the time of the national Bicentennial titled *In the Hearts and Minds of the People*. In more recent years, new biographies of Adams, including a notable one by John K. Alexander of the University of Cincinnati, have given me a fresh understanding of his and Otis's inventive policies.

But as I reconsidered those policies of the 1760s, they seemed to exist at a strange remove from the waterfront concerns that had powered Boston politics earlier in the century. Was something else going on? Fortunately, at this moment Pat Leehey steered me toward a stack of the periodicals issued over the years by the Paul Revere House. Many issues of this *Revere House Gazette* presented up-close vignettes of actual political life within the venerable taverns and houses of North Boston. Secretly, in that neighborhood's blocked-off upper rooms and elsewhere across town, the caucuses originally organized by Deacon Samuel Adams and Elisha Cooke and strengthened by Samuel Adams Jr. drew together a heady mix of waterfront characters and eager upstarts from the artisan class. Pat also obtained for me a rare copy of E. H. Goss's 1891 biography of Revere, in the appendix of which are dutifully recorded the caucus clubs' monthly meetings. There, I found that many of the members were ship captains.

Yet those captains were hardly pressing in the direction of democracy; what they most desired at this point was the creation of a pressure group of mutually interested parties. Four books proved of particular help in explaining how those captains, positioned between the merchant hierarchy and the waterfront muscle, became a willful part of governmental change: Richard B. Morris's *Government and Labor in Early America* (with Professor Morris, I had produced *The American Worker* for the U.S. Labor Department in 1976), Ray Raphael's *A People's History of the American Revolution*, Robert St. George's *Conversing by Signs*, and Edmund S. Morgan's *Inventing the*

*People.* The last two books also stress the reshaping of many old English folkways not usually considered as political expressions—such as Guy Fawkes Day celebrations—into new patterns reflecting American sentiments.

It was not, however, until Al Young led me in the direction of a biographical sketch of Ebenezer Mackintosh written by George P. Anderson in 1924 that I could put a face on what a dockside laborer in this period had to endure and how he would have become involved in mob actions. Similarly, it was only when John Bell introduced me to the Pope Day drawings of Pierre Eugène du Simitière that I could visualize the excitement of that nighttime celebration and appreciate what a key role Boston's children—who made up more than half of the town's population—played in it. Then I began to see who this new generation of not-yet Americans were, ready to assert themselves through riots and crowd actions as politicized citizens. This permitted me to read Edmund and Helen Morgan's classic work of 1953, *The Stamp Act Crisis*, with a new eye—not, that is, as merely a study of the "emergence of constitutional principles," but also as a drama of individuals bold enough to make certain revolutionary choices.

For chapters 6 and 7, it was necessary to resolve conflicting opinions about whether the actions of Boston's waterfront mobs, which intensified during the Stamp Act riots and carried on through the alleged Boston Massacre of 1770, were spontaneous (and possibly traditional) protests or were organized and knowing strikes at political authority. And if organized, by whom? In this analysis, the rough behavior of small bands of New England seamen—specifically, the tarring and feathering of an increasing number of British officials—emerged as a key action. The detailed study of that practice given to me by historian Ben Irvin (later published in the *New England Quarterly*) allowed an up-close view of this peculiarly Yankee way of punishing the perceived enemy and of creating an atmosphere of terror.

It was also necessary to keep a weather eye on what was happening both at the upper levels of Boston's merchant-dominated government and at the level of contact between those merchants and the awakened people of the artisan and the working classes. The most fascinating figure in making those connections, even more effective in promoting crowd actions than the so-called Loyal Nine, was William Molineux. Both a smuggler and a benefactor of unemployed women and men, this salty character has long been a mystery to historians. Although no biography of Molineux has yet been written, researcher John Bell is in the process of gathering much fresh material on him; John was gracious enough to share pertinent bits of that information with me.

Partially because of that fresh information and also because of other research on Boston's working-class people, I have preferred not to favor interpretations of the pre-Revolutionary events in Boston that emphasize upper-level machinations. Here I am thinking of Hiller B. Zobel's otherwise meticulous 1970 book on the Boston Massacre. I am also thinking of the diary of Boston merchant John Rowe, as edited by his descendant Anne Rowe Cunningham. Although it provides many fascinating glimpses into political life in the 1760–1776 period, the edited diary fails to shed light on the powerful push toward liberty provided by the men and the women of Boston in the streets and at their rallying places.

Rather, I preferred to heed interpretations that dealt with the work and the struggles of everyday people, particularly the maritime workers. My depiction of the all-important ropewalk workers in chapter 7 was made possible through the research made available by Boston's Historical Park and by that agency's expert in the subject, Louis Hutchins. To him, I must express special thanks. I also owe thanks to author James Neyland and others who concentrated on the presence of Native American and African American workers in the tensions leading up to the Boston Massacre.

For chapters 8 and 9, the line of inquiry had to change. It was not just a matter of whether the maritime mobs of Boston provided the essential push toward Revolution but also whether the men of the mobs would continue to be influential factors as the explosions in Boston evolved into a war for national liberation. Benjamin W. Labaree brought out his answer to the first of these questions in *The Boston Tea Party* (1964). Like all of Professor Labaree's works, this one considers the seamen first, finding them to be consciously involved in daring acts against the Crown, whether in their own gangs or on the orders of their captains. As Professor Labaree explains, the men who split open the tea chests were not simply thugs, "Mohawks," rounded up for this duty by the clever Samuel Adams. On the contrary, they were responsible seamen and other workers who believed, along with their captains, that the British actions closing down the port had to be countered.

Among those vigorous men was a certain dockside shoemaker named Robert George Twelves Hewes. He is the main character in Al Young's pathfinding book *The Shoemaker and the Tea Party* (1999), a book that probes to the heart of that famous "party." The event was not just the expression of merchant-class hostility to Hutchinson's regime but a joint affair in which self-conscious working people took leading parts. Other New England researchers, including Carol Ely, have also done important work to identify and tell the story of waterfront families from Boston's North and South Ends who became intimately and effectively involved in the drama of the Tea Party.

Yet another vital link in the story of the evolution of the maritime mobs into fighting forces was provided by Ray Raphael in his *The First American Revolution,* in which he makes the connection between revolutionaries in the interior towns of Massachusetts with those in the barricaded port of Boston. This link was also established by David Hackett Fischer in his justly renowned *Paul Revere's Ride.* Robert A. Gross's *The Minutemen and Their World* and Louis Birnbaum's *Red Dawn at Lexington* also provided other valuable clues to the communications network that was being established by patriots across New England and eventually across the colonies.

When, after Concord and Lexington, it became clear that a rebellion had become a war, the siege of Boston commenced—a siege conducted both by the militia men outside the port's gates who hemmed in the British troops and by the royal forces inside the wall who harassed left-behind patriots. That story was originally told in Richard Frothingham's 1873 *Siege of Boston* but acquired more impact when presented in Richard Ketchum's *Decisive Day.* This intricate picture of how the people of Boston at various levels strove to defend themselves and take the fight to the enemy became all the more interesting and complex when I learned from John Bell of the work performed by the boys of the Boston Latin School in helping to subvert the British. I also benefited from the research of my friend and classmate Garrison Valentine into the contribution of the forces from New Hampshire that streamed in to help besieged Boston.

But the most astonishing insight into who did the real warriors' work in the ultimate battles of Breed's Hill and Bunker Hill was provided by author George Quintal, whose unpublished paper "Patriots of Color" was made available to me by Phil Hunt at the Boston Navy Yard. From that paper, as well as from Jayne Triber's paper titled "Historical Background on the Siege of Boston," I derived an unforgettable sense of the determination of men and women at the lowest levels of Boston society to risk all and to join the Revolution (if that's what it was to be).

The bloody sacrifice of five Boston seamen and waterfront laborers in the massacre on King Street—here, I think particularly of

*The North End's Green Dragon Tavern, where caucus members plotted the Boston Tea Party, looks mysterious in this 1773 ink-and-watercolor drawing. Before it stands a carriage such as Paul Revere might have selected for a foray; above it floats a Masonic symbol and a pipe-smoking man-in-the-moon. The solid-brick building was unfortunately torn down after the Revolution.*

American Antiquarian Society

the violent whaler Crispus Attucks and the caught-in-the-crossfire sailor James Caldwell—would be recapitulated by many other Americans on land and sea until victory was won. I am immensely indebted to those historians and archivists who brought me to that broadened recognition of how it happened that the maritime community was so intensely involved in that initial event of the American Revolution.

I am also grateful to the men and the women of various institutions who helped to bring forth this book's illustrations. Here I refer to the directors and the staff members not only of the previously mentioned Massachusetts Historical Society but also of Historic New England (previously, the Society for the Preservation of New England Antiquities), the Bostonian Society, the Boston Museum of Fine Arts, the Boston Athenaeum, the American Antiquarian Society in Worcester, the Peabody Essex Museum in Salem, the New York Public Library, the John Carter Brown Library in Providence, the Library Company of Philadelphia, and the Yale University Art Gallery.

Thanks of a very profound sort are owed to my agent, Kirsten Mangess of Curtis Brown Ltd., and to my editor Stephen Power of John Wiley, for their initial and continuing assistance in the shaping of this book. Finally and most fondly, I want to express my gratitude to my wife, Dora Flash Bourne, not only for her expert editing of each and every chapter but also for her willingness to experience this book, like all of our voyages, as in a partner ship.

# Bibliography

## Books

Albion, Robert G., William A. Baker, and Benjamin W. Labaree. *New England and the Sea.* Mystic, Conn.: Mystic Seaport Museum, 1972.

Alexander, John K. *Samuel Adams: America's Revolutionary Politician.* Lanham, Md.: Rowman and Littlefield, 2002.

Allis, Frederick S., Jr., ed. *Seafaring in Colonial Massachusetts.* Boston: Colonial Society of Massachusetts, 1980.

Applewhite, Harriet B., and Darline G. Levy, eds. *Women and Politics in the Age of Democratic Revolution.* Anne Arbor: University of Michigan Press, 1990.

Bacon, Edwin M. *Rambles around Old Boston.* Boston: Little Brown, 1914.

Bailyn, Bernard. *The Ordeal of Thomas Hutchinson.* Cambridge, Mass.: Harvard University Press, 1974.

Baxter, W. T. *The House of Hancock.* Cambridge, Mass.: Harvard University Press, 1945.

Birnbaum, Louis. *Red Dawn at Lexington.* Boston: Houghton Mifflin, 1986.

Bolster, W. Jeffrey. *Black Jacks: African-American Seamen in the Age of Sail.* Cambridge, Mass.: Harvard University Press, 1997.

Bridenbaugh, Carl. *Cities in Revolt: Urban Life in America, 1743–1776.* New York: Harper, 1955.

Brigham, Clarence S. *Paul Revere's Engravings*. New York: Atheneum, 1969.

Bruchey, Stuart. *The Colonial Merchant: Sources and Readings*. New York: Harcourt, 1966.

Cook, George Allan. *John Wise: Early American Democrat*. New York: Octagon, 1966.

Fischer, David Hackett. *Liberty and Freedom: A Visual History of America's Founding Ideas*. New York: Oxford University Press, 2005.

———. *Paul Revere's Ride*. New York: Oxford University Press, 1994.

Forbes, Esther. *Paul Revere and the World He Lived In*. Boston: Houghton Mifflin, 1942.

Fowler, William M., Jr. *The Baron of Beacon Hill*. Boston: Houghton Mifflin, 1980.

Frothingham, Richard. *The History of the Siege of Boston*. Boston: Little Brown, 1873.

Gilje, Paul A. *Liberty on the Waterfront: American Maritime Culture in the Age of Revolution*. Philadelphia: University of Pennsylvania Press, 2004.

———. *Rioting in America*. Burlington: University of Indiana Press, 1996.

Goss, Elbridge Henry. *The Life of Colonel Paul Revere*. Freeport, N.Y.: Books for Libraries, 1891.

Gross, Robert A. *The Minutemen and Their World*. New York: Hill & Wang, 1976.

Henretta, James A. *The Evolution of American Society, 1700–1815*. Lexington, Mass.: Heath, 1973.

Hoerder, Dirk. *Crowd Action in Revolutionary America, 1765–1780*. New York: Academic Press, 1977.

Hofstadter, Richard. *America at 1750: A Social Portrait*. New York: Random House, 1973.

Holton, Woody. *Forced Founders: Indians, Debtors, Slaves, and the Making of the American Revolution in Virginia*. Chapel Hill: University of North Carolina Press, 1999.

Howard, Brett. *Boston: A Social History*. New York: Hawthorne, 1976.

Howell, Colin, and Richard J. Twomey, eds. *Jack Tar in History: Essays in the History of Maritime Life and Labour*. Fredericton: University of New Brunswick Press, 1991.

Irvin, Benjamin H. *Samuel Adams: Son of Liberty, Father of Revolution.* New York: Oxford University Press, 2002.

Jehlen, Myra. *American Incarnation: The Individual, the Nation, and the Continent.* Cambridge, Mass.: Harvard University Press, 1986.

Jones, Douglas Lamar. *Village and Seaport: Migration and Society in Eighteenth-Century Massachusetts.* Hanover, N.H.: University Press of New England, 1981.

Kammen, Michael. *Empire and Interest: The American Colonies and the Politics of Mercantilism.* New York: Lippincott, 1970.

Ketchum, Richard M. *Decisive Day: The Battle of Bunker Hill.* New York: Holt, 1962.

Krieger, Alex, and David Cobb, eds. *Mapping Boston.* Cambridge, Mass.: The MIT Press, 1999.

Leehey, Patrick M. *Paul Revere—Artisan, Businessman, and Patriot: The Man behind the Myth.* Boston: Paul Revere Memorial Association, 1988.

Lemisch, Jesse. *Jack Tar vs. John Bull: The Role of New York's Seamen in Precipitating the Revolution.* New York: Garland, 1997.

Linebaugh, Peter, and Marcus Rediker. *The Many-Headed Hydra: Sailors, Slaves, Commoners and the Hidden History of the Revolutionary Atlantic.* Boston: Beacon, 2000.

Lustig, Mary Lou. *The Imperial Executive in America: Sir Edmund Andros, 1637–1714.* Madison, N.J.: Fairleigh Dickinson University Press, 2002.

Maclay, Edward S. *A History of American Privateers.* New York: Burt Franklin, 1899.

Maier, Pauline. *The Old Revolutionaries: Political Lives in the Age of Samuel Adams.* New York: Knopf, 1980.

——. *From Resistance to Revolution: Colonial Radicalism and the Development of Opposition to Britain, 1705–1776.* New York: Knopf, 1972.

McClellan, T. K. *Smuggling in the American Colonies at the Outbreak of the Revolution.* New York: Moffat Yard, 1912.

McLennan, John S. *Louisbourg: From Its Foundation to Its Fall, 1713–1758.* Halifax: Book Room, 1979.

Merrill, Mildred, and Sam Wilnetz. *The Key of Liberty: The Life and Dramatic Writings of William Manning, "A Laborer," 1747–1814.* Cambridge, Mass.: Harvard University Press, 1993.

Miller, John C. *Sam Adams: Pioneer in Propaganda.* Calif.: Palo Alto University Press, 1936.

Morgan, Edmund S. *Inventing the People: The Rise of Popular Sovereignty in England and America.* New York: W. W. Norton, 1988.

——, and Helen M. Morgan. *The Stamp Act Crisis.* Chapel Hill: University of North Carolina Press, 1953.

Morison, Samuel E. *The Maritime History of Massachusetts.* Boston: Houghton Mifflin, 1921.

Nash, Gary B. *The Urban Crucible. The Northern Seaports and the Origins of the American Revolution.* Cambridge, Mass.: Harvard University Press, 1986.

Neyland, James. *Crispus Attucks: Patriot.* Los Angeles: Melrose Square, 1995.

O'Connor, Thomas H. *Bibles, Brahmins, and Bosses: A Short History of Boston.* Boston: Trustees of the Public Library of Boston, 1976.

Pencak, William, ed. *Riot and Revelry in Early America.* University Park: Pennsylvania State University Press, 2002.

——. *War, Politics, and Revolution in Provincial Massachusetts.* Boston: Northeastern University Press, 1981.

Raphael, Ray. *The First American Revolution: Before Lexington and Concord.* New York: New Press, 2002.

——. *A People's History of the American Revolution.* New York: New Press, 2001.

Rediker, Marcus. *Between the Devil and the Deep Blue Sea: Merchant Seamen, Pirates, and the Anglo-American Maritime World, 1700–1750.* Cambridge, Mass.: Cambridge University Press, 1987.

Schlesinger, Arthur M. *The Colonial Merchants and the American Revolution, 1763–1776.* New York: Columbia University Press, 1918.

Seasholes, Nancy S. *Gaining Ground: A History of Landmaking in Boston.* Cambridge, Mass.: The MIT Press, 2003.

Shurtleff, Nathaniel B. *A Topographical and Historical Description of Boston.* Boston: Rockwell and Churchill, 1891.

St. George, Robert Blair. *Conversing by Signs: Poetics of Implication in Colonial New England Culture.* Chapel Hill: University of North Carolina Press, 1998.

Sweetser, M. F. *King's Hand Book of Boston Harbor.* Cambridge, Mass.: Applewood, 1882.

Tager, Jack. *Boston Riots: Three Centuries of Social Violence.* Boston: Northeastern University Press, 2001.

Triber, Jayne E. *A True Republican: The Life of Paul Revere.* Amherst: University of Massachusetts Press, 1998.

Tyler, John W. *Smugglers and Patriots: Boston Merchants and the Advent of the American Revolution.* Boston: Northeastern University Press, 1986.

Unger, Harlow Giles. *John Hancock: Merchant King and American Patriot.* New York: Wiley, 2000.

Wertenbaker, Thomas Jefferson. *The Puritan Oligarchy: The Founding of American Civilization.* New York: Scribner's, 1947.

Winsor, Justin. *The Memorial History of Boston* (4 vols.). Boston: Osgood, 1883.

Wood, Gordon S. *The Creation of the American Republic, 1776–1787.* Chapel Hill: University of North Carolina Press, 1969.

——. *The Radicalism of the American Revolution.* New York: Knopf, 1992.

Young, Alfred F., ed. *The American Revolution: Explorations in the History of American Radicalism.* DeKalb: Northern Illinois University Press, 1976.

——, ed. *Beyond the American Revolution: Explorations in the History of American Radicalism.* DeKalb: Northern Illinois University Press, 1993.

——. *Ordinary People and the American Revolution.* New York: New York University Press, forthcoming.

——. *The Shoemaker and the Tea Party.* Boston: Beacon, 1999.

Zobel, Hiller B. *The Boston Massacre.* New York: Norton, 1970.

## Diaries, Articles, and Unpublished Material

Anderson, George P. "Ebenezer Mackintosh: Stamp Act Rioter and Patriot." *Publications of the Colonial Society of Massachusetts*, vol. 26 (1924): 15–64.

Bell, J. L. "'Behold the Guns Were Gone!': Did Four Brass Cannon Set Off the American Revolution?" Paper presented in the Boston Area Early American History seminar series, Massachusetts Historical Society, Boston, 2001.

——. "Du Simitière's Sketches of Pope Day in Boston, 1767," in *The Worlds of Children, 1620–1920: Proceedings of Dublin Seminar for New England Folklife, 2002,* edited by Peter Benes and Jane Montague Benes. Boston: Boston University Press, 2004.

——. "Latin School Gentlemen in Revolutionary Times: The Culture of Boston's South Latin School under the Lovells." Paper prepared for the annual conference of the New England Popular Culture Association, Boston, 2002.

Cunningham, Anne Rowe. *Letters and Diary of John Rowe, Boston Merchant.* Boston: W. W. Clark, 1903.

Doggett, John, Jr. "A Short Narrative of the Horrid Massacre in Boston." Printed by Order of the Town of Boston, New York, 1849.

Ely, Carol. "North Square: A Boston Neighborhood in the Revolutionary Era." Boston: The Paul Revere Memorial Association, 1983.

Grundset, Eric G., ed. *African American and American Indian Patriots of the Revolutionary War.* Washington, D.C.: National Society of the Daughters of the American Revolution, 1992.

Heath, William. *Memoirs of Major-General Heath.* Boston: Thomas & Andrews, 1798.

Hoffman, Ronald, ed. "In Search of Early America." Williamsburg, Va.: *William and Mary Quarterly* (1993).

Hutchins, Louis P. "Work, Culture, and Resistance to Mechanization in the American Rope Making Industry, 1830–1850." Boston: Boston National Historical Park, 1999.

Irvin, Benjamin H. "Tar, Feathers, and the Enemies of American Liberties, 1768–1776." *New England Quarterly* (June 2003).

Lax, John, and William Pencak. "The Knowles Riot and the Crisis of the 1740s in Massachusetts." *Perspectives in American History* 10 (1976): 161–214.

Longley, R. S. "Mob Activities in Revolutionary America." *New England Quarterly* 6 (1933): 98–130.

Morgan, Edmund S. *Paul Revere's Ride: Three Accounts of His Famous Ride.* Boston: Massachusetts Historical Society, 2000.

Quintal, George, Jr. *Patriots of Color: A Peculiar Beauty and Merit, African Americans and Native Americans at Battle Road and Bunker Hill.* Boston: National Historical Park, 2002.

Triber, Jayne E. "Historical Background on Siege of Boston and Adolescence in Revolutionary Period." Produced for "Bringing History Home," project of the Paul Revere House, Boston, 1999.

Wood, Gordon S. "A Note on Mobs in the American Revolution." Williamsburg, Va.: *William and Mary Quarterly*, 3rd series (1966): 635–642.

# *Index*

Page numbers in italics refer to illustrations.

9 781684 421527